D0195779

A SHORT HISTORY
OF THE WESTERN LITURGY

A SHORT HISTORY
OF THE WESTERN LITURGY

An Account and Some Reflections

THEODOR KLAUSER

Translated from the German by John Halliburton

SECOND EDITION

Oxford New York Toronto Melbourne
OXFORD UNIVERSITY PRESS

Oxford University Press, Walton Street, Oxford OX2 6DP

OXFORD LONDON GLASGOW
NEW YORK TORONTO MELBOURNE WELLINGTON
KUALA LUMPUR SINGAPORE HONG KONG TOKYO
DELHI BOMBAY CALCUTTA MADRAS KARACHI
NAIROBI DAR ES SALAAM CAPE TOWN

Published in German as
Kleine abendländische Liturgiegeschichte
© Peter Hanstein Verlag, 1965

English translation from the fifth German edition

Second edition © Oxford University Press 1979

First edition 1969
Second edition first published in paperback 1979, 1981

All rights reserved. No part of this publication may be
reproduced, stored in a retrieval system, or transmitted, in any
form or by any means, electronic, mechanical, photocopying,
recording or otherwise, without the prior permission of
Oxford University Press

British Library Cataloguing in Publication Data
Klauser, Theodor
  A short history of the western liturgy.—2nd ed.
  1 Roman Catholic Church. Liturgy and ritual—
History. 2. Public worship—History
  I. Title
  264′.02′009   BX1970   78–41053
  ISBN 0–19–213224–5
  ISBN 0–19–213223–7 Pbk

Printed in Great Britain by Fakenham Press Ltd,
Fakenham, Norfolk

Translator's Note to the Second Edition

Fourteen years have now passed since the appearance of Dr. Klauser's fifth German edition and ten since the publication of the English translation. Much has happened in the liturgical life of the Church since 1965. I have therefore with Dr. Klauser's permission added (in Appendix IV) a brief guide to these developments and a select supplementary bibliography.

Chichester,   R.J.H.
August 1978

Translator's Note to the First Edition

Thanks are due to the late Dr. Leslie Cross, who sponsored and encouraged this translation, and to Dr. William Rusch, who kindly put his own translation of this work at my disposal. The publishers' thanks are due to Mrs. Brenda Hall for compiling the index.

Oxford,   R.J.H.
July 1969

Acknowledgements

Acknowledgement is due to the Aschendorff Verlag, Munster, for permission to reprint in translation the 'Guiding Principles for Designing and Building a Church in the spirit of the Roman Liturgy' *(Richtlinien für die Gestaltung des Gotteshavses aus dem Geiste der römischen Liturgie)* compiled by Theodor Klauser under the direction and with the collaboration of the Liturgical Commission, first published by them in 1949, and re-issued in 1955; also to Burns Oates Ltd. for permission to reprint the translation of the Canon, the Hymn of the Angels, and the Deacon's Hymn of Praise from *The Missal in Latin and English* (London, 1962); also to Geoffrey Chapman Ltd., and to the Rev. J. D. Crichton for permission to use extracts from Fr. Crichton's translation of the Constitution 'On the Sacred Liturgy'.

Preface

This *Short History of the Western Liturgy* represents an attempt to introduce a wider circle of readers to the most important facts and problems of the history of the Western liturgy, and to awaken in them an understanding of those things with which liturgical reform is concerned. The book first appeared in December 1943 as the 'Bonn Correspondence Course for Students on Active Service', and later (in two editions) as a correspondence course for prisoners of war. The present greatly enlarged and revised work represents the fifth edition; the previous version has been available some years now in English, American, French, Italian, and Spanish translations.

The 'Guiding Principles for Designing and Building a Church in the Spirit of the Roman Liturgy', which is printed as an Appendix, was drawn up by order of and with the assistance of the liturgical commission that was convened by the conference of bishops at Fulda. It appeared first in 1949 in the fourth issue of *Kathedrale*, a series of papers dealing with the restoration of German cathedrals and churches. We have reprinted it here by kind permission of the Aschendorff Press at Münster.

The bibliography at the end of the book provides some necessary directives for all those who wish to go deeper into this subject. By the addition of some critical notes, this has developed into a kind of *bibliographie raisonée*, which not infrequently complements the text. Those who would like to know more, especially about the celebration of the eucharist, should refer to Jungmann's *Missarum Sollemnia*. Never before has research in the field of liturgical history been carried out with greater thoroughness and one would like to hope that no future publication in this specialist field will fall below the standard of this model study. First-rate guidance in other aspects of the liturgical cosmos can be obtained from Leichner's *Liturgik*. If the editions of this excellent manual were to follow one another in quicker succession, this book could become for liturgical history what Altaner's *Patrology* has long since been for patristics—a standard guide for everyone.

The author wishes to thank very much several colleagues at the Franz Dölger-Institut zur Erforschung der Spätantike in Bonn for some essential references and technical assistance but he is especially grateful for the valuable advice of his friend Alfred Stuiber.

THEODOR KLAUSER

Ippendorf bei Bonn

Contents

Introduction

Our ancient cathedral churches, which were originally designed as buildings with well-defined outlines in the Romanesque or Gothic style, have in many cases long since become confusing structures. Each century has left in them traces of its own particular forms and spiritual and aesthetic interests. In the course of time the choir and side-aisles have been garlanded with a wreath of chapels of various kinds. The walls have gradually been covered with monuments to the dead. The framework of the windows, which has constantly undergone alterations, has been filled with stained glass of widely differing periods. Statues and free-standing tombs of the founders, lights and lecterns, sacrament-houses and stalls everywhere break up the gently flowing lines of the body of the church, and the few altars surviving from the earliest period have lost their prominence to their numerous, richly ornamented successors. Today it is only the few trained experts who can survey these ancient episcopal churches as a whole and grasp their spiritual meaning; and the fruits of their investigations almost fill to overflowing the massive volumes of the official inventories of public monuments.

Similarly involved, though much more complex, is the Western Roman liturgy in its present state. Its history spans not a single millennium, but almost two. It bears the deep and ineradicable scars of the spiritual development not of a single people, but of several. The most diverse influences, in constantly renewed onslaughts, have played their part in the moulding and structuring of our liturgy. Such are the sober but masculine temper of the early Christian popes; the devotion of the early monasteries, for whose members, in their wholehearted attachment to the *opus Dei*, time was a matter of no concern; the enthusiastic delight with which the clerics of the Merovingian and Carolingian eras exercised their ingenuity in the use of symbols and allegorical interpretations; the emotional devotion to the Passion of the medieval mystic, and contemporaneous with it, the analytical intellect of the scholastic theologian. Later came the linguistic purism of the humanists, and the almost ecstatic demand for splendour of the baroque period; and the final, yet strong influence was that of the dispassionate, juridical mentality of the rubricists of more recent times, who were indifferent to considerations of liturgical history. Who indeed can hope to be equal to the task of surveying, expounding, and interpreting the final result of this long process of formation with its many and closely interwoven threads of development.

But, in spite of all this, the liturgy must be understood. For, day by day, it is our duty to live within it and by means of it. At the very least, we must acquaint ourselves with its historical changes and developments in such a way as to furnish ourselves with a key to a rudimentary understanding of its basic elements. The purpose of this book will be to survey and describe these changes and developments in the liturgy as they appear to a student of the subject at the present time.

The liturgical history of the West may be divided into four periods. The first takes us down to Gregory the Great, i.e. to 590; the second to Gregory VII, i.e. to 1073; the third to the Council of Trent, i.e. to 1545; and, finally, the fourth to the Second Vatican Council. For we can already safely say that, with this Council, which is still in session, a new epoch has dawned in the history of the liturgy.[1]

Of the four periods we have just mentioned, the first may be described as the period of creative beginnings; the second as that of expansion under Franco-German leadership; the third, the era of luxuriant growth in which the liturgy was both re-interpreted and also misinterpreted; and the fourth as the age of a rigid unified liturgy and of rubricism.

I shall first give a brief survey of these periods. Then I shall sketch into this rough outline those firmly established features of

[1] The German edition of this book was published in 1965.

the liturgy which have been brought to light by the extensive and intensive research that has been carried out in this field since the end of the First World War. Finally I shall attempt (in the spirit of the sub-title—'An Account and Some Reflections') to compare the events and developments I describe with the ideal picture of the Western liturgy as it emerges from the pages of history.

I

Creative Beginnings:
From the Ascension of Jesus to
Gregory the Great

i. OUTLINE OF THE PERIOD

A brief description of what is known today about the earliest period of the Christian liturgy may be set out as follows:

The fundamental acts of worship of the early Church—the celebration of the eucharist, the rites of the sacraments, prayer in common, and the liturgical sermon—all go back to the express command of Jesus, or at least are based on his example and commendation. Jesus, however, did not originate these liturgical acts, but took them over from the practice of late Judaism. The primitive church continued this policy; to a limited extent it created of its own accord forms of worship which had not already been laid down by Jesus; but to a much greater extent it fashioned its worship according to the liturgical customs of Judaism. In Gentile congregations, borrowings were made increasingly from the religious practices of the Graeco-Roman world.

I shall now examine what is Jewish and what is Greek in the worship of the early Church.

From Jewish sources comes the substance of the Service of the Word which survives in the first part of our mass, i.e. the two lections, the psalmody which comes between them, and the sermon which concludes the service. These three elements were taken over from the sabbath morning service at the synagogue. Of Jewish origin too is the essential structure of the ancient eucharistic prayer, which is preserved today (albeit very fragmentarily) in the Preface and Canon. It was derived on the one

hand from the hymn of praise and thanksgiving which concluded
the Jewish ritual celebrations at the family meal which also formed
a part of the liturgy; and on the other hand from the hymn of
praise for creation and for God's gracious guidance of Israel
which was intoned each sabbath morning at the service in the
synagogue. From Jewish sources comes the great intercessory
prayer, which used to introduce every Mass of the Faithful and
which, until a short time ago, was only used on Good Friday. It
was modelled on the Prayer of Eighteen Intercessions which was
said at the beginning of the synagogue service. Of Jewish origin
too is the seven-day week, and the weekly day of worship which
the Church soon transferred from the sabbath to Sunday, the day
of the Resurrection. The festivals of Easter and Pentecost derive
from Jewish sources, as indeed does the idea of the 'Church's
Year', i.e. the sanctification of the secular year by a succession of
religious festivals. The cult of the martyrs is also Jewish in origin.
So too are some important elements in the liturgical hours of
prayer, viz., the morning and evening devotions (today called
Lauds and Vespers), the triple number of the day hours (known
today as Terce, Sext, and None), the division into three of the
night prayers (the Nocturns of our Mattins), and (which it is
important to make clear) the reckoning of the liturgical day from
evening to evening, i.e. from Vespers to Vespers. From Judaism
came the use of the Laudate Psalms at the morning office; and the
custom of introducing liturgical prayers by an invitatory formula
such as 'Sursum Corda', 'Oremus', and 'Gratias Agamus' is also
Jewish in origin. From Jewish sources comes the doxology, i.e.
the custom of ending the prayer with an ascription of praise, like
our 'Gloria Patri'. Of Jewish origin is the use in the liturgy of the
Tersanctus, the Hymn of the Seraphim from Isaiah 6.3. This
ultimately goes back to the Qedusha of Jewish morning devotions. Similarly derived are some of the congregational responses
or 'acclamations' (as they are called), i.e. 'Amen', 'Alleluia',
'Hosanna', and 'Et cum spiritu tuo'. From Judaism comes the
pattern for the so-called 'paradigmatic prayer' which implores
God for help and salvation by appealing to the great examples
(paradigms) of his mercy in salvation history. Finally from Jewish

sources comes one of the most important ritual actions in Christian worship—the laying on of hands.

From the Hellenistic world on the other hand—in part probably from its mystery religions—come undoubtedly the decisive influences in the shaping of the Christian rite of initiation, baptism, by the addition of exorcisms and anointings. From Hellenism too comes the idea of transferring the celebration of baptism to the night of Easter, and with it the keeping of the vigil. Again from Hellenism is derived the *disciplina arcani*, i.e. the Christian custom (which was not, it is true, generally enforced until the fourth century) of observing silence about what lay at the heart of the sacred rites and especially concerning the sacred formulas. Hellenistic in origin is the tendency to make the formulas of prayer conform to the laws of ancient rhetoric, especially to the law of symmetry and that which governed the rhythmic ending of sentences. From Hellenism comes the Christian custom of turning east for prayer (foreshadowed in the Jewish practice of praying towards the Temple) and, by the same principle, the building of Christian churches so that they run from east to west. From Hellenism, once again, come innumerable liturgical technical terms, among them the word 'liturgy' itself as well as such words as 'eucharist', 'eulogy', 'mystery', 'preface', 'canon', 'anamnesis', 'epiclesis', 'agape', 'epiphany', 'advent', 'exorcism', 'doxology' ,'acclamation', 'hymn', 'vigil', etc. Lastly, from the same source come certain forms of prayer, including those of the type of the Litany of the Saints, and formulas such as 'for all eternity' and 'throughout all ages, world without end'; similarly derived are the other 'acclamations', 'Kyrie eleison', 'Dignum et justum est', and 'Deo gratias'.

Now in drawing on these two sources—primarily on the Jewish and to a lesser extent on the Hellenistic—and by adding something of its own, the early Christian liturgy underwent roughly the following development.

At the outset there were two forms of divine service: first, the Service of the Word consisting of readings, a sermon, and prayer, which was probably held originally on Saturday mornings and then later transferred to Sunday morning; and then the liturgical meal, held on Friday evenings and later perhaps on Saturday evenings, consisting of the celebration of the eucharist within the context of a full-scale meal. At an early date, the meal was separated from the eucharist proper and called the agape (i.e. love feast), which was presumably done because congregations had increased in size and technical and disciplinary difficulties had become insuperable (cf. I Cor. 11.20-2, 33-4). In the course of the fourth century, the meal that had constituted the agape finally died out altogether. The celebration of the eucharist, on the other hand, now no longer bound up with the agape, ceased to look quite so much like a meal under the influence of a general effort to make worship more spiritual (cf. John 4.23), The 'Prayer of Thanksgiving', the 'eucharisteia', henceforth was the determinant factor in its structure and also gave to it its name. Probably from the beginning of the second century onwards, the celebration of the eucharist was gradually transferred to the Sunday morning and combined with the Service of the Word, which from now on formed, so to speak, the introduction to the eucharistic action.

There was a time when the faithful, each according to his means and following an ancient and widespread custom, used to bring their own contributions to the evening meal. After the separation of the eucharist from the agape, they continued to bring their gifts to each of these two liturgical meals; and in this custom, as well as in the regular practice of the ancient world, whereby members of the community themselves presented the sacrificial offerings, lie the roots of the so-called offertory procession, i.e. the presentation of gifts by the faithful.

The eucharistic prayers were at first improvised freely on the basis of traditional patterns by the bishop, the normal leader of the liturgical assembly. As the early Christians conceived it, the ability to do this was one of the signs of a person being endowed with the charismatic gifts necessary for holding the office of a bishop. When the demand for bishops could no longer be met from the number of those possessing such charismatic gifts, it became customary to prepare the prayers beforehand at home and finally to make use of set texts composed by someone other than the bishop.

In Rome as in the countries which bordered on the Mediterranean, the universally recognized language of the liturgy in the first centuries was Greek, apart from a short preliminary period during which Aramaic was used. Aramaic remained in use only in the remoter parts of Syria. But in Rome, the gradual transition from Greek to Latin took place about the middle of the third century; for approximately at this time, Greek began to disappear from the civic life of the Imperial capital. In the Roman province of Africa, the use of Latin in the liturgy seems to have been imposed somewhat earlier.

The Easter festival, together with its extension over the ensuing fifty days and its weekly repetition on Sundays, was celebrated almost from the very beginning. To this were added further liturgical commemorations, namely (in the declining years of the second century and in the third) the first feasts of the martyrs, and, in the fourth, the festivals of Christmas and the Epiphany. The elaboration of this basic structure to a religious ordering of the whole year from Advent to Pentecost and hence the development of the so-called 'Church's Year' was completed in its essentials by the end of the sixth century.

Besides the Service of the Word and the celebration of the eucharist, there was the administration of the sacraments, which to begin with was not confined to any fixed season or day. But these seasons and days must soon have been decided upon at an early period; for baptism was administered during the Easter Vigil and the consecration of bishops took place on Sunday. In the case of ordination, the essential ritual act was the laying on of hands; and at baptism the central action was the washing (hardly submersion!) of the candidate in running water.

From the beginning of the fourth century, the daily hours of prayer which had originally been observed only in private became established in monastic houses as a communal observance. In these the new hours of Prime and Compline were added and to a certain extent the monastic custom of reciting the hours of prayer together was from the fourth century onwards adopted also by non-monastic communities. At the offices, the Psalms which originally had been used simply as lections had now become the staple element in prayer, a development which had been effected long before the foundation of the first monasteries.

In the primitive church the Christians were counting on an early return of the Risen Christ and indeed were with some impatience awaiting the day of His Second Coming. The eucharistic meal was therefore felt to be a joyful foretaste of the eschatological banquet in the Kingdom of Christ, the more so since Jesus Himself seems to have given it this meaning (cf. Mark 14.25; Luke 22.16). Probably on account of this atmosphere of expectation, there developed in the early days of the first Christian community the liturgical 'acclamation' 'Maranatha' an Aramaic expression meaning 'Come, Lord, come' (I Cor. 16.22; Didache 10.6). In Greek-speaking countries a similar acclamation, 'May the grace of Christ come, and may this world pass away', was introduced (Didache 10.6); and when the expectation of an early Second Coming gradually died out around the year 100, both of these acclamations disappeared and were remembered no more.

Such in general terms is the picture normally sketched by those who have studied the development of the primitive Christian liturgy. The remarkable intensity with which studies in this field have been pursued in recent years enables us to make it more precise and to amplify it at certain points. Some particularly important aspects will, therefore, as I have promised, now be dealt with in greater detail in the pages which follow.

ii. THE ROMAN LITURGY *c.* AD 220 ACCORDING TO THE CHURCH ORDER OF HIPPOLYTUS

Until the First World War, the so-called Leonine Sacramentary—a private collection of mass prayers, which, written over a considerable period of time by individual popes and preserved in the papal archives, was completed *c.* AD 550—was considered to be the oldest Roman liturgical book. But in the years 1910 and 1916 respectively, the German philologist Edward Schwartz and the English Benedictine Dom Hugh Connolly conclusively established the fact that the document hitherto known as the 'Egyptian Church Order' embodied a yet more ancient book from the City of Rome than the Leonine Sacramentary just mentioned and that this book indeed was none other than the manual which Hippolytus, the Roman anti-Pope who later died in the mines of Sardinia, compiled *c.* AD 220 under the title of the 'Apostolic Tradition'. It had been known for a long time that Hippolytus had written such a work. For in 1551 a marble statue of this remarkable man was discovered which represents him seated in a professorial chair, on the right hand side of which is inscribed a list of his writings. The list includes a book with the title, in Greek, ἡ Ἀποστολικὴ παράδοσις, i.e. the 'Apostolic Tradition', which has now been identified and restored to us.

The significance of this discovery can hardly be overestimated. At a single stroke we have secured a fixed point in the somewhat obscure early history of the Roman liturgy. The account of the rite of baptism and of the celebration of the eucharist which the philosopher Justin Martyr, who lived in Rome, had inserted seventy years earlier in his *Apology* (ch. 61, 65–7) is indeed extremely valuable by reason of its early date, but nevertheless too meagre. By contrast, Hippolytus enables us to see the entire compass of the liturgy of the age of the martyrs. The objection might be raised that perhaps Hippolytus, the head of a schismatic community, did not incorporate in his book the traditional practices of Rome, but gave us a wholly new Order drawn up by himself or even (as J. M. Hanssens has suggested) one which had been imported from Alexandria. But this objection overlooks the fact that in his struggle with Pope Callistus, Hippolytus was pre-eminently the one to defend tradition, the ardent spokesman of conservative circles in Rome. Moreover the fact that, shortly after its composition, Hippolytus's treatise was in use for several centuries in the most widely separated provinces of the Church, not only in the West but predominantly in the East, either in the original text, in translation, or in the form of adaptations in varying degrees of closeness to the original—all this is proof that it was considered a wholly orthodox collection of liturgical regulations and one consonant with tradition. We may even conclude from the extensive use made of it over several centuries that it met a deeply felt need. It seems probable that Hippolytus's work was the first book to supply not merely the main themes of the prayer to be improvised upon, but rather a pattern of fixed prayer formulas for the liturgy.

If we are correct in making such an assumption, then Hippolytus's book marks a decisive turning point in the history of the liturgy. The age of the predominance of charismatic leaders of the liturgy who spoke by the inspiration of the Holy Ghost was coming to an end, especially (as is understandable) in the smaller communities whose bishops were not so well educated and less conscious of the authority that had been conferred upon them. These gladly renounced their right to improvise, a task to which they did not feel themselves equal, and now began the era of more or less fixed formulas and formularies, and with it the era of statutory liturgical regulations and ever-increasing uniformity. The multiformity of local custom yielded gradually to uniformity over a wider area.

It is sad for us that Hippolytus's book has not been preserved in the original Greek, but only in Latin, Sahidic, Bohairic, Arabian and Ethiopian translations, as well as in Greek, Syrian, and Arabic adaptations. Great efforts are being made in research to reconstruct the original text, as far as is possible, by means of a careful collation of the evidence. The first attempt at a critical edition, presented to us in 1937 by the Anglican Benedictine, Dom Gregory Dix, was followed in 1963 by another which we owe to the Belgian Benedictine, Dom Bernard Botte, a philologically very satisfying edition which will remain a standard one for some time. At all events, we know all that we need to know about this text for our purposes today. We know how Hippolytus's book was constructed and are in a position to enumerate the set liturgical forms which the book prescribed and say what each of these looked like. And whereas in the oldest Church Order known to us —the *Teaching of the Twelve Apostles* (the Didache, which must have originated *c.* AD 100 in the region of Antioch, the capital of Syria)—disciplinary instructions had far outweighed liturgical directives, in Hippolytus the situation is reversed, for the liturgical interest is predominant, and discipline takes only a secondary place.

His book, we find, contains the ordination of bishops, presbyters, and deacons, the appointment of widows, lectors, and subdeacons, and the consecration of virgins (widowhood and virginity were particular ecclesiastical states). Further on, it deals with the catechumenate, baptism, and confirmation, and finally with fasting, the agapes, and the hours of prayer.

Candidates for baptism in Rome in those days underwent a catechumenate lasting three years. No one was admitted to the catechumenate without someone to testify as to his good conduct, and these sponsors were probably those very persons whom Hippolytus mentions, whose duty it was to keep a watching eye on the behaviour of the candidates and, if need be, advise against their admission to baptism. Already by Hippolytus's time the fixed day for baptism was the Easter Vigil. Among the ceremonies connected with the catechumenate and baptism which he describes are to be found already the breathings of the rite of exorcism, the laying-on of hands and the signing with the Cross, and the renunciations and anointings, all of which form a part of our baptismal ceremonies today and which make our rite so difficult for modern man to understand. The baptism itself was already preceded by the blessing of the baptismal water.

On the other hand baptism in the name of the Trinity (which is our practice today) was as yet unknown, and was to remain so until the Middle Ages. By contrast, baptism was administered at the moment when the candidate made his threefold confession of faith, and this confession was arranged in the form of questions and answers. This form will have lain close at hand in the usages of the Roman law of contract. For baptism is indeed the sealing of the reception of the convert into the community of the faithful and, according to the legal mentality of the Romans, such an act included the making of a contract between the neophyte and Christ; this was his oath (*sacramentum*), his baptismal promise. And the Romans liked to clothe such pledges in the form of a carefully worked-out question-and-answer dialogue.

By the time Hippolytus was writing, infant baptism was by no means an unusual phenomenon. Even babes in arms were not excluded from baptism and their parents or some member of the family made the baptismal promises on their behalf. The latter in all probability took the child from the font and saw to his religious and moral upbringing; hence the origin of the Church's system of godparents.

We learn also from Hippolytus that at the evening agapes, the ceremony of bringing in lighted lamps played an important part. A special prayer of thanksgiving was said over the lamps, and, as Franz Joseph Dölger has so admirably demonstrated, the solemn welcome of the 'Lumen Christi' during the liturgy of the Paschal Vigil is a rite which stands in direct line of succession to the custom described by Hippolytus.

The account of the ceremonies of the celebration of the eucharist occurs twice, once within the context of the rite for the ordination of a bishop, and again, in a shorter form, in the description of the rite of baptism, though with supplements added to suit this special occasion. In the first of these accounts, mention is made of the thanksgiving pronounced not only over the oblations of bread and wine, but also over other gifts, namely oil, cheese and olives. In a later section of the book, Hippolytus mentions the presentation of offerings other than bread and wine, i.e. the first fruits, flowers, etc., and also the thanksgiving. It is not made clear, however, whether or not this thanksgiving was a part of the eucharistic prayer itself or whether it was a different thanksgiving pronounced separately over the other gifts.

Hippolytus gives the following indications and directions as to how the eucharist is to be celebrated:

1. The faithful offer their gifts. From these gifts the deacons take bread and wine and present them to the bishop.
2. The bishop pronounces over these gifts the solemn eucharistic prayer (Eucharisteia) which opens with the dialogue which we still use today. According to Hippolytus's text, the eucharistic prayer includes a short 'institution narrative', an anamnesis (i.e. the making of a memorial of the death and resurrection of

the Lord), an epiclesis (the calling-down of the Holy Spirit upon the bread and wine), and a concluding doxology, to which the congregation responds 'Amen'.

3. The bread over which eucharist has been made is then broken and distributed; in the same manner, the consecrated wine is given to everyone. At the eucharist of the Easter Vigil, the newly baptized drink, in addition, from other chalices which are filled with milk sweetened with honey, and with water, both of which have had a thanksgiving pronounced over them earlier in the service.

From Hippolytus's description, we may judge that the three actions of the eucharist which we have enumerated were performed quite simply without any special attention to ceremonial formalities. It is noteworthy that Hippolytus makes no mention of the deacon's summoning the attention of the people with the words 'Listen, attend' (προσχῶμεν), nor of the deacon's admonition, 'Sancta sanctis'—'the holy things [only] for the holy people!' It is possible, nevertheless, that both of these (or something similar) were in use at this time. It is expressly stated that Sunday is the day for celebrating the eucharist.

It is remarkable too that Hippolytus's description of the eucharistic liturgy agrees, as to its positive statements, in every respect with the short account given by Justin Martyr; it appears however to be silent on the subject of two elements in the introduction to the rite, both of which are expressly mentioned by Justin, namely the intercessory Prayer of the Faithful which is said before the celebration proper begins, and the exchange of the kiss of peace which comes at the end of this prayer. Neither of these elements is in fact lacking, as is revealed by certain indications in both of the sections of Hippolytus's book that we have been considering.

According to Justin Martyr, immediately before the eucharist there was a Service of the Word with lections and a sermon. Hippolytus, it is true, makes mention of clerical groups of lectors, and of catechizings which often took place in the early morning on weekdays. But how and when the lectors went about their business, and whether or not at least part of the catechizing was connected with the Sunday morning eucharist, remains wholly uncertain. For Hippolytus's book, as is only too evident, is by no means a complete Church Order.

The basic features of the Roman Canon today are already discernible in Hippolytus's eucharistic prayer of thanksgiving. Hans Lietzmann, the Berlin liturgical historian who died in 1942, in analysing Hippolytus's eucharistic prayer, came to the conclusion that this prayer is in fact a direct development from the eucharistic prayer which circulated in the churches of Saint Paul. Whether or not he is right in drawing such a conclusion is a matter which remains to be resolved. But Hippolytus's text is in any case so important that it deserves to be given here in full.

Bishop: The Lord be with you.
People: And with thy Spirit.
Bishop: Lift up your hearts.
People: We have raised them up to the Lord.
Bishop: Let us give thanks to the Lord.
People: It is right and fitting.
Bishop: We give Thee thanks, O God, through Thy beloved Son, Jesus Christ, whom in these last times Thou didst send to us to be a Saviour, and Redeemer and the Messenger of Thy counsel,

Who is Thy Word inseparable from Thee, through Whom Thou madest all things and in Whom Thou wast well-pleased,

Whom Thou didst send from heaven into the Virgin's womb,

Who being made Flesh was demonstrated to be Thy Son, being born of the Holy Spirit and the Virgin,

Who fulfilling Thy will and obtaining for Thee a holy people, stretched forth His hands in suffering that He might release from sufferings those who believe in Thee,

Who, when He surrendered Himself to voluntary suffering that He might break the power of death and tear asunder the bonds of the devil, tread Hell under foot, enlighten the righteous, bring their captivity to an end, and show them the Resurrection,

Took bread, and giving thanks unto Thee said: 'Take and eat. This is my body which will be broken for you.'

Likewise also, He took the cup and said: 'This is my blood which is shed for you.

As often as you do this, do it in remembrance of me.'

Having therefore in remembrance His death and Resurrection we offer unto Thee the Bread and the cup and thank Thee that Thou hast found us worthy to stand before Thee and to minister unto Thee, and we pray Thee to send Thy Holy Spirit upon the oblation of Thy Holy Church and grant to all Thy Saints [i.e. Christians] who partake of these that they may be one and filled with the Holy Spirit and confirmed in the true faith.

That they may praise Thee and glorify Thee through Thy Son, Jesus Christ,

Through Whom glory and honour be unto Thee, the Father, and the Son, with the Holy Ghost in Thy holy Church

Now and for ever and world without end.

People: Amen.

As the text reveals, in Hippolytus's time there was still no Sanctus, which when it was later introduced (in the fourth century?) probably led to the gradual breaking-up of the eucharistic prayer. But there can be found no trace in Hippolytus of certain other elements in the Canon which we use today, no Mementos of the living and the dead and no double commemoration of the saints. But, on the other hand, we certainly find in it the traditional elements of the Christian eucharistic prayer; the giving of thanks for the mighty acts of creation and redemption, the institution narrative, the anamnesis, the epiclesis, and the doxology. In fact the eucharistic prayer, as those who read it will have sensed, was, in essence, then exactly what it is today. We are therefore able, thanks to the discovery of Schwartz and Connolly, to survey at least the main outlines of the growth of the eucharistic prayer over a period of 1,900 years.

It must be left to the reader to reflect on what bearing these insights have on the manner in which each of us takes his part in the liturgy. I would however particularly like to draw attention to some fine observations made by Anton Baumstark at the beginning of his short book, *The History of the Development of the Liturgy*, in a passage which he devotes to the subject of 'that sense of community which transcends the limitations of time' (*überzeitliches Gemeinschaftsbewusstsein*). Baumstark says that he who prays liturgically, sees himself

as one of a great multitude of people who at one and the same moment lift their hands in praise, thanks, and supplication, offer the eucharistic sacrifice or take part in its offering. . . . At the same time he feels himself to be at the point which links those who before him, since the very earliest days of Christianity, have offered prayer and sacrifice with those who in time to come will be offering the same prayer and the same sacrifice, long after the last fragments of his mortal remains have crumbled to dust.

iii. FROM GREEK TO LATIN AS THE LANGUAGE OF THE LITURGY

It is clear from the list of Hippolytus's writings and those books of his which we still possess that the language spoken by the Roman Christian congregation of his day was still Greek. This is not to be wondered at; for down to the middle of the third century, a considerable section of the Roman population spoke or at least understood Greek. Nor must we forget that of those who lived in the Eternal City only a minority were Roman in origin or born and bred in the Italian provinces. For the most part they were freemen or slaves who had come to the Eternal City from the Middle East. Moreover, the upper classes of society had set a high value on acquiring for themselves a Greek education, and were fully convinced of its superiority. The liturgy of the Roman church, therefore, was also in Greek. How long, we may ask, did this continue?

A hundred and fifty years after Hippolytus, the Roman writer Marius Victorinus quoted a fragment of the Roman Canon in a work of his, written in Latin. In the middle of his Latin text, when he comes to the Canon, he goes over without comment to Greek (*PL* 8, 1094D), which is a sure sign that at that date at least, the Canon, if not indeed all the mass prayers, was said, or rather 'recited'—we would say 'sung'—in Greek. Only twenty years after this, another Roman writer, the so-called Ambrosiaster, again quoted a fragment of the Canon, but this time in Latin (*CSEL* 50, 268). If we further observe that there is a close affinity between the language of the Latin Canon and the style and expressions of certain Roman writers of the end of the fourth century, we may assert with some certainty that around the year 380 (i.e. in the time of Pope Damasus) the Latin tongue worked its way into the very heart of the Roman mass, the Canon itself, and it seems likely that before this the Latin tongue had already established itself as the language of the Service of the Word and of the liturgy for the other sacraments.

Was, however, the Latin Canon which came into being in the fourth century something completely new? Or did it arise from the translation of a Greek original? Some years ago Anton Baumstark endeavoured to defend the latter thesis. He argued that the phrase in the Canon, 'summus sacerdos tuus Melchisedech', may have been worded in this strange way (which differs from the text of the Bible) owing to an error in translation. To be more precise, when the Greek Canon was translated into Latin, the translator, foundering on the difficulties of the Greek modes of expression, made of a 'Priest of God Most High', a 'Most High Priest of God'.

But, however perceptive and compelling Baumstark's argument may once have seemed (Albert Erhard, himself a first-rate scholar, considered Baumstark's discovery to be as inspired as it was correct), it cannot now stand up to a more radical testing. For even if we suppose that an error of translation underlies this phrase in the Canon, must it have been the author of the Canon who made the mistake? May not in fact the writer of the Canon have taken the expression from an already existing text, i.e. from the Latin Bible? A conclusive observation, however, has been made by Dom Bernard Botte. He was the first person to recognize that *c.* 380 Melchisedech was already termed 'High Priest', even in the Greek-speaking East. Hence the Latin rendering in question certainly need not have arisen from an erroneous translation of the Canon, and probably corresponded at that time to a designation already generally current of the Old Testament Priest-King.

On the other hand, the Latin Canon in use during the declining years of the fourth century, the full text of which we unfortunately do not know, was certainly not something wholly new. Over the centuries, a fixed pattern for the Eucharisteia, the great prayer of thanksgiving which gave the rite its name, had been constructed, a pattern moreover which was followed in the East and West alike. It was the universal practice to incorporate into the Eucharisteia the institution narrative, as well as an epiclesis (i.e. a prayer calling the Holy Ghost down upon the Bread and Wine), an anamnesis (i.e. a prayer which, coming after the institution narrative, declares the eucharist to be a commemoration of the Passion, Resurrection, and Ascension), a prayer asking that the oblations may be received (i.e. the actual prayer which offers the sacrifice), and finally a reference to the angels who surround the altar. Together with those elements of the pattern of the prayer we have just mentioned, there were also certain formulas and expressions which had become the common property of churches almost everywhere. It was the accepted rule that one began with the dialogue between bishops and people ('Lift up your hearts', 'We have raised them up to the Lord', 'Let us give thanks to the Lord our God', 'It is right and fitting'), that the transition from the institution narrative to the anamnesis was made with the expression, 'having in remembrance therefore' that the eucharistic gifts were described as a 'pneumatic (spiritual) sacrifice', and that the whole of this solemn prayer was concluded with a doxology. Most of these ideas and expressions were already contained in the eucharistic prayer at the time of Hippolytus (a conclusion which may be drawn from the text we have already quoted), and only a few were added at a later date.

Hence we may sum up by saying that when the transition was made from Greek to Latin in the eucharistic prayer and the text was given a new form, the traditional stream of thought was preserved, while certain expressions newly composed in the spirit of the Latin tongue and consecrated by previous usage, were adopted. This account of what happened would be a sufficient explanation of the similarities which we have already noticed between the Canon of Hippolytus and our own.

In this connection, Dom Odo Casel, the well-known Benedictine scholar who died some years ago, made the very significant observation that the peculiar description of the eucharistic sacrifice as *oblatio rationabilis*, i.e. as a 'pneumatic', or spiritual' sacrifice', which is already met with in the Roman Canon of the fourth century finds its only linguistic parallel in Saint Ambrose of Milan. This important observation, together with our knowledge that the earliest evidence for the existence of our Latin Canon comes from Milan (*De Sacramentis* 4, 21–7), forms the basis of the conjecture (which receives additional support from other considerations) that the Latin Canon which came into being in the fourth century and is still in use today was the creation not of a Bishop of Rome but of the greater restorer of the liturgy at Milan. In this case it would follow that the complete transition from Greek to Latin as the language of the liturgy was first carried through, not at Rome but at Milan. Ambrose and not Damasus would have to be accounted the pioneer of the Latin liturgy on Italian soil, though we should still owe a great deal to Damasus for having secured general recognition for the bold step taken by the Bishop of Milan by giving it the authoritative support of the Roman See. There are, however, some chronological difficulties, and some observations have been made concerning the language of these texts which compel us to abandon this theory.

On the other hand, there are many who favour the theory that the earliest attempts at a Latin liturgy were made neither in Rome nor in Milan but in the Roman provinces of North Africa, principally in Carthage. For at a time when the bishops and theologians of Italy were still speaking and writing in Greek (i.e. at the beginning of the third century) the church of North Africa had already made the transition to the use of the Latin tongue. In these circumstances, is it reasonable to expect that they should have continued to use Greek as the language of their worship? At present we have not sufficient evidence to provide an answer to this question.

When we reflect, however, that the Latin language began to predominate in the cities of the West at the latest in about 300, i.e. roughly at the date at which the popes began to set Latin instead of Greek inscriptions on the tombs of their predecessors, we must necessarily conclude that for at least eighty years, the language of the liturgy in the West was at variance with that of the people. In those days, too, there had already come into being that cleft between the language of the liturgy and the language of the people which is giving us such trouble today. Many bewail this as an unhappy event, whereas others see it as the work of Providence, since this distinction between the language of the liturgy and every-day speech gives people a far greater sense of the mysterious character of the liturgy.

We can, however, learn a great deal from the fact that the early Church only tolerated this cleft between the language of the liturgy and that of the people as a passing phenomenon. In the end it had no hesitation in abandoning Greek which had been the language of religious worship in the apostolic age and the age of the martyrs in favour of the Latin vernacular.

The observations recorded by Ambrosiaster (*PL* 17, 269) at the time clearly reveal that the authorities in the Church were conscious that in making this change, they were acting along the lines laid down by Saint Paul. Saint Paul had made it a rule, having in mind chiefly the role played by the charismatics in the liturgy of the community, that liturgical prayer should be intelligible to the congregation, on the ground that the congregation should make it its own, should assent to it with its 'Amen', and should also be able to derive from it a measure of edification.

I will pray with the spirit (i.e. moved by the Holy Spirit) [he writes], and I will pray with the understanding also. . . . Otherwise, if you bless with the spirit [i.e. with the unintelligible ecstatic sounds of those filled with the Spirit], how can anyone in the position of an outsider say the 'Amen' to your thanksgiving when he does not know what you are saying? For you may give thanks well enough, but the other man is not edified (I Cor. 14.15–17).

Nobody, however, in the more sober atmosphere of fourth-century Rome, realized that the strange sounds uttered by the charismatics at Corinth when celebrating the liturgy were simply an expression of the fact that they were in an ecstatic state. Further, according to the opinion of the Roman theologians of this time, if Saint Paul took exception to the 'speaking with tongues' of the charismatic celebrants, he must have meant that they spoke in a foreign language which nobody could understand. Presumably Saint Paul would never have objected to such an interpretation of his views, for neither speaking with tongues, nor the use of a foreign language, was compatible with the liturgy as he understood it.

It is important that we do not lose sight of the facts we have just set out, especially at a time when the question of the use of the vernacular in the liturgy is occupying people's minds. We are only following the example of the liturgy in the classical age and the principles established by Saint Paul if we support the demand that the liturgy must also be comprehensible to the man in the street. This applies especially to the instructional part of the service, i.e. to the lections, which ought in themselves to serve as a means of religious instruction for the people, and ought therefore to be heard in such a way that they can be understood. They should moreover be read by the celebrant direct, and not heard in a roundabout way by means of a simultaneous translation. This demand for comprehensibility applies also to the prayers of the liturgy, first and foremost to its most prominent and central part, the eucharistic prayer, for it is to this that Saint Paul's comments (which we have already mentioned) refer. Just as the Latin-speaking Church of the third and fourth centuries was not afraid to forsake altogether the Greek eucharistic prayer which had been handed down to them, and to construct an entirely new 'Canon', so too we today cannot continue to evade making such a decision, the less so since, in our present liturgy, we no longer possess the text of the Canon which was composed in the fourth century, nor can we even make a reliable reconstruction of it. The original text undoubtedly revealed all that was best in the Latin prayers which were written at that time; it certainly reproduced the traditional elements of the eucharistic prayer in a clear yet at the same time elegant Latin style. The remnants of this text in our modern Missal reveal that, not only has much been added to it during the centuries which led up to Gregory the Great, in a way which accorded neither with its basic pattern of thought nor with its grammatical construction (i.e. by the introduction of an intercession for the Church and her leaders, the Memento of the living and the dead, and the double commemoration of the saints), but also, over the centuries which followed, it has been the victim of some clumsy reforms (i.e. prayer endings and 'Amens' have been inserted together with signs of the cross). No longer do we see before us today that majestic and orderly inner sanctuary which at one time crowned the structure of the eucharistic liturgy, but a chapel whose architecture has run wild and is cluttered with turrets and bays in such a way that the untrained eye can scarcely detect its basic outline. The historian will retain his affection for such a building despite all this since it can tell him much about trends in the liturgy of centuries past. But our congregations are not made up of historians; they need a holy temple in which each may feel at home and by means of which they can feel themselves, in the Pauline sense, to be genuinely edified.

We must, then, be careful of abandoning too quickly the Latin Canon that has been in use up till now as with the ancient church, it may take us a full century of reflection and experimentation to acquire a new and fully mature form of the Canon.

iv. WAS THE ROMAN LITURGY A MYSTERY RITE?

The liturgical Greek of Hippolytus and still more the Latin of the so-called Leonine Sacramentary and of the other early collections is interspersed with expressions which, as the philologists recognize, derive from the language of the pagan rites of antiquity and especially that of the mystery religions. We refer here to words such as *mysterium, actio, memoria, illuminatio, invocatio*, and their Greek equivalents. We are bound therefore to inquire whether these expressions, when taken over into the Christian liturgy, retained the concrete meaning associated with them in ancient pagan worship, or whether, on the other hand, at the moment of their adoption by the Church they acquired a new and perhaps abstract and spiritual significance. To make the problem clear by an example: had the word *mysterium* in these early liturgical prayers already come to mean a 'secret', or did it still retain its classical meaning of a 'sacred consecratory action'?

Dom Odo Casel, who examined this question in numerous studies (mainly of a philosophical nature), soon came to the conclusion that the expressions in question continued to retain their traditional meaning even within the framework of the Christian liturgy. On the basis of these philological investigations, he concluded that the compilers of the Roman liturgy must have regarded the celebration of the eucharist and the administration of the sacraments as sacred mystery rites (in the sense in which that term was currently understood in antiquity), that is to say as rites which beneath a symbolical exterior renewed the salvific actions of the Saviour-God, giving them a mystical yet real presence. Casel thought he could establish by means of an extensive list of references that this view of the matter represented no mere passing current of opinion of the third and fourth centuries, but was the universally held conviction of the Church from the time of Saint Paul down to the classical age of Scholasticism.

According to Casel's so-called 'mystery-doctrine' (*Mysterienlehre*), we should now interpret the liturgy in the following manner: all liturgical actions, the celebration of the eucharist as well as the rites of the sacraments, the Church's year as a whole, and each separate festival—all are in essence 'mysteries' (*Kultmysterien*), in the sense in which that term was understood in the ancient world. Each of these actions in its own particular way serves to make real and present once more the saving activity of Jesus Christ which itself is the 'primal mystery' (*Urmysterium*). But it is not only the person of the ascended Lord who becomes present in these rites: together with Him is made present all that he has taken upon himself for our redemption, his incarnation, his life of humility, his death on the Cross, and his resurrection. Now the reality of this act of bringing these mysteries into the present is of a very special kind; it is a reality to which one can only have access by faith, and not by reason. One is therefore justified in speaking of a 'sacramental' or 'mystical' reality, and of a 'presence in a mystery' of the saving events. By saying that the saving events were 'present in a mystery', we do not mean, however, that the Lord's acts of redemption in history were re-enacted in the mystery cults; still less does this mean that the saving activity of Jesus is made present simply by a subjective act of remembering. Rather should we say that these events, together with the person of the Lord are in their entirety objectively and really present, even though there is something hidden about their reality. The purpose of this 'mystery presence' of the saving work of Christ in the rites of the mysteries is to allow the faithful to participate directly in the life, death, and resurrection of the Lord, and so to effect an intimate association between them and their Lord. It has already been suggested that the function of the mystery rites is to make accessible to the faithful the fruits of the redemption, i.e. the grace of salvation, and such, as is well known, traditional sacramental theology is considered to be the proper sense of all liturgical rites. But according to Casel, the meaning of liturgical actions is not exhausted by saying that their function is to apply to us the grace of salvation; their purpose is further to effect the mystical presence of the Lord with his saving activity, so that by bringing this 'mystery presence' close to the believer, there is also brought close to him and made accessible for him the grace of salvation; for grace flows, so to speak, to the believer from the Lord himself who has been made present together with his redeeming activity.

Let us now apply what we have said in a more concrete fashion to at least some of the mystery cults. In the eucharistic mystery rite, for example, it is primarily the sacrifice of Christ on the Cross that is made present in a mystery, though included with this simultaneously are all his other acts of redemption. In the baptismal mystery cult, it is primarily the death of Christ that is made present (as Saint Paul teaches in Romans 6.2–11), in order that the candidate may become involved in this dying and rising again, and thus be endowed with divine grace; in this case also, though the death of Jesus forms the basic content of the mystery rite, his other saving activities are also made present. The purpose of the liturgical year and its feasts is to unfold in all its richness the mystery of our redemption and to make it mystically present for us by giving each liturgical day a special emphasis at the celebration of the eucharist.

Casel has set out this theory in an immense number of articles and books and has both expanded it and defended it against his critics. Any who immerse themselves in these writings will be amazed at the scope of the author's learning, the richness of his ideas, as well as at his eloquence in setting them forth. Nor can they fail to be moved by the warm though well-controlled enthusiasm which comes out in everything that he writes. We soon feel that we are here dealing not so much with a philologist or top-ranking historian who is defending a technical discovery which is of merely relative significance, but rather with a prophet who is proclaiming a hidden knowledge which has been granted to him by the special grace of heaven and which it is his solemn duty to pass on. Filled with an unshakeable sense of mission, and not in the least daunted by the number or importance of his critics, Casel to the very last held firmly to the conviction that it was his duty to make available once more to his Church the treasures of doctrine that had been buried over the course of centuries, a doctrine moreover for which the Divine Teacher had prepared mankind by means of the pagan mystery religions. Like all prophetic personalities, Casel attracted a great following in his day; his influence was considerable and it still continues to be felt. The other side of the picture is that Casel, like other prophets, could be impatient and intolerant, especially when he sensed a lack of followers and when he underwent criticism; there are many of his contemporaries alive today who could enlarge on this aspect of his life. But, at the same time, gifted men of this kind and of this stature are much needed both in the world and in the Church. They shake us up and show us new paths and we must be thankful for the effect they have on us, even if we cannot always follow them.

After these preliminary observations we must come now to the key question. Is Casel's 'mystery doctrine' in fact historically correct? It must be admitted that he has not succeeded in his attempt to provide overwhelming proof for his theory that the 'mystery doctrine' was in fact taught in the early Church. It has been shown that this idea of mystery occurs only in a few places in the early Church and is found in only à very few of the Fathers. For example, even John Chrysostom, who is àn important witness of the teachings of tradition, remains quite untouched by the mystery doctrine in Casel's sense of the term, as Gerhard Fittkau has shown in a careful piece of research. Nor is there any trace of this teaching even in the Latin prayers of the Roman liturgy. Casel has defended with particular obstinacy the view that the Proper of the mass for the ninth Sunday after Pentecost shows quite clearly in the Secret the mark of the mystery doctrine. There it reads: 'Concede nobis, quae sumus Domine, haec digne frequentare mysteria, quia, quoties huius hostiae commemoratio celebratur, opus nostrae redemptionis exercetur'. Casel, and with him Urban Bomm in his Missal, translates this as follows: 'Grant to us, Lord, we beseech thee, that we may perform these mysteries as frequently as they deserve to be celebrated; for as often as we celebrate the memorial of this sacrifice, the work of our redemption is effected.' This translation of Casel and Bomm, however, reads into the text something which is not actually there. As Walter Diezinger has finally shown, the prayer only purports to say that the celebration of the memorial of Jesus's sacrifice on the Cross, which is performed in the eucharist ('huius hostiae commemoratio'), effects the redemption of mankind ('opus nostrae redemptionis exercetur'). Other Latin formularies adduced by Casel are still less suited to a proof of the presence of his mystery doctrine in the primitive Church.

After what has just been said, there can be no question of Casel's 'mystery theology' having been a doctrine which was taught universally by the Church from the beginning, and therefore it cannot claim to be recognized as a basic element which together with Holy Scripture is the source and standard of our faith. What Casel proposes is simply the opinion of a modern theologian, a 'theologoumenon' which indeed is not entirely without precedent in the early Church and perhaps even a matter with which Saint Paul was concerned. Theological debates of the future will have the task of determining how much (despite what we have said) can be taken from Casel's theories and built into the Church's sacramental theology. Certainly it would appear that in the future we shall never be able to speak about the liturgy in general and the sacraments in particular in quite the same way as we used to speak about them before Casel made his ideas known. This is not to say, however, that before him our teaching on this subject had been riddled with errors. But over the years the Church, under the influence of specific currents of thought in certain periods, has concentrated its attention in its teaching all too much on the question of the validity and objective efficacity of those rites which we commonly call the 'means of grace', and has allowed more important matters to fall gradually into the background. So too insufficient consideration has been given to the fact that not only the eucharist, but also the sacraments, the sacramentals, the liturgical year and its feasts, each in its own particular way, constitute an encounter between mankind and the ascended Christ, and lays mankind open to the activity of Christ Himself in our salvation. At one time the traditional teaching of the Church did not properly take into account the fact that in virtue of this unifying factor which binds all the elements of the liturgy together (i.e. the personal activity of Christ Himself), liturgical rites and especially the sacraments do not exist in isolation from and independently of one another, but constitute a closed and harmonious system. And it is this that Casel has once more enabled us to see.

It must not be overlooked, however, that Casel has another great merit which he acquired from his schooling in a style of classical philology which was particularly patient of application to the history of religion. He managed by dint of careful research to restore to many a liturgical phrase, rite, and feast its full original meaning. It is to be hoped that his scattered series of published articles on this subject will soon be made available in a collected edition (i.e. his treatises on the formula *oblatio rationabilis*, on the liturgical words *actio* and *munus*, on the symbolism of pearls and light, on the 'Exultet' and the Blessing of the New Fire, and on the discipline of silence).

Finally we must recall once more a more general sense in which we are in Casel's debt, one to which we have already drawn attention. Casel, more than anyone else, by his prophetic warnings and by his pertinacity shook up the Catholic theology of his day, had fermented in it a state of healthy unrest. It is to be hoped that his influence will have far-reaching effects for some considerable time and will continue to bear fruit.

v. THE POSITION OF CHRIST IN THE PRAYERS OF THE LITURGY

Joseph Andreas Jungmann, the author of that great work on the mass, began, in his younger days, some research on the position of Christ in the prayers of the liturgy which has since proved very fruitful. It had long been observed that though it is true that primitive Christian acclamations like 'Kyrie eleison' and the 'Gloria in excelsis Deo' (which is in fact a series of acclamations that have been strung together) are addressed to Christ, yet the actual prayers of the liturgy are directed almost exclusively to God the Father and that Christ is only allowed to take His place in them as the high-priestly Mediator. These early Christian prayers, therefore, are arranged according to a basic and invariable pattern as follows: 'Deus qui . . .; concede, ut . . . per dominum nostrum Jesum Christum, qui tecum vivit et regnat . . .' (O God, who . . . grant that . . . through Jesus Christ Our Lord who liveth and reigneth . . .). The situation is reversed in the prayers of the Middle Ages and more recent times, which are addressed by preference to Christ Himself. The pattern for these is as follows: 'Domine Jesu Christe, qui . . .; concede, ut . . ., qui vivis et regnas cum Deo Patre . . .' (O Lord Jesus Christ, who . . . grant that . . ., who livest and reignest with God the Father . . .).

When and in what circumstances did this change in the arrangement of the prayers take place? This question has often been asked, but no one has really known how to answer it. Jungmann

proved conclusively on the basis of a careful collation of all relative liturgical texts that the impulse to this change came from the
struggle which occupied the greater part of the fourth century
with the Arians. These heretics were contesting the fact that
the Son was equal in essence to the Father. This quarrel with
the Arians resulted in a stronger emphasis being placed upon the
divinity of Christ and at the same time brought about a weaken-
ing of the conception of the high priesthood of the Man Christ
Jesus and of his role as mediator, which has been so strongly
stressed by the Lord Himself (John 16.23, etc.) and with just as
much emphasis by the Apostles (I Tim. 2.5; I John 2.2; Hebr.
4.14, etc.). It so happened, therefore, that first in the East and
then (under eastern influence) gradually in Gaul and in other
parts of the West, the prayers of the liturgy were by preference
addressed to Christ. Two African synods which met at Hippo in
393 and at Carthage in 397 (both of which were, no doubt, heavily
influenced by Saint Augustine) vigorously opposed this innovation and held categorically to the view (canon 21 cf. 23) that 'at
the service of the altar, prayer shall always be addressed to the
Father'. But this objection, though rooted in Scripture and
tradition, was in the long run to be of no avail. Certainly the
Roman Church at least remained loyal to this older tradition right
up to the end of the first millennium, though this was due more
to its innate dislike for change in liturgical matters than to the fact
that it had consciously and theologically made up its mind. But
when, in the second half of the ninth century, the variants that
had developed in the Roman liturgy on Gallo-Frankish territory
were officially adopted (I shall have more to say later about this
historical process), there appeared at the same time in Rome as
well liturgical prayers which began with an address to Christ.
This general loosening up of the formal style of the prayers
helped (together with other factors) to prepare the ground for a
kind of piety both personal and liturgical which centred on Jesus,
His incarnate life and Passion, and His presence in the eucharist,
which blossomed extensively in the Middle Ages and which
persists up to the present day.

Now it is true that we should not and indeed cannot reverse the course of the development I have just described. But, as Karl Adam has convincingly shown, if we cultivate once more the prayer 'through Jesus Christ Our Lord', we shall not only become conscious again of the order in which the Church's prayers used to be written, but will also recover some religious values which have become almost buried. The especial value of this kind of prayer can be illustrated by a quotation from *Liturgy for the Layman* by Ludwig A. Winterswyl (who follows closely in Casel's footsteps): 'The Christian who prays through Christ to God the Father [he writes] is not just calling upon Christ but is, as it were, placing himself beside Christ who as Man is our brother. Furthermore, when he prays, he enters Christ, he prays from within Christ of whom he is a member by baptism. Prayer through Christ is true Christian prayer and through Christ this prayer is sure to reach the Father. For Christ our Mediator lives and reigns with the Father, one God for ever and ever. And therefore prayer through Christ leads the Christian straight to the Heart of God, to the Holy Trinity in which the Father and the Son in the unity of the Holy Spirit are united from all eternity in the fullness of life and love.'

vi. LITURGICAL DRESS, INSIGNIA, AND PRIVILEGES

There is little of a conclusive nature that recent investigation can tell us about the beginnings of liturgical dress and insignia and about the origins of the ceremonial with which the celebration of pontifical high mass (i.e. mass celebrated by the bishop) is invested. The oldest ritual authorities, the so-called 'Ordines' take us back only as far as the seventh century, and at this stage we find that the development is already far advanced or if we take as our sole authority the development that had taken place in the city of Rome, then it was in fact by this time complete. These 'Ordines' do not, however, provide us with an answer as to when genuflexion to the Pope, the kissing of his foot and hand, the practice of covering the hands for certain actions, the throne, incense, and lights made their way into the liturgy, nor as to when the bishop and priests first wore their characteristic vestments and insignia such as the ring, the *pallium*, the *mappula* (maniple), and the stole.

About thirty years ago, however, a Hungarian classical historian, Andreas Alfoldi, who is now working in the United States, gave us for the first time a coherent account of the official ceremonial in use at the court of the Roman Emperors. It is indeed surprising how close are the points of contact between the ceremonial of the Roman-Byzantine court and the rules for the papal mass of the seventh century, i.e. the ceremonial which still survives in every pontifical rite and to a more limited extent in every high mass with deacon and subdeacon. The similarities are so great that we cannot escape drawing the conclusion that the privileges and ceremonial belonging to the imperial court and the highest ranking officials were at some time or other transferred to the bishops and other clergy and thus made their way into the liturgy; in association with this, no doubt, there arose the system of insignia and special liturgical dress. It is not quite so easy to explain in detail how this development came about. But I have myself gone to the length of giving at least some account of the origins of this process in an address to the university of Bonn.

To begin with, we ought to be quite safe in saying that the beginnings of this process are to be sought for during the reign of the Emperor Constantine, i.e. between 312 and 337. When Church and State went into partnership under the first Christian emperor, the ruler persuaded the bishops to take over and to exercise some of his own prerogatives. In 318, he handed over to them the power of jurisdiction in civil proceedings between Christians and other Christians, and also between Christians and non-Christians, and no one was allowed to appeal against their judgements. In 316 and 321 he enlisted their help over the question of the legal force of those acts which granted manumission to Christian slaves and in association with this the granting of the rights of citizenship to those who had been made freemen. In all this, however, the pedantic and bureaucratic Roman State saw itself faced with the necessity of assigning to the bishops and to a certain extent their assistants (the priests and deacons) their proper place in the carefully graded social scale of the State and equally of granting them a proper priority when it came to questions of protocol in court. In the process of putting this into practice, the State had also logically to grant to the bishops the titles, insignia, and privileges which corresponded to the rank with which they had been supplied. And since for the most part the bishops were made equal to the highest dignitaries in the land, the *illustres*, they received in addition a number of insignia such as the *lorum* (the *pallium*), the *mappula* (a ceremonial napkin), the *campagi* (a special kind of footwear), the *camalaucum* (a distinctive head-gear), and probably also the golden ring. In the same way, they held certain privileges such as the right to a throne whose height and design were carefully prescribed, the right to be accompanied by lights and incense, and the privilege of being greeted with a kiss of the hand. And since the Bishop of Rome himself had acquired almost the same degree of dignity as the Emperor, like the Emperor he could claim the right to have his portrait hung in public buildings (i.e. in churches), to be greeted on his arrival at church by a choir of singers (whence the origins of the Introit in the eucharist today), to be waited on at the throne and the altar with covered hands and to have people genuflect to him and kiss his foot. Hence it was due to the State that all those privileges which the ceremonial of court provided for the Emperor and the highest of dignitaries were now possessed by the Bishop of Rome and also in correspondingly lesser degrees by his assistants, in so far as these were taken on by the State as judges at law or keepers of the records.

It was understandably a matter for the Church to decide whether and to what extent her dignitaries were to be allowed to make use of such insignia and privileges that had been granted them by the State. When in the third century Paul of Samosata, who functioned as Bishop of Antioch and at the same time held an important position of State in the kingdom of Palmyra, set up in his cathedral a 'podium with a high throne' and built an 'audience room like that of the secular authorities' in his episcopal palace; and when he arranged to be greeted on entering his basilica church, by the chant of a choir of virgins, he aroused great bitterness amongst his fellow-bishops in Syria. He was deposed by a synod at Antioch (Euseb, *H.E.* 7.30-9) though this was not solely on account of this offence. But when, on the other hand, similar privileges were granted to a great number of bishops by the Roman State in the fourth century, views on the matter had changed considerably. So far as we know, only a few bishops were doubtful of ascribing great importance to their official insignia and privileges and of making use of them in worship. These few were certainly among the best of their time: Hilary of Poitiers, Martin of Tours, Fulgentius of Ruspe, and Augustine. The majority were of the opinion, however, that it could only enhance the Church's authority if those who exercised this authority were invested with official badges of rank and surrounded with the splendour of the ceremonies of state.

It lies beyond the scope of this book to provide an answer to that problem of church history as to whether or not the Church did right in binding herself so closely to the State by taking on civil duties and civil privileges. We are concerned however with the question as to what our attitude today ought to be towards the considerable number of elements in our liturgy which have their roots in the imperial privileges granted in the fourth century. But those who want to state their position with regard to this question should be careful not to forget one important thing. And that is that after the fall of the Roman empire, the original insignia and privileges underwent a radical transformation in style, almost to the extent of becoming unrecognizable and moreover, 'spiritualized', i.e. given a religious significance. Hence none of us today when we see a bishop complete with mitre, *pallium*, pastoral staff, ring, and bishop's shoes, accompanied by lights and incense and presiding from canopied throne, has the feeling that here we have a dignitary who is caught up in worldly affairs. On the contrary, in the course of a process which has gone on for centuries the insignia and privileges which were once the symbol of secular power have been so transformed that they now suppress the individuality of the human person who temporarily holds the office and brings to the forefront of our attention the spiritual nature of the high office which he holds. At the most, it is only the bishop's throne which could remind us still of temporal power; and we should therefore welcome the fact that in some cathedral and abbey churches, the throne has been moved back from the position it formerly occupied at the side of the high altar, where it was so noticeable, to the place where at one time the simple bishop's chair used to stand and from which he instructed his people, i.e. to the focal point of the apse and therefor behind the altar. In this position it is no longer equal in importance to the altar, but is made less important.

All things considered, then, this insight into the secular origin of all those elements in our liturgy I have mentioned should make us very wary of ascribing to them too great an importance. One often gets the impression that far too much emphasis is laid today on outward ceremonial at pontifical high mass, a ceremonial which is after all only founded upon the privileges of state of an earlier epoch; and it seems also that the attention of the congregation is distracted more than it should be by this ceremonial from seeing the essential of the liturgy.

We shall be returning to this theme (i.e. the influence of court ceremonial on the ceremonies of the bishop's mass) in the second part of this book. I should in passing, however, once more draw attention to the fact that the feeling which had been awakened in the fourth-century Church for the outward formalities of the imperial court, for the social grades of Court and State with their insignia and privileges, and for the careful distinctions and niceties of palace etiquette, did not have an effect merely on the liturgy. It also served to transform permanently the way in which the person of Jesus Christ was represented. For it was in this century that Christ began to be looked upon as a ruler who as the 'Pantocrator' governed the whole of creation. As a result of this conception whenever Jesus was portrayed in the art of that period he assumed the outward marks of imperial rank; he was the ruler who sat on a throne adorned with jewels and purple cushions, who wore the royal halo, whose foot and hand were kissed, who was surrounded with a heavenly cortege of palace officials and much else besides. This meant that the way in which Mary, the apostles, the angels, and the saints were represented had to be altered to accord with this new development. Hence Mary became the Mother and Empress, the apostles were turned into a senate, the angels now constituted the household of a heavenly court, and the saints were represented as guests seeking audience and bringing their offerings. A change occurred also in the way in which people spoke about such matters. Heaven, the resting place of the glorified Son of God and of his people, become now a *curia* or *palatium*, the heavenly court and palace, of which the imperial palace on earth is basically but a shadowy reflection. Hence there arose a new view of the world which found its fulfilment in the theocratic systems of the Byzantine Empire of the East and of the mediaeval Roman Empire of the West.

vii. THE CHARACTERISTICS OF PRAYER-FORMULAS IN THE ROMAN LITURGY

Research into the earliest period of the history of the Roman liturgy has in the end helped us also towards a clearer conception of the characteristics of this liturgy today. We owe this achievement primarily to the fact that we are now in a position to distinguish between those elements in the prayers and ceremonies which were composed actually in Rome from those which were added from non-Roman sources, and we have even succeeded to a large extent in being able to name the bishops who composed many of the Roman formulas and formularies. Of these bishops, Leo the Great and Gelasius stand out from all the rest by reason of the quantity of their liturgical compositions.

True liturgy should not be the expression in words of the individual's subjective thoughts and feelings, nor of the devotional temperature of his soul; since it is the worship of a community, it should on every occasion consist only of that which the community can make its own. Now the Romans possessed a special gift which they used to create a liturgy of this kind. This gift consisted of their ability to compose ordered and well-constructed formularies. It was manifested equally in their dislike of an excess of emotion and vague sentimentality, of their severe though powerful sense of style, and in the dignified manner in which they publicly presented their liturgy, both inside and outside the Church. During the fourth, fifth, and sixth centuries, the bishops of Rome, by constantly applying themselves to the task, compiled a veritable treasury of liturgical prayers, which in so far as it is objective, clearly thought out, monumental in its structure, concentrates on dogmatic and fundamental truths and expresses man's basic religious aspirations, must be recognized as one of the great classics of mankind.

Now in order to demonstrate the skill of the compilers of this liturgy, yet at the same time to make clear their limitations, we shall give here by way of illustration a Roman Collect for Easter, which runs as follows:

> Deus,
> qui hodierna die per Unigenitum tuum
>   aeternitatis nobis aditum
>   devicta morte reserasti,
> vota nostra
>   quae praeveniendo adspiras
>   etiam adiuvando prosequere—
> per Dominum nostrum Jesum Christum . . .

In the first part of this prayer is contained, in carefully balanced phrases, what Edward Norden (who has studied the history of the forms of religious language) would call a 'relative predicate' (*relativische Prädikation*) applied to God the Father, i.e. an ascription of praise to the Almighty, arranged in the form of a relative clause. The meaning of this predicate, if we express it quite simply, is roughly as follows: 'Thou, O God, on this Easter Day which we commemorate, hast redeemed mankind by Thy Son.' But this reference to and extolling of God's primary act of salvation is not expressed in quite so abstract a fashion, but presents an image like this: 'Thou, O God, hast on this day by Thine only begotten Son, overcome Death (which is here personified) and opened unto us the entrance to heaven.'

Here, however, it should be noticed that in the composition of this picture, the rather plastic expression 'to open up again' is not used of the 'gate of heaven' but rather of an entirely abstract 'way into eternity'. Furthermore, the task of 'opening up', like that of 'overcoming' is not described as being the work of the 'only begotten Son' but as a work which (as dogmatic theology teaches) He has been commissioned to perform and which itself belongs to the Father. Now both these details in the composition of the prayer prevent the faithful from being presented (for them to behold, as it were, with their spiritual eyes) with a picture of Christ the Conqueror, who, having just vanquished Death, walks over him and opens up the gate of heaven with a key. The Roman bishop who composed this Easter Collect has in fact assembled together all those elements necessary for composing a most striking picture, but finally has not actually put them together to make this picture. For in the last resort, he is only concerned to give clear expression to a matter of dogma, and appeals therefore to people's reason and not to their imagination.

If we now look at the second part of the Collect (an earlier edition of which is to be found in the Gelasian Sacramentary, ed. Mohlberg, No. 463), we shall find that our conclusions are confirmed. This second part consists of a request that God the Father, who on the Day of the Resurrection has done such great things for us through His Son, may, in addition to this mighty act, grant to us another, though lesser gift; by His prevenient grace (the prayer says) He has inspired His people to the making of their *vota* (prayer and sacrifice) this Easter Sunday; may he now crown His work and make His people turn their act of piety to good effect.

After our experiences with the first part of the Collect, we naturally hunt around on this occasion also for some traces of imagery. But our search is in vain; for the bishop who composed this prayer is only concerned to set out clearly and precisely Saint Augustine's anti-Pelagian teaching on grace (perhaps because further controversy about this had arisen). So the prayer says that in order for the faithful Christian to be able to present his *vota* at the service, he needs first the prevenient and secondly the accompanying or subsequent grace of God (cf. Sacr. Greg., ed. Lietzmann, 44.7).

To give an accurate representation of the author's ideas and opinions, we ought perhaps to translate this Easter Collect in the following manner:

O God
> Who today through Thine only begotten Son hast overcome death
> and opened unto us again the way into eternity
grant that our prayers and sacrifices
> which by Thy prevenient grace Thou has moved us to offer unto Thee,
> may also be further accompanied by the assistance of Thy grace

Now this single example is, I think, sufficient to make clear the merits and the weaknesses of the prayers of the Roman liturgy. First, the good parts: the Roman Collects give expression in the opening predicatory section to basic dogmatic truths, which they pronounce with great (one might almost say juridical) precision. It is these same truths of the faith which underlie and dictate the theme of the actual prayer which follows. So it seems in our example: because God has done such great things for us on that first Easter Day, He will surely on this anniversary of Easter which we are now celebrating grant us that (by comparison) small mercy, for which we intend now to approach Him. Again it is dogma, viewed clearly and unemotionally, which determines the precise manner in which the request is formulated: without God's grace we cannot turn our Easter prayer and sacrifice to a good purpose: therefore (the prayer says) we earnestly ask for this grace.

The authors of the Collects, however, in giving expression to this teaching, followed the rules of the most cultivated Roman rhetoric and used the modes of expression of a liturgical language which had developed over the course of centuries and not only in Christian circles, since the beginning of Christianity. They expressed their teaching in well-balanced sentences with resonant phrases and a majestic rhythm. They addressed all this also (following the prevailing rule of early Christian liturgy) to God the Father ('Deus . . .') and ended by calling upon the high-priestly Mediator who stands before the throne of God ('per Dominum nostrum . . .').

Nor can we overlook the fact (if we want to appreciate all the merits of the Roman liturgy) that this style of prayer, which in the course of the liturgical year naturally varies as to its dogmatic theme, is designed to impress the most important teachings of the faith upon the understanding and memory of the faithful. At the same time, this style of prayer serves to make the faithful conscious once more of the eternal majesty of God and at the same time of the insignificance and dependence of those whom He has both created and redeemed.

On the other hand, however, all these advantages are overshadowed by a whole host of weaknesses which cannot be overlooked. The Roman Collects (and indeed all the Roman prayers) appeal, as we have already seen, to the intellect; the faithful's powers of imagination are scarcely exercised and their feelings are at most only indirectly called into play. In a service which is composed exclusively of such prayers, and in which no other expressions of worship are used to provide a balance, no place is left for those important and powerful forces to be found in the hearts of religious men. The consequence of constructing prayers according to the laws of Roman rhetoric and using the ancient sacred language of Rome has been that not only is the way in which these prayers are written far above our everyday language (to a certain extent this is necessary in every liturgy), but indeed is so far above it that it is certain that the average Roman Christian of the fourth, fifth, and sixth centuries was not always able to follow the prayers. Finally we must take account of the following weakness in the style of the Roman prayers. The religious discourse of the Fathers of the Latin-speaking West, say, of Saint Ambrose or Saint Augustine, possesses a peculiar quality, a quality which has the power to soothe our feelings, the soothing power in fact of the inspired Word of Holy Scripture. For the Fathers lived to such an extent in and with the books of the Old and New Testaments upon which they meditated again and again, that invariably biblical ideas and biblical usages came readily to them when speaking or writing. There is none of this in the Roman Collects, and only occasionally does one find traces of it in the other Roman prayers. I hope I shall not be misunderstood if I say that, fundamentally, the Roman liturgy is far removed from the Bible.

In the foregoing discussion of the advantages and weaknesses of the Roman prayers, with especial reference to the Collects, I have already expressed the opinion that it was not always easy for the Roman Christians in late antiquity to grasp the full meaning of the prayers whose solemn cadences the Pope pronounced at the liturgy. For the expressions he used were for the most part not those of everyday language and they were moreover frequently open to a variety of interpretations. Seldom indeed could this ambiguity be dispensed with by referring to the actual context of the sentence; and the brevity and formality of the language only served to make matters still more obscure.

We of today should not be at all surprised if we too stumble again and again upon the same difficulty. Even the expert who has been schooled in the Latin tongue encounters a lot of trouble with these Roman prayers when he wants to interpret them for himself or to others. (The compilers of vernacular missals for the layman have many a tale to tell about this.) What in fact we need most of all is this new branch of philology, the philology of the Latin liturgical language, whose task it is to make clear by means of painstaking and detailed research the concrete meaning of many ambiguous and obscure words in Roman liturgical language. Then for the first time we shall know how to re-express these words in the vernacular, though presumably in many cases we shall only after all this be able to establish the fact that the actual Latin liturgical word we are dealing with is basically untranslatable.

When I was discussing the Easter Collect, I stumbled for a moment over the question how we should translate the word *vota* into the vernacular. It means much more than 'oath' or 'prayer' or 'wish'. But what after all does it mean—all three? We encounter similar problems with *actio, clementia, confiteri, devotio, dignitas, disciplina, dispensatio, effectus, fides, fiducia, gloria, imago, incolumitas, initiare, munus, opus, pax, pietas, pignus, praefatio, refrigerium, remedium, sacramentum, salus, solatium, suffragium,* etc.

We should however be grateful for the fact that since the Benedictine Dom Augustinus Daniel carried out his investigations into the word *devotio*, many scholars have taken much trouble to enlarge and deepen our knowledge of liturgical vocabulary. It is with particular satisfaction that one sees that recently a research centre for this kind of philology has been developed at the University of Nijmegen, under the expert direction of Christine Mohrmann. And the theologians Joseph Pascher and Walter Dürig from Munich, following the Belgian Benedictines Dom Bernard Cappelle and Dom Bernard Botte, have turned their attention to the same kind of work.

Those, however, who despite all this would like to improve their sense of the great qualities of the Roman liturgy would do well to read carefully Romano Guardini's classic little book *The Spirit of the Liturgy*. This work has contributed substantially towards the education of the present generation in an understanding of the liturgy in general and of the Roman liturgy in particular. It will continue to fulfil this function in the future. But perhaps one would also do well to complement what one learns from Guardini by comparing the oldest collection of prayers of the Roman Church, the so-called Leonine Sacramentary, with the later Gregorian Sacramentary. We shall be able to see from this comparison what it was that later Roman bishops objected to in the prayers produced by their predecessors and subsequently rejected. So too we shall learn from this what (in the opinion of these men) was contrary to the strict laws of sacred language and the yet stricter ones of the Christian liturgy. And, in his illuminating research into the prefaces which have been collected together in the Leonine Sacramentary, Alfred Stuiber has been able to show how gross were the errors that even bishops of Rome were capable on occasion of perpetrating.

In this way the important fact that the bishops who revised the substance of the earlier Roman liturgy at the end of the sixth century had in front of them the Canon in a form which is very close to the form in which we know it today will gradually become clear to us. We must undoubtedly conclude from the fact that they did not consider that they were permitted to interfere with the text that they were no longer sensitive to the difference between the eucharistic prayer, whose thought and form were so compact (one thinks here of Hippolytus's Church Order), and the patchwork character of the text of the Canon which they actually used. It certainly did not occur to them to admit to themselves the weaknesses of the text and to make a move to purge them, because the way in which the Latin Canon had arisen in the fourth century had in the meanwhile been forgotten and it was now looked upon as part of the most sacred apostolic tradition.

It is sad to have to acknowledge the fact that the most important prayer in the liturgy, the very heart in fact of the worship of the universal Church, which was once so magnificent a piece of composition, was handed down to later generations via the framework of the Roman liturgy in such a pitiable state of dilapidation. We ought not therefore (as we have already observed earlier in another connection) in the last resort to put off any longer a complete reconstruction of this text; for, as I have already shown, during the Middle Ages, by the addition of meaningless 'conclusions' and 'Amens' at the end of each section, and by the equally meaningless signs of the cross (which in part were probably manual acts altered into signs of the cross), the Canon underwent yet further distortion.

II

Franco-German Leadership:
From Gregory the Great to Gregory VII

i. OUTLINE OF THE PERIOD

The second period in the development of the Roman liturgy
which, according to our plan, covers the years 590–1073, may be
described in outline roughly as follows:

The liturgy of the Roman church had, in its new Latin form,
been gradually developed and expanded by the labours of the
popes in writing prayers, in particular by Leo the Great and Gelasius I. Under Gregory the Great and his immediate successors, it
received its final form which found its concrete embodiment in
the so-called Gregorian Sacramentary, the so-called Gregorian
Antiphonary, the 'Capitulare evangeliorum', and the 'Ordines'.
The Gregorian Sacramentary contains the prayers to be recited by
the celebrant at mass throughout the liturgical year, and those to
be said at the administration of the sacraments. The Antiphonary
provided the 'Schola' of singers with its part in the worship of the
eucharist. The 'Capitulare evangeliorum' showed the deacon
which section of the four gospels he had to read on each liturgical
day (a corresponding list of those *pericopes* which were not taken
from the gospel for the use of the sub-deacon does not seem to
have existed, probably because a choice of lections had not at that
time been decided upon). And, finally, the Ordines give directions
to the clergy concerning the ritual procedure to be observed at
each liturgical function. Whether or not the basic elements in the
hours of prayer had been fixed by this time by means of revising
or even editing for the first time the psalter, the collections of the
lives of the saints, the lectionaries, and the homilies, and so on, is

something we still do not know; for research into this question is not as yet sufficiently far advanced.

In this form, which was finally established by Gregory and his immediate successors (especially, perhaps, by Honorius I) and was thereafter known as 'Gregorian', the Roman liturgy made its home first in England and then under Pippin and Charlemagne in the Franco-German world. Here it came into contact with the remains of the ancient Gallican liturgy as well as with an older Roman version, which was ascribed to Pope Gelasius and had crossed the Alps at some earlier date. Out of the conflict between these three traditions—the Roman-Gelasian, the Roman-Gregorian, and the Gallican—there came into being a mixed version of all three. This became domiciled at Rome around AD 1000 or shortly afterwards.

There is no trace of any real advance in the development of the Roman liturgy during this period. It is probable that a counter-balancing of the first part of the liturgical year, which, covering as it did the period from Christmas to Whitsuntide, reflected in broad outline the events of salvation history as recorded in the New Testament, with a similar scheme for the second half of the year, was not far off; this part of the year could have been given the function of recalling the principal events of salvation history as recorded in the Old Testament. An attempt of this sort, i.e. to organize the period between Whitsun and Christmas according to a single theme, seems to have occupied the attention of clerics both before Gregory the Great and during his time, as is evident from the thematic arrangement of the four or five Sundays of Advent. In Rome, however, this idea could not be followed up owing to lack of interest and ability to put it into practice.

The other things that were undertaken are of little importance. The need to give the Lord's Prayer a suitably dignified place in the liturgy of the mass caused Gregory the Great to put it immediately at the end of the canon (Ep. 9.6), since up till then it had fulfilled the function of a prayer of preparation for communion, and had therefore come just before the communion, together with the sentence which introduced it and the prayer which followed it, that is, the embolism. Gregory the Great certainly intended that the Lord's Prayer should retain its character as a communion devotion. A further act of preparation was added by Pope Sergius I, who came from a Syrian family living in Sicily, who arranged that the faithful should sing the 'Agnus Dei' during the fraction (Lib. pont. 1,376 D).

The liturgical spirituality of this period was conditioned primarily by the fact that the allegorical interpretation of the rites and texts was developed in a decisive if not always a very fortunate manner by Amalar the Frank and, despite passionate opposition on the part of the deacon, Florus of Lyons, started off on the road to victory. At the same time, in accordance with the new type of popular devotion, the Christ of the Passion and the Christ of the Eucharistic Presence became increasingly prominent as a feature of liturgical piety (cf. page 30 above and page 135 below).

Into this somewhat hazy picture of our second period we shall now sketch some important details in rather stronger outlines.

ii. THE DECLINE OF THE 'PRAYER OF THE FAITHFUL'

Recent research has put into our hands a variety of facts which lend support to the theory that the primary object of Gregory the Great in his final attempt at the arrangement and ordering of the liturgical inheritance was to abbreviate those parts of the liturgy which had grown too long and thus to lighten what had become an excessive burden on both celebrant and people, a burden moreover which scarcely served to increase their devotion. Unless I am wholly mistaken, one item in the older Roman liturgy of the mass which fell a victim to Gregory's endeavours to make the service shorter (which in this case we have every reason to regret) was the so-called Intercessory Prayer, also known as the 'General Prayer of the Church'. I shall give a brief account of the history of this prayer in support of this assertion.

In Rome, as elsewhere, that part of the mass known as the Service of the Word, ended with the dismissal of the catechumens, for at the second part of the liturgy, i.e. at the offertory procession, the consecration, and the communion, only the baptized, the *fideles*, were allowed to be present. However, before this second part (the *missa fidelium*—Mass of the Faithful) began with the offertory procession, the assembled company first prayed for the general needs of the community. This is the prayer which the sources term the *oratio fidelium*, i.e. the Prayer of the Faithful to whose origins in the Prayer of Eighteen Intercessions from the liturgy of the synagogue we have already referred (p. 6). This was the first common prayer to be said at the service; for the faithful were not allowed to pray in common with the catechumens or with the unbaptized. Hippolytus had already said as much in his Church Order (ed. Botte, p. 55).

In Rome the form of this prayer was invariable. Whoever led the service invited those present to pray with him to God, making use of a formula which in its basic outlines was always the same. He introduced in this manner, for example, a common prayer for the whole Church which runs as follows: 'Let us pray, dearly beloved, for the Holy Church of God, that our God and Lord may be pleased to endow it throughout the world with His grace, peace, and protection that He may put in subjection to it the (demonic) principalities and powers, and that He may bestow on us the means of glorifying the Almighty Father by a quiet and untroubled life. Let us pray.'

In response to this bidding of the officiant, the congregation devoted themselves for a while to silent prayer. Then the celebrant again raised his voice to gather together the petitions of all those present in a short prayer, which was later called the 'collecting prayer' (*collecta*). The Collect corresponding to the bidding we have quoted above runs as follows: 'Almighty and everlasting God, Who hast in Christ manifested Thy glory to all people, preserve the works of Thy mercy, so that Thy Church which is spread throughout the whole world may continue steadfast in faith and in the praise of Thy name, through the same Lord Jesus Christ, who . . .'. The congregation, together with the celebrant, who during the Collect stood looking eastwards, his eyes raised to heaven, his arms extended in the attitude of prayer, expressed their assent with a loud 'Amen'.

In this way, prayer was made in turn for all the members of the community; for the members of the hierarchy, for the confessors, for the virgins and widows, for the emperor, for the catechumens, for the sick and suffering, for heretics and schismatics, for Jews and heathen. When it happened to be a penitential day, the silent prayer was said kneeling instead of standing, but the congregation stood again for the concluding prayer. The deacon (the successor of the 'herald' in the cultic rites of antiquity) gave the sign for kneeling and standing up again by announcing 'Flectamus genua' ('Let us kneel down') and 'Levate' ('Arise').

It is probably correct to say that this form of prayer successfully combined the silent devotion of the individual and the vocal prayer of the congregation and in addition also helped the people to give themselves both in body and soul to the service of God. But it had one considerable limitation: it was a little long drawn-out and could, by frequent repetition, i.e. if the wording remained unchanged, become wearisome. In addition it so happened that this form of intercessory prayer took up a great deal of time in relation to the rest of the service. This was a serious problem for the bishops of congregations in large towns; the service, apart from the lections and the intercessions already entailed the prescribing and ordering of a ceremonious offertory procession of all the many faithful who were present, the presenting of the oblations, the eucharistic prayer itself, and the time-consuming process of giving communion in both kinds to the whole congregation; how then, it was asked, could the bishops so regulate the length of the services that it might still be endurable for those taking part?

In the East and also (under the Eastern influence) in Gaul and Northern Italy, there was current another and shorter form of the intercessory prayer. The deacon announced the subject of the intercession, using a very short form, and the congregation itself finished off the petition, giving it a very simple conclusion. So, for example, the deacon summoned the people to pray for the whole Church in the words 'Let us pray for an abundance of divine blessings on the immaculate Church of the living God, dispersed throughout the world'; and the congregation responded

'Kyrie eleison'. This type of prayer is known to us by the name of a litany (which derives from the Greek word λιτανεία, a petitionary prayer). Its particular merit derives from the fact that it combines the qualities of being short and very easy to understand and has a very lively rhythm. Its weakness is that it does not give the faithful opportunity to pray silently, which together with the vocal prayer of the congregation constitutes, in our opinion, an indispensable element in this kind of prayer.

Pope Gelasius I, who was an important bishop of Rome at the end of the fifth century, took a liking to this short Eastern form of the intercessory prayer. As Dom Bernard Capelle, formerly Abbot of Mont César, has proved with such ingenuity, Gelasius translated it into Latin, and we still possess the full text of this translation under the title 'Deprecatio Gelasii'. He then introduced it into the Roman mass in place of the older, indigenous form of the intercessory prayer. It is probable that at the same time the position of the prayer was changed, being moved from its place at the beginning of the Mass of the Faithful to the beginning of the Mass of the Catechumens. By so doing, the division between the two parts of the eucharist was dispensed with altogether. Since at that time there were normally scarcely any adult catechumens, it seemed perhaps to the Pope that there was no longer any sense in barring the unbaptized from the main part of the service.

Only on two days in the year, both in Holy Week, did Gelasius allow the old practice to continue. On the Wednesday in Holy Week and on Good Friday the eucharist began straight away (as it always used to) with the lections, and not until these were finished did the intercessory prayer follow in the old Roman form. This is incidentally a good example of an important law of liturgical development, discovered by Anton Baumstark, and which he describes somewhat formally as 'the law of the preservation of the traditional at important liturgical seasons' (*das Gesetz der Erhaltung des Alten in liturgisch hochwertiger Zeit*). But also on the other days of the year there remained, unbeknown to Pope Gelasius and certainly not intended by him, faint, remaining traces of the primitive arrangement, namely that curious 'Oremus' which comes at the beginning of the Mass of the Faithful and to which no corresponding prayer is attached.

It was, then, precisely this Gelasian form of the Roman intercessory prayer, and not the older form of it which survived in Holy Week, which Gregory the Great modified in his work of abbreviation. We learn from a complaint made in passing by the Pope when he was ill (Epistle 10.14) that the service which he himself conducted on festivals lasted in those days up to three hours. Clearly something had to be done to remedy the situation. Gregory saw that a suitable way out of this predicament lay not in doing without the sermon, as most of his predecessors and successors had done, but in shortening the litany, which moreover, since the time of Pope Gelasius, had been developed so that now together with the supplication 'Kyrie eleison', the acclamation 'Christe eleison' was also used. Gregory also dispensed with the deacon's part in the litany on ferias, and allowed only a last reminder, i.e. the congregational responses (a repeated 'Kyrie eleison' and 'Christe eleison'), to remain. Only on Easter Sunday did everything remain as it used to be in the days before Gelasius (in accordance once more with the law we have mentioned). Down to the present time, the mass on this day begins with a complete litany in which, it is true, the petitioning of the saints (at one time non-existent, then gradually intruding into the litany) has in the course of time become so prominent, that one no longer feels that this is an intercessory prayer directed to God or Christ, but solely a supplication to the saints; for this reason it is customarily known as the litany of the Saints.

Furthermore, Gregory or one of his immediate successors must soon have taken another step in this process of abbreviation. The practice of omitting the biddings in the litany was eventually no longer confined to ferias but extended also to feast days (cf. Ordo Romanus Primus, 51 A). In the mass of the Easter Vigil, however, everything remained unchanged.

People in the age of Saint Gregory may well have consoled themselves about the abandonment of the intercessory prayer by reflecting that enough attention was already paid to the needs of the Church in the Canon of the mass. But the intercessions in the eucharistic prayer, especially those prayers for the living and the dead which begin with the word 'Memento', are expressed in very general terms. Moreover, in view of the fact that for a long time it had been a rule never to make any alteration in the Canon, these intercessions did not permit any elastic adjustment to suit circumstances which change from day to day. And lastly they did not allow for any direct participation on the part of the congregation. Consequently they were unable in the long run to satisfy the needs of everyone. This point is made clear enough by later developments. We need only recall the following facts: In many congregations, it was (and still is) the practice at Sunday worship to provide either before or after the sermon an extra-liturgical 'General prayer for the Church' written in the vernacular. In Masses for the Dead, it is the custom in many places to interpolate before the beginning of the sacrifice special prayers in the vernacular for the departed who are mentioned by name. Finally, in times of stress, specially composed non-Latin prayers have to be introduced either after the gospel or at the end of the mass to act as bridges as it were to the personal concerns of members of the congregation.

The last two kinds of vernacular prayer we have mentioned consist as a rule of the announcement of a particular intention which is followed by the Lord's Prayer repeated several times. It is indeed a truly tragic stroke of fortune that the same Pope Gregory who wanted to restore to the Lord's Prayer its proper dignity by placing it immediately after the Canon, should have unsuspectingly caused this same Lord's Prayer to be lamentably debased by silencing the deacon's litany. Today it is used, together with the 'Ave Maria' as an 'all-purpose prayer', with which it is attempted to cover all those exigencies which are insufficiently provided for in the liturgy itself.

At this juncture, we should remind ourselves of a practical example which is very instructive, i.e. of the vernacular intercession which until a short time ago had to be said after every low mass. It consisted of three 'Ave Maria's', the antiphon of Our Lady, 'Salve Regina', and the prayer which went with this, a prayer to Michael the Archangel, and a threefold supplication of the Most Sacred Heart of Jesus. The prayers to Our Lady at the beginning of this intercession were prescribed by Pope Pius IX at a time when the Papal states were in danger, but only for this particular territory. Leo XIII, who was perturbed by the devilish activities devised by Leo Taxil, added the prayer to Michael the Archangel, and bound the whole Church to take over this now much-lengthened intercession; and Pius X extended it further to include the supplications to the Sacred Heart of Jesus. We should indeed be grateful to the Second Vatican Council for doing away altogether with this appendage to the private mass which has no organic connection with it and which in course of time has grown so large.

Here then is clearly outlined for us an important task in the reform of the liturgy. The short prayers which come before the eucharist proper must once more be closely related as they used to be to the people's needs of the moment, to their sorrows, their joys, and their hopes, just as this close relationship was formerly guaranteed by the intercessory prayer and later, to a lesser extent, by the litany. For a liturgy which, by over-straining the principle that it must be objective, has lost all touch with the concrete situation of the Church as a whole and of the local congregation runs the risk of losing the inward participation of the people. It could in fact transpire that the faithful may come to public worship by way of fulfilling their duty to be present, and therefore seek to satisfy their actual devotional needs in extra or non-liturgical forms of devotion to bring their personal request to God.

Any reform of the liturgy should therefore have the intercessory prayer revived in its original place. But one should beware of prescribing a fixed form for this prayer to be used everywhere, which expresses only in general terms the requests of the Church as a whole and of the local congregation. What we need is an intercessory prayer which arouses the attention of the faithful at the service, because it expresses concretely what they are concerned about at the moment. So, for example, the intercessory prayer in Germany should perhaps mention clearly by name the division of our country, which is something that concerns us all, and make it a particular intention in the prayer. Moreover, we

would have great difficulty in accepting the form of the intercessory prayer that we need unless great variability and extensive
freedom of choice were permitted.

iii. THE COMPILATION OF THE LITURGICAL BOOKS

In our introductory survey of this period of the Western liturgy,
we spoke briefly about the composition of the liturgical books
during the years 530–650, a period which in other respects also is
rich in works of codification. We heard that Gregory the Great
undertook the task of making a collection of the prayers of the
liturgy, which was probably not completed until the reign of one
of his immediate successors and which moreover was henceforth
to determine the manner in which the eucharist was to be celebrated and the sacraments administered. The book we are speaking of is that known as the 'Sacramentarium Gregorianum',
which had an extremely important part to play in the liturgy of
future generations. But just after this, we learned that side by
side with this Gregorian collection of liturgical prayers, there
existed yet another, which since the ninth century at least (according to a reference in the Liber Pontificalis 1, 255 D) has been
attributed to Pope Gelasius I, who reigned from 492–6, i.e. at
least a hundred years before Saint Gregory.

What kind of a book, then, is this 'Sacramentarium Gelasianum'? Was it really something to do with the Pope whose
name has later been associated with it? Or are we here dealing
with a collection which has incorrectly been ascribed to this fifth-
century Pope but which in fact was made by some other Pope
who reigned at some time during the period between Gelasius I
and Gregory I? Or, alternatively, is the Gelasian Sacramentary
nothing less than a preliminary attempt made by Gregory the
Great which he later abandoned in favour of the book which
bears his name? Such and similar conjectures come to mind
whenever we find ourselves faced with the problem of the history
of the origins of the Gelasian Sacramentary.

Scholars have long sought in vain to elucidate the mystery of this book. It shares a peculiarity with the (incorrectly) so-called Leonine Sacramentary inasmuch as we possess only a single manuscript of both of these; in the case of the Gelasianum, this manuscript is the Codex Reginensis 316 of the Vatican Library. Now the place where this manuscript is kept today might well lead the uninitiated to conclude that it must also have been written at Rome; but this would be to draw an over-hasty conclusion. For the Codex only came into the possession of the Vatican when the Vatican acquired the library of Queen Christina of Sweden, the convert daughter of Gustavus Adolphus; and the country of its origin is more likely to have been France. Palaeographers of the standing of Elias Avery Lowe and Bernhard Bischoff have shown that the manuscript must have been written there about 750, probably in a convent called Chelles near Paris.

We get another surprise when we examine the contents of the manuscript. Certainly, the bulk of the prayers in the Codex quite clearly come from the city of Rome; but side by side with these we find many texts which could not possibly be native to Rome. This is true, for example, of the prayers for Saints Nabor and Nazarius, who were venerated at Milan, and equally of those for Saint Vitalis of Spoleto, of the Southern Italian saints, Juliana, Vitus, and Magnus, and of a variety of other prayers also.

If we examine the text even more closely, we find yet another series of peculiar characteristics in this manuscript which cannot be reconciled with a conclusion that the text originated in Rome. Such are, for example, the formularies for certain rites which could not possibly have been in existence in Rome at the time when the manuscript was written, and in respect of these, the instructions drawn from canon law which have been added betray the fact that the forms must be Gallican in origin. So, too, certain details in the Calendar of the Saints refer us once more to Gaul.

It is yet more remarkable that many of the Roman formularies in this Codex reveal quite clearly that they were not composed (or at least not primarily composed) with a view to fulfilling the liturgical requirements of the bishop of Rome. They must have been intended in the first place for the titular churches of Rome (the forerunners of what were later to be parish churches); and their purpose therefore was to provide the presbyters who ministered in these churches with the necessary texts. Some sections also seem to have been designed for use in Roman monasteries.

The peculiar structure of each particular set of prayers is deserving of special attention. The so-called 'Oratio super populum', that ancient Roman prayer for blessing the people, which still appears in our Missal today, as in the Gregorian Sacramentary, on all weekdays during Lent, is met with in the Codex we are dealing with throughout the remainder of the liturgical year and also, though not with quite such consistency, in the Leonine Sacramentary. Moreover, in the Codex we are concerned with, we discover another prayer which has been inserted between the Collect and the Secret, which is quite alien to the Leonine Sacramentary and which again is missing from the Gregorian Sacramentary. This is the 'Oratio super sindonem'; and it is possible that this prayer was said when, by way of preparation for the offertory procession, a cloth called a *sindon* was spread over the altar.

The observations I have just made lead me to conclude that the Roman collection which forms the basis of the Codex we have been dealing with reflects the state of the liturgy as it was in Rome before the time of the Gregorian Sacramentary, but after that of the Leonine. Since, however, the Leonine Sacramentary itself takes us right into the second half of the sixth century, the Roman core of the Gelasian Sacramentary cannot have originated much before the Gregorian Sacramentary. Now it is on the basis of such observations, coupled with some research of a more detailed nature, that Antoine Chavasse first enlightened us about the basic details of the origins of this Sacramentary and its later fortunes.

A few years before Chavasse, Alfred Stuiber, by using the same methods of internal and external criticism, was able to throw some light on the history of the origins of the so-called Leonine Sacramentary, and pointed out that this collection had grown out of a number of sheets of parchment (*libelli*) containing liturgical prayers which the presbyters who ministered at the titular churches in Rome had compiled for themselves, thus making use of the liturgical sketches the Popes had made for their own use and then laid down in the papal archives of the Lateran Palace. Chavasse was now able to show that the Gelasian Sacramentary too derives from similar sheets of parchment used by the presbyters, the difference being that these were of a later date. But whereas in the Leonine Sacramentary the *libelli* that were used were arranged in only a very arbitrary fashion, in the Gelasianum we find that the material has been so carefully edited that we are fully justified in giving the end product of this process the name of sacramentary. Only, as we have seen, this Sacramentary has nothing whatsoever to do with Pope Gelasius, nor moreover with a papal editor, for both those who composed it and those who used it were Roman presbyters; and therefore we could more than justifiably call it a Roman presbyters' sacramentary and thereby make a clear distinction between it and the papal sacramentary which is set out for us in the Gregorian Sacramentary.

What is now so remarkable is that this presbyters' sacramentary (as an analysis of the Codex Reginensis reveals) continued to be used in Rome even after the composition of the Gregorian Sacramentary. From this we may conclude that the Gregorian Sacramentary was only used when the Pope himself celebrated the liturgy, i.e. at services led by him at the Lateran or in the stational churches; and the presbyters were free to use the book which had been compiled by them for their own use and for their own churches. Now we have already seen that there are also formularies from other parts of Italy in this book. This compels us to draw yet another conclusion, namely that the Roman presbyters were by no means reluctant to incorporate into the book which they used for the mass feasts and prayers they had become acquainted with on their travels in other parts of Italy; and the fact that we also find traces of monastic services in the Codex Reginensis proves conclusively that those priests who officiated in the monasteries of Rome also made use of this presbyters' sacramentary.

It is thanks also to Chavasse's keen insight that we can see now that in Rome the papal sacramentary and that used by the presbyters were not wholly and entirely divorced from one another, for a copy of the Gregorian Sacramentary used at Saint Peter's has undergone changes to make it agree with the presbyters' sacramentary. This in turn solves the mystery that surrounds an early 'mixed' sacramentary which is today kept in Padua and which in the past has given scholars a great deal of trouble.

Around the year 700, the Roman presbyters' sacramentary, in common with many other liturgical books, including the Gregorian Sacramentary, was imported into France by Frankish clergy. There it became a rival to the ancient Gallican collections, principally the Gregorian Sacramentary. Since the latter from the very beginning had been concerned solely with papal services, it was now felt to be insufficient and the presbyters' sacramentary was therefore used as a basis from which to make good its inadequacies. Hence there arose in France a 'mixed' sacramentary to which scholars usually give the title 'Sacramentarium Gelasianum saeculi octavi'.

Thus this account of the origins and fortunes of the Roman presbyters' sacramentary help us to see for the first time that neither Gregory the Great nor his immediate successors foresaw or required that their liturgical books should alone and everywhere be regarded as authoritative. In Rome people were generous enough to permit the titular churches to keep their books and their liturgy which deviated somewhat from the normal practice. During the whole of the sixth and seventh centuries, in fact, it is impossible to speak of an absolute unity as regards the liturgy of the city of Rome; for the bishop used the Gregorian Sacramentary, and the presbyters kept to their own book.

This information moreover should serve to comfort all those who are shocked by the fact that as a result of the Second Vatican Council the centuries-old, cast-iron uniformity of liturgical books and prayers has been abandoned in favour of an attempt to make the liturgy correspond more closely to the needs of different people and different countries. For surely, if the Church was able to tolerate variations in the liturgy even within the one city of

Rome and moreover was not ashamed of this, then in the same way she will also be able to tolerate the fact that in the future the liturgy will only be universally the same in respect of its fundamental principles, but will differ widely as to the manner in which it is put into practice.

iv. THE ROMAN BISHOP'S MASS *c.* AD 700

As I have already mentioned, among the liturgical books compiled during the Gregorian period were the so-called 'Ordines Romani', i.e. *libelli* or notebooks in which were set out instructions as to how each of the liturgical rites was to be performed. Like the other new books, these Ordines have understandably been copied over and over again, especially in places other than the Eternal City itself. This resulted in frequent alterations of the original text, since regional or local pecularities had to be taken into account. It is, therefore, not easy to recapture from the rich manuscript tradition the original Roman version of the Ordines. Michel Andrieu, the Strasbourg liturgical historian who died in 1956, devoted his life to this Sisyphean task. The result of his life's work is set out in his monumental critical edition of the Ordines which contains besides the texts a large number of important investigations in which he makes an evaluation of his material. From the way Andrieu had chosen to arrange the texts in his edition, we can get a clear picture of all those matters for which the Roman *libelli* and their immediate successors made regulations. An account of this arrangement follows according to the numbering given by Andrieu.

Ordines I–X in Andrieu's edition concern the mass as celebrated by the bishop of Rome; XI deals with the rite of baptism; XII–XIV contains prescriptions for the chant and lections of the liturgical hours; Ordo XV has a special title 'Capitulare ecclesiastici ordinis' and constitutes a rearrangement of Ordines I–XI, made with a view to conditions in France; Ordo XVI which is called an *Instructio* adapts Ordines XIV and XV to suit the needs of a monastery; Ordo XVII is again a monastic adaptation of XV and XVI. XVIII and XIV come into the same category and comprise regulations for the hours of prayer and for the meals in the monasteries of Rome. Ordines XX–XXXIII prescribe certain details of the liturgical years; XXXIV–XL concern the ordination of bishops and clerics and also the liturgy of the Ember season in the framework of which ordinations are performed to this very day. In Ordines XLI–XLIII there is a description of the manner of consecrating churches at Rome and also of the closely associated practice of the deposition of relics. Ordo XLIV concerns the ritual cleansing (*diligentia*) of the 'Confessio' in Saint Peter's. Ordines XLV–XLVIII provide regulations for the crowning of the emperor and may well, therefore, have not originated until long after the 'Gregorian' period; presumably they come from the ninth and tenth centuries. Ordo XLIX deals with the liturgy for the dying and prescribes what is to be done with the body. Ordo L did not come into being until *c.* 950 in the church of Saint Alban at Mainz. It follows the course of the liturgical year, and puts together in a practical manner all the material contained in the Roman Ordines; it adds some prayers which belong to the Roman sacramentaries; in addition it contains some illuminating texts from Frankish commentaries on the liturgy and also some hymns. This fiftieth Ordo, as may readily be understood, was the most sought-after and most influential of all. It constituted an important part of the Romano-German Pontifical (which originated at the same time) and between the years 951 and 972 accompanied the Emperor Otto I and his entourage of German bishops to Italy on many occasions.

We shall next, following Ordo I in Andrieu's edition, give a short account of the papal mass as it was celebrated at Rome *c.* AD 700. It is not possible in this account to pay attention to all the details of ceremonial, but we can in so doing give the reader a sufficiently clear picture of how the eucharistic rite was performed in Rome at the end of the Gregorian period of liturgical codification.

Early in the morning, the Pope rode with a great following from his residence in the Lateran to the church, which at the previous day's mass had been announced as the place (or *statio*) where the papal mass was to be held. (In the Roman Missal today these *stationes* are still printed at the beginning of the relevant Propers of the mass.) The Pope was accompanied on the one hand by those who held high office in his administration, and on the other hand by the deacons, sub-deacons, and acolytes who were to act as ministers at the liturgy. They took with them from the Lateran treasury liturgical books, vessels, linen, and other equipment. When they arrived at the stational church, the Pope, supported ritually on either side by two deacons (this was in fact the *sustenatio* of court ceremonial), went to the sacristy or *secretarium* which was situated at the front of the basilica. Here his followers, following the rules laid down in Byzantine court ceremonial, stood round and assisted him in the removal of his outer garments in order that they might then clothe him in the liturgical vestments. These were identical with those in use today, namely the linen alb which was girded at the waist with the *cingulum*; then the cloth which went over the neck or shoulders, the *amictus*. Next came the two dalamtics (the short one underneath, the longer one on top); and then the chasuble (*planeta*). Finally two insignia were handed to the Pope, the *pallium*, which was laid loosely round his neck and over the chasuble and held in place with pins; and the *mappula* the ceremonial napkin which he held in his right hand. There is no mention in the year 700 of other insignia such as the bishop's shoes, the pectoral cross, the ring, the pastoral staff, or the tiara. But it is certain that in those days, the Pope wore a ring, the bishop's shoes and the *camelaucum* (i.e. the distinctive kind of headgear from which eventually developed the mitre—the *phrygium*—and the tiara). Nothing is said about these in the Ordo, on account of the fact that the Pope had already put them on while he was still at the Lateran. What is important, however, is that there is no sign of a stole among the papal insignia which probably indicates that the stole was only the mark of the lower grades of clergy while the corresponding mark for the higher grades of clergy was the *pallium* here mentioned as being the special insignia of the Pope.

Meanwhile, all those taking part in the service, having processed from the church which had been announced as the place of assembly, had now for some considerable time been in their carefully allotted places in the basilica. The suburban bishops and the presbyters sat round the apse on their *subsellia* next to the throne; the choir (*schola cantorum*), consisting of men and boys, stood in a square partition on the nave side of the altar; and in the centre of the nave itself was the congregation which was strictly divided with the men on one side, the women on the other, and the aristocracy in the front rows. The period during which they waited was interrupted by a solemn ceremony; an acolyte (with his hands covered) carried the Book of the Gospels into the basilica, and a sub-deacon laid it reverently (*honorifice*) on the altar. In the sacristy, the Pope was informed as to which sub-deacon was to proclaim the *apostolus* (i.e. the epistle) and which member of the choir was to lead the singing; it was not permitted to make any alterations in this arrangement afterwards. Finally, the Pope gave a signal. Whereupon the candles on the seven candlesticks (*cerostatae*) were lit, the sub-deacon concerned put incense on the *thymiaterium*, and the choir, on the instructions of a messenger, began the Introit antiphon. (Lights, incense, and music at the Introit were, as we know, some of the privileges of secular origin to which the Pope also had a claim.) The Pope then, once more ritually supported, entered the church at the end of a solemn procession. At the head walked the sub-deacon with the thurible, then followed the seven torch-bearers, and last came the deacons and sub-deacons. They met on their way to the altar a sub-deacon and two acolytes who presented to the Pope an open *capsa* containing fragments of the eucharistic bread (the so-called *sancta*) from the most recent papal mass. The Pope greeted them by merely inclining his head and then decided how much of this he would use at the mass he was going to celebrate and how much was to be brought back and put in the *conditorium* (perhaps this means a cupboard in the sacristy of the Lateran basilica). The *sancta* which he kept was later to be put into the eucharistic chalice to act as a *fermentum*, i.e. a kind of leaven. It served equally to illustrate the connection between the two masses held on different occasions. And in order also to show how the services which were held in different places were really all part of one papal service, before the communion a fragment of the bread consecrated by the Pope was carried by the acolytes to each of the Roman parish churches (*tituli*) in order that the presbyters who were ministering there might put it in the chalice at their own celebration of the eucharist.

When they arrived in front of the altar, four of the seven torch-bearers went to the right, and three to the left. The Pope reverenced the altar with a bow, made the sign of the cross on his forehead, and gave the kiss of peace to his assistant ministers down to and including the deacon. He then gave a signal, where-upon the *schola* brought the Introit psalm to an end with the 'Gloria Patri', and the Pope waited for this to finish, kneeling on the apse side of the altar. At the 'sicut erat', he kissed the Book of the Gospels, then the altar, and went to his throne in the centre of the apse, where, turning east, he followed the singing of the 'litany' (i.e. the 'Kyrie eleison'). When it seemed to him that a sufficient number of Kyries had been sung, he commanded the choir to cease. Turning now to the congregation (facing, there-fore, west), he intoned the hymn 'Gloria in excelsis Deo'; and while this was being sung, he again faced eastwards. When this was over, he turned round once more and greeted the people with the salutation 'Pax vobis'. Immediately after this, facing east once more, he gave the bidding for prayer 'Oremus' and straight away said the Collect, leaving no time at all for silent prayer. From this we may judge that the silent prayer which used to precede the 'collecting prayer' had also by this time already fallen victim to efforts to shorten the service. After the Collect, the Pope sat down on his throne and all present sat down also. They listened to the lection which the sub-deacon who had been appointed read from the ambo. As soon as he had finished, a singer, as had been previously arranged, stood up with his music book, the *can-tatorium*, to sing the *responsum* (which we call the Gradual). The 'Alleluia' which followed this seems for the most part to have been omitted. Then the deacon who had been appointed to read the Gospel came to the throne, kissed the Pope's feet (in accord-ance with Byzantine court ceremonial), and had the blessing 'Dominus sit in corde tuo' given to him. After this he went to the altar and he kissed the book of the gospels lying on the altar, and with the book in his hands proceeded at the end of a short procession, consisting of the two sub-deacons carrying the thurible and two acolytes with torches, to the ambo which he mounted alone, marking with his finger the relevant place in the book from which he was to read. After the reading, one of the two sub-deacons, holding with covered hands the book of the gospels in front of him, went to all the clergy in the sanctuary in turn, in order of rank, so that they might kiss the book. Whereupon the book was put back in its *capsa*, which was then sealed for safety's sake, for its binding was ornamented with precious stones.

With this, the Service of the Word was abruptly brought to an end. As we have seen, however, this part of the service was no longer limited solely as it used to be to just the Word of God. For in front of the lections, a series of prayers had been inserted, consisting of the Litany, the hymn 'Gloria in excelsis', and a Collect. But what, we may ask, had happened to that other basic element which together with the lections used to form a part of the original Service of the Word, i.e. the sermon? In the Ordo, this has been omitted altogether. It looks as if on account of the dimensions of the stational churches, and equally by reason of the length of the service, which was already excessive without a sermon, the Pope had given up the practice of having a liturgical address at every eucharist. Was there nevertheless still a sermon in the titular churches of Rome? We cannot tell. From about the year 700 onwards the original ending to the Service of the Word is also missing, i.e. the dismissal of the catechumens from which its name 'the mass of the catechumens' had been derived. It seems clear that the universal introduction of the practice of infant baptism and the decline in the number of adult converts had been the occasion of this act of dismissal falling into disuse. We should not be surprised that no mention is made of the 'Credo' (the creed), for this did not become a constituent part of the Roman liturgy until the eleventh century under Franco-German influence.

The second part of the eucharistic celebration used at one time to open with the primitive Common Prayer of the baptized or *fideles* (i.e. the faithful), who at this stage were the only ones present. But this primitive prayer, as we have already heard, had been abandoned in its traditional form two hundred years earlier, and had been replaced by the Litany with which we are already familiar. This moreover had been removed to the beginning of the Service of the Word, so that the second part of the eucharistic liturgy could now begin with the offertory procession.

This was performed in the following manner: first the seven acolytes laid their torches on the ground in a row in front (on the nave side) of the altar, for they had to have their hands free to perform the duties for which they were required during the offertory procession. At one time all the faithful who were present used themselves to carry to the altar whatever gifts they had chosen to bring from home. This practice had proved to be both time-consuming and disturbing, so now the oblations were collected by the clergy from each section of the congregation, and they were only allowed to bring bread and wine. The Pope himself took part in this newly arranged 'offertory procession' by collecting the gifts of the aristocracy; the suburban bishops and the presbyters collected the *oblata* from the rest of the congregation. The loaves were put in large linen cloths (*sindones*) which were carried by the acolytes behind the Pope and his assistants. The flasks of wine (*amulae*) were emptied into a chalice, which when full was poured out into a large vessel (*scyphus*). Despite all efforts at simplification, this ceremony certainly took a great deal of time; but when it had been performed the Pope and his assistants washed their hands. Then the Pope laid his own offering of bread on the altar and the archdeacon selected from the rest of the oblations as much as should be necessary for the communion, and arranged them all on the altar. Next to them he placed the large chalice with handles, into which was poured the wine which the Pope and his deacons had brought as an offering and also a little water. During the offertory procession and the preparation of the oblations, the choir had been singing the antiphon and psalm prescribed for the *offertorium* of the day. Their singing was terminated by a signal from the Pope who then pronounced the *oratio super oblata* which is also called the *oratio secreta* since it is now said in a whisper and no longer, as at one time, aloud.

The liturgical action was now nearing its climax, the Eucharisteia or Canon. All the clergy now took up their position in the sanctuary which they were to occupy until the communion. The sub-deacons stood on the nave side in front of and facing the altar. The deacons organized themselves in two ranks behind the altar; next to them came the acolytes, some of them carrying linen sacks, others the *scyphus* containing the wine offered by the congregation. The bishops and presbyters stood in the apse by their bench (*subsellia*). The Pope was now at the altar itself, facing the people and therefore looking west. He once more greeted the assembly with the salutation 'Dominus vobiscum', called out to them 'Sursum corda', and received in reply the acclamations. Then he sang the first and variable part of the great prayer of thanksgiving which today we call the Preface. At the end of this, the sub-deacons, and presumably also the singers, joined together in singing the Tersanctus (the congregation at Papal masses did not take part in any chants). As soon as it was finished, the Pope began the Canon which was no longer sung but said, and moreover had to be said in such a way that he could be understood at the very least by those in the sanctuary. While the Pope said the Canon, everybody else stood with bowed heads. There was as yet no elevation after the two sections of the Institution Narrative, still less was there any genuflexion. During the final prayer, 'Per quem haec omnia', the archdeacon lifted up the chalice by its handles while the Pope held the oblations on the edge of the chalice. Clearly by this ceremonial act it was intended to make the consecrated bread and wine visible to all the congregation. After the Canon and its solemn conclusion the Pope said or sang the Lord's Prayer which had been put in this place by Gregory the Great, together with the prayer which came immediately afterwards. Saying the salutation, 'Pax Domini sit semper vobiscum', the Pope then immersed the particle which came from the previous day's mass in the chalice and at the same time broke off a piece of bread which he had consecrated, and which was to serve as a *fermentum* at the next service. After this, the Pope returned to his throne and sat down.

Now began the communion which had to be preceded by the breaking up of the bread, for the bread then used came from ordinary Roman households and was not quite small enough. Perhaps it was shaped like a small wreath; it had anyhow to be reduced in size. During the fraction of the bread, the 'Agnus Dei' was sung which had been borrowed by Pope Sergius I from the Greek liturgy shortly before the composition of Ordo I— thus introducing a completely new sound into the Roman liturgy. The archdeacon took the consecrated bread from the altar, and put it in the small sacks held by the acolytes, who then carried it to the bishops and presbyters seated in the apse. These broke up the loaves and put the pieces back in the sacks. The Pope's own oblation had meanwhile been brought to him on a paten at the throne so that he might perform the fraction. When they had all finished breaking the bread, the chalice containing the consecrated wine was also brought to the throne. The Pope then broke off a piece of the consecrated bread, and dropped it into the chalice while saying the prayer 'Fiat commixtio et consecratio'. The purpose of this prayer was to make clear that the bread and wine represented the One Lord; and the fact that Ordo I gives this text in full perhaps indicates it had only recently been incorporated into the Roman liturgy; it is possible also that this prayer, together with the rite which accompanied it, was of Syrian origin. The Pope then ate the bread which remained and drank from the chalice handed to him by the archdeacon. Immediately after this, the archdeacon carried the chalice back to the altar and poured a little of the consecrated wine into the *scyphus* filled with the wine which had been offered by the faithful, and which was brought to him by the acolytes. And, according to the teaching of that time, this mixing was considered sufficient to consecrate the wine in the *scyphus*. Immediately after the Pope had communicated, the archdeacon announced the time and place of the next papal mass (*statio*), probably because all those who did not wish to communicate were accustomed to leave the church before the actual communion. There followed next the communion of the clergy. The bishops, presbyters, and deacons, and with them the high-ranking officials of the Lateran, received the eucharistic bread from the hands of the Pope, who was seated on his throne, whereas they went to the altar to drink from the consecrated chalice. The wine which was left over in this chalice was poured back into the large *scyphus*.

Then the Pope, together with the assisting bishops, presbyters, and deacons proceeded with the communion of the people at which the same priorities were observed as at the collection of the oblations. The bread was taken from the acolyte's sacks, the wine was given from the chalice which was refilled again and again from the *scyphus*. The bread was at this time still placed in the hands of the faithful and they themselves put it in their mouth. It is not clear whether the people came up to the altar rails for their communion, or were communicated in their own places. It seems on the whole that, around the year 700, it was considered important to limit the movements of the faithful in church to the very minimum. And, therefore, the double side aisles which the architects of the Lateran basilica in the time of Constantine had made for processions had become superfluous. During the whole of the communion, the choir sang the antiphon and psalm proper to this part of the liturgy.

It was the Pope who again decided when the communion anthem which the choir was singing should be ended. He went once more to the altar and, turning east, said the *oratio ad complendum* (which we call the Postcommunion). Then a deacon called out to the congregation 'Ite missa est', the congregation replied with the response 'Deo gratias', and the Pope then proceeded in a solemn procession back to the sacristy, giving his blessing to each section of the congregation on the way.

The reader will probably have gathered from the foregoing account of the Roman bishop's mass as it is described in Ordo Romanus I that the simple eucharistic rite with which the primitive Roman church was acquainted and which we can read about in the descriptions of it by Justin Martyr and Hippolytus, had, during the intervening period, undergone some enormous changes and extensions. Whether all these changes in the liturgy were for the good, however, is a matter about which we may rightly have some doubts. Let us remind ourselves once more about some of the more questionable alterations.

The clear-cut division that there used to be between the Service of the Word and the eucharist proper, whose history we have already learned, had now been abandoned altogether. For in the intervening period certain prayers had been absorbed into the Service of the Word, which formerly had been kept strictly to the second part of the celebration. On the other hand, the Service of the Word (at the papal mass at least) had suffered the loss of an important element, namely the sermon. So too the pressure of conditions in large towns had brought about a stunting of some of the impressive ritual ceremonies of the eucharistic part of the service; for example, the offertory procession had been transformed into a mere collection of the gifts by the clergy (a ceremony which foreshadows the present-day collection of alms) and the going up to receive communion had been replaced by the practice of giving the bread and wine to the faithful either in the chancel or in their own places. Above all, the whole of the sacred action had become enmeshed in a network of complicated rites drawn from court ceremonial; we need only think of the solemn chant with which the bishop was greeted when he entered the basilica, the solemn assembling of his spiritual and temporal assistants, of their complicated ceremonial movements, and of the accumulation of elaborate gestures of reverence towards the Pope, ranging from kissing his hand to kissing his foot (though in the account we have given here these are not all mentioned). In fact we can scarcely recognize this overburdened liturgy for what it was supposed to be—an imitation and a recalling of that simple memorial meal instituted by Our Lord. One might make the rather pointed observation that the Last Supper had clearly been the victim of the long history of the Roman church and, especially in the realm of ceremonial, of its aspiring to political power; and the fact that these aspirations were just as alive in the eighth century as they were in the fourth is shown by the propagation in Rome *c.* 760 of the forged document known as the 'Donation of Constantine' (quoted in full on pages 92-3).

Now many a reader who has been disturbed by his study of the complicated shape of the papal mass will turn with a sigh of relief to a consideration of the Roman titular churches, where on Sundays a single presbyter, either on his own or assisted by a sub-deacon or acolytes, had to cope with the celebration of the eucharist for the faithful in his parish. Many people might think that in these churches the liturgy was of necessity performed according to the very simple forms of the primitive period. Here too (they think) they will encounter that simple celebration of the Last Supper which was denied to the bishop of Rome, at least at his public appearances in the stational churches, bound as he was by the chains of courtly ceremonial which alas he had forged for himself. Certainly, there was such a thing as this simple form of the mass celebrated by a presbyter. But in Rome this was not considered to be the regular form of the liturgy, because the early Christians considered the bishop alone to be the proper celebrant of the eucharist for the congregation. Since therefore this pres-byteral liturgy was not the normal form, as far as we can see, not very much attention was paid to it at the Lateran, apart from the fact that the *fermentum* was despatched to churches where it was celebrated. The presbyters themselves were given the responsi-bility of providing the basic texts for their services (we have already heard how they attempted to solve this problem); and as regards the rite which they used in their liturgy, it was probably considered just as much their own affair to find out, by relying on the papal liturgy, how they should conduct their celebrations of the eucharist. But whereas we still possess the sacramentary which they compiled for their own purposes, we do not know anything about their Ordo; and even supposing they formulated such a document, it has not at all events come down to us. It is possible also that it was not considered necessary at the Lateran to include such an Ordo in the series of Ordines Romani, because this simple rite was presumably familiar to everyone, and because also the presbyteral mass as compared with the papal mass was only a makeshift. By contrast, apparently, people took notice of the baptismal Ordo in use in the titular churches (Ordo XI in Andrieu's edition deals with this) which could connect with the fact that in Rome, apart from exceptional cases, baptism which for a long time had generally speaking only to be conferred upon infants, was a task which had been handed over by the Pope to the titular churches. Its ceremonies, moreover, which were now as complicated as they ever had been, were in urgent need of explanation. Hence there were constant inquiries from outside concerning the rite of baptism, which may well be the reason for one of the Ordines being devoted especially to this subject.

Now we might well think that the complicated and cumbersome rite of the mass celebrated by the bishop of Rome, which we have learned about, would have undergone a thorough process of simplification when it was taken over by the churches of France. How otherwise, one might conclude, could they carry out within the narrower confines of conditions in that country liturgical directives which assumed a well-populated metropolis possessing numerous clergy and whose members had for centuries been accustomed to the etiquette of the imperial court. But a sentence at the end of Ordo II, which was probably added by an editor commissioned by the Frankish court or by a Synod, states quite clearly that Ordo I must be followed just as faithfully in the episcopal cities of France as in Rome itself: 'Episcopi, qui civitatibus praesident, ut summus pontifex ita omnia agant', i.e. 'The bishops who preside over congregations in towns must perform everything in the same way as the Pope' (Andrieu 2.116, No. 10). Ordo I, therefore (apart from the ceremony of kissing the feet, which was probably considered a special privilege of the Pope), was considered to be binding on all the bishops of France. Only the town and country presbyters were allowed to celebrate their eucharist more simply. Apparently they followed the example of the Roman presbyters, the ceremonies of whose mass they could have become acquainted with from the narratives of clerical pilgrims who had made a journey to Rome.

The consequences of this Frankish instruction we have just quoted were that, in the centuries to come, Ordo I remained completely unaltered as to its essentials. First the Romanized

Celts of the cities and then the Franks of town and country accustomed themselves to its use. It became the measure according to which the bishop's mass (pontifical high mass) was celebrated and has continued to be so to the present day. We should not be surprised, therefore, if we are reminded of Ordo Romanus I when we are present at pontifical high mass in our cathedrals and abbey churches. It is true that side by side with this, the presbyteral mass of the old days in its various forms, which have been determined by the mistakes or interests of clergy, or by the lack of or presence of other clerics, is today much more in the foreground of the life of the church mass than it used to be. Today, the bishop does not celebrate pontifical high mass every Sunday, as Ordo I says he should, and this solemn ceremony is reserved for specially important festivals. That things have come to such a pass is in fact the consequence of the growth of the daily 'private' mass; for as soon as the bishop was compelled to celebrate the eucharist not only on Sundays and high festivals but every day, he had to take refuge in the form prescribed for the presbyteral mass. To celebrate pontifical high mass every day according to Ordo I would have been far too much for him.

v. THE DEVELOPMENT OF THE ROMAN LITURGY

The research of the past forty-five years on the subject of the sacramentaries, *pericopes*, and the Ordines which has been carried on with such extraordinary vigour and has proved so fruitful has enabled us to have a far more clear-cut picture of the development of the Roman liturgy and of the active part which was played in its development by the Franco-German dioceses than was possible for scholars of the pre-1920 period, even for the most perceptive of these, Louis Duchesne. We know now that it was not Charlemagne, but Pepin before him, who first introduced the Gregorian liturgy of Rome into his kingdom and made it obligatory by royal decree, and that he did this on the occasion of his coronation in the presence of the Pope in the year 754.

The motives which lay behind Pepin's taking this step were not only political and ecclesiastico-political, but also religious. He wanted to be in closer contact with the porter of the gate of heaven, Saint Peter, with his tomb, with his city, and with his liturgy. Probably more than anything, however, it was hoped also that the rivalry between the Roman and Gallican liturgies which had lasted for more than a hundred years could be brought to an end, and with it the division in liturgical matters which this rivalry had occasioned. And if hitherto only some isolated bishops and abbots had worked at the Romanization of the liturgy, now the supreme authority of the King himself was set to work to achieve the same end. Under Pepin, owing to technical difficulties, they failed to attain their objective. It was impossible even to provide all the churches of the land with the requisite new books at the right time, since the Roman copies they needed were either not available at all, or at least not in sufficient numbers. The clergy from the episcopal seats of the land were compelled to carry on using the older books. We can see now that in the Frankish empire, instead of there being a uniform Missal which corresponded to the Roman liturgy in its most up-to-date form, i.e. the Sacramentarium Gregorianum, there came into circulation that 'mixed' form of the liturgy we have already mentioned, in which Gelasian, Gregorian, and to a limited extent Old Gallican elements were combined into a single unit. This is the type of sacramentary known (as we have already learned) as the 'Gelasianum saeculi octavi'. On account of its success in Pepin's time, it has also been called the 'Pepin Sacramentary'; and if those who give it his name mean by this that the 'Gelasianum saeculi octavi' was the officially recognized 'Roman' Missal used in the reform of the liturgy under Pepin, then certainly they are claiming far more than can actually be proved.

It was Charlemagne's intention to complete his father's work. He once again made it obligatory for the churches of his realm to accept and use the pure Roman liturgy. At the same time, he asked Pope Hadrian for books which could be relied upon, i.e. those which conformed to the most up-to-date form of the Roman liturgy which had been rearranged by the much-admired

Pope Gregory (J. 2473). When Charlemagne finally received these after a long wait (probably in 785), he placed them in his palace library at Aachen to serve as patterns for others to copy (*codices authentici*). Henceforward, such copies as were needed to supply the Frankish churches were to be made from these.

It has been possible to make a reconstruction of the presumably 'authentic' Sacramentarium Gregorianum at that time in Aachen from some surviving early copies of it which have been only slightly edited. This is a problem which was definitively solved by Hans Lietzmann in 1921. A careful examination of the text revealed that all the Sundays after Pentecost and the Sundays after Christmas were missing, and also some of the feasts that had been recently introduced in Rome during the seventh and eighth centuries. The explanation for this deficiency is an easy one. Because the intention was to send the ruler of the Franks a book which was properly representative and because also by reason of the collapse of the Roman scriptoria nothing better could be produced in the short space of time available, a somewhat antiquated but certainly lavishly inscribed and just as expensively bound book from the papal sacristy was chosen. This book, however, made provision only for those services performed by the Pope himself at the stational churches, and therefore, so far as the liturgical year was concerned, it was, as might be expected, incomplete.

If the authorities in Rome had given some serious thought to Charlemagne's intentions and the situation he was faced with, and if considerations of prestige and the lack of scribes had not been factors which stood in their way, then it might well have occurred to them to append to the papal sacramentary all the forms from the Roman presbyteral sacramentary which were not to be found in the papal book, and the small number of new sets of prayers for feast days which had not yet been added. The measures which were now taken in Aachen itself prove that this would have been the right way to help the ruler of the Franks.

It was from his counsellor, the Anglo-Saxon Alcuin, that Charlemagne learned that the book which had been sent from Rome could not fully satisfy the liturgical needs of the Frankish churches, quite apart from the fact that it made no provision for certain blessings and feasts which were at that time customary in France. With Charlemagne's authority, Alcuin invented substitutes for everything that Rome had neglected to include. Drawing principally on the mixed sacramentary which had been in circulation since Pepin's reign, he put together all the forms which were not to be found in the magnificent book from Rome. In the Preface, he directed that his supplementary collection was only to be added as an appendix to copies of the Roman book. Later generations, however, no longer took any notice of this directive of Alcuin's, which so clearly illustrates his scrupulous approach. For the convenience of the users of the book, they inserted the pages of Alcuin's appendix in their appropriate liturgical places in the Sacramentary itself. With Alcuin's help the objective after which Charlemagne had striven had now been achieved. The Roman liturgy in the form in which it had been compiled by the much admired Gregory the Great (though we have already shown above that Gregory the Great was far from being the sole originator of this compilation) was now the standard liturgy of the Frankish church, even though many kinds of non-Roman prayers had been intermingled with it from Alcuin's appendix.

As is well known, chaotic conditions prevailed in Rome from the end of the ninth century onwards. The office of the Roman bishop fell into the clutches of some unworthy characters; and since these men fulfilled their liturgical duties in a slovenly manner, or alternatively did not fulfil them at all, the clergy of Rome and the Roman people lost all interest in the liturgical life of the Church. After a short time, things had come to such a pass, that the sense of the liturgy in Rome threatened to die out altogether. Small wonder then that the few scriptoria which still functioned did not produce any liturgical books at all; for such books were no longer in demand. It is possible that the liturgical life of the Eternal City would have died out altogether had it not been that at least some of the new Roman monasteries founded by the Cluniacs in the tenth century had begun to cultivate it with great conscientiousness in accordance with the strong traditions of their order.

At the end of the tenth century, however, a surprising turn of events took place. In various places in Italy and also in Rome itself, liturgical texts began to appear (Michel Andrieu was the first to see this in his extensive researches on the Ordines) which did not reflect the old Roman forms for the administration of the sacraments, but rather new rites, such as had developed in the eighth, ninth, and tenth centuries in France. Andrieu established that in Rome they suddenly ceased to confer ordination on clergy in the concise, austere manner of the ancient Roman rite, but started to use a much richer ceremonial which during the intervening period had been adopted in Franco-German circles.

How is this to be explained? Certainly, the Roman Cluniac monasteries we have spoken about made the most fundamental contribution to this change. They cultivated the liturgy in a form that was current in the monks' own country, France, and secured the enthusiasm of both clergy and people in Rome for this form of the liturgy. They also certainly gave copies of the Frankish books they used themselves to anyone who asked for them. But what was in fact decisive in effecting the change-over was without doubt primarily the attacks of the Saxon rulers, Otto I and Otto II. On their journeys to Rome, they sometimes attempted to deal also with the reform of the church in the Eternal City; for the low ebb which religion and worship had reached in Rome made these religious men shudder. They demanded a careful nurturing of liturgical life, and provided such liturgical books as were necessary where these were lacking. These books were of course the same as those which were in use on the other side of the Alps.

This work of restoration must have been nearly completed soon after the year 1000. The Eternal City, home of the Roman liturgy, had received its liturgy back, but in the form which it had acquired in the north; it was a liturgy radically altered, at least so far as the liturgy of Holy Week and Easter and that of the sacraments and sacramentals was concerned.

The fact that the emperors after the turn of the millennium did not cease to keep a watching eye on the liturgical life of Rome and, if it seemed necessary to them to make improvements in it, is shown by a report made by the Abbot Berno of Reichenau, who witnessed the coronation of Henry II by Pope Benedict VIII. It occurred to the Emperor that the Credo was omitted at the coronation mass, something he was accustomed to hear when he was at home. Quite unmoved by the appeal made by the Roman clergy to their own traditions, Henry demanded that they should follow the Franco–German custom which had recently been introduced from the East, i.e. of making the confession of faith follow immediately after the reading of the Gospel. (The Franco-German custom of reciting the Credo in the mass derived ultimately from Greek or oriental influences.) Neither Emperor nor Pope could have foreseen, however, that this very Credo would in the age of polyphonic church music lead to a lamentable shift of emphasis within the celebration of the eucharist. For in their time the Creed was still recited or sung by the congregation as a whole.

It would be no exaggeration to say in conclusion that during a critical period, the Franco-German Church succeeded in saving the Roman liturgy not only for Rome itself but for the entire Christian world of the Middle Ages. By doing this, she was able to repay her debt of gratitude for the valuable religious and humanistic values which since the time of Gregory the Great had, through the Roman liturgy, been heaped upon her.

vi. THE FRANCO-GERMAN CONTRIBUTION

As we have already explained, we ought to be grateful to the Franco-German Church not only for having salvaged the Roman liturgy, but also for having enriched it. In more recent years, the old idea that under Gregory the Great and his successors (i.e. between 600 and 700) the Roman liturgy was codified and given a structure which has held good to the present day, and that after this time nothing of importance was added, has now been shown to be erroneous. It is certainly true that after Gregory the Great liturgical activity came to a halt in Rome itself. A few more feasts were added to the calendar, about which I shall have something to

say later. There was also added to the Good Friday rite a very
simple form of the veneration of the Cross, probably due to
pressure brought to bear by pilgrims to Jerusalem. Under
Eastern influence, as we have already heard, the practice was
begun of arranging for the 'Agnus Dei' to be sung during the
fraction. But the impulse to greater efforts and further construction
was wholly lacking. In particular there was (as we have already
said) no impulse to an organic development of the post-Pentecostal
portion of the liturgical year nor any incentive to a working out
of the liturgy of the other sacraments. In this connection, the
monotonous uniformity of the Sundays after Pentecost and the
disparity that had existed at least since the turn of the third
century between the lavishly devised baptismal liturgy and that
of the other sacraments ought to have aroused the Roman litur-
gists to some degree of creative activity. But this challenge met
with no response in Rome.

Things were quite different, however, in the new home of the
Roman liturgy. The Franco-German clergy did not look upon
their new liturgy as a treasure which was not to be meddled with
and which they merely had to pass on. Nor did they confine
themselves to making a thorough and careful examination of it, as
is shown by the questionnaire sent out by Charlemagne to
inquire into how the faithful were being instructed on the meaning of the ceremonies of baptism, by the answers which were given
in return, and to a greater extent by the liturgical writings of
Amalar, Agobard, Walafrid, the pseudo-Alcuin, and others.
Recent investigations have been able to show in detail that,
during the eighth and ninth centuries, the Franks boldly developed the liturgy they had inherited, exercising at the same time
a high degree of creative ability. It is true that the Sundays
after Pentecost were not influenced by this urge to do something about the liturgy, it affected rather the solemn days which
fell between Palm Sunday and Easter and the rites of the
sacraments.

We shall in a moment be hearing in detail how successful and
how important were the consequences of these efforts made by
the Frankish clergy in respect of the Roman liturgy. But we must

first of all draw attention briefly to a special initiative taken by the Franks, but which was something of a temporary affair, because it was eventually swallowed up in the development of the church's organization.

Visitors to the Eternal City were certainly impressed over and over again by the system of the Roman stational masses, that is to say by the attempt made by the Christian community of a large metropolis to arrange for the bishop to celebrate the liturgy according to a fixed plan sometimes in one church, sometimes in another, in order to preserve at least to some extent the fundamental unity of the people. Rome, however, was not alone in possessing such a system. We know that this custom of the bishop travelling from church to church to celebrate mass was current also in Oxyrhynchus in Egypt, in Jerusalem, in Antioch, and in Constantinople. Generally speaking it was only in Rome, however, that Frankish bishops and clergy would have got to know this arrangement. And when they returned home, some of them who lived in a town with a large number of churches attempted to imitate the Roman pattern in the interests of preserving the unity of their people. It has been possible for a long time to point to the traces of such attempts in Tours, Metz, and Strasbourg. But in more recent times, the chance discovery of two manuscripts has suddenly thrown more light on the growth and decline of the stational system at Metz. In the eighth century, there were already more than two dozen churches in this town. It appears that it was Bishop Chrodegang (742–66) who attempted to counteract the splitting up of the Christian community at Metz by introducing the system of stational masses. In the year 753 Chrodegang, on orders from Pepin, had travelled to Rome, and had moreover accompanied Pope Stephen II on his journey to France. On this visit to Rome, he must have got to know the Roman liturgy and Roman church music so thoroughly that he was able on his return to carry out a successful reform of worship, following the pattern he had learned in Rome. It is thanks to him that Metz became so famous as a centre for the cultivation of liturgical music that people came from abroad to Metz to seek instruction. This organization of the stational masses, together with his organization of the community life of the canons, seems to have been an important link in the chain of his efforts to reform the liturgy.

All that had been achieved in Chrodegang's day in this particular field, however, fell into a state of neglect under his next but one successor, Bishop Angilramus (768–91). Angilramus celebrated the stational Mass in person only on the more important days of the year, and on the remainder he arranged for members of a specially created group of clergy called *stationarii* to take turns in standing in for him. He provided also a special honorarium for these *stationarii*, as well as for the clergy who took part in the stational services. That the Bishop himself withdrew from these stational masses probably has something to do with the fact that he was frequently kept in Aachen by his duties at Court, and in the end remained there for almost all the year (he had been chaplain to Charlemagne since 784). And that the clergy of Metz had to be lured into taking part in the stational services by the prospect of an honorarium can only be attributed to the fact that they no longer appreciated the usefulness of the system of stational masses.

Are we justified, we may ask, in seeing in this development the beginnings of the process whereby the parish was first consolidated, both legally and actually? For as soon as there were parishes, it followed automatically that the parochial clergy wanted to perform their liturgical duties in their own churches, rather than elsewhere. And the development of the parochial system meant moreover that on the practical level an even sharper division was made between the bishop and his congregation and their clergy in the cathedral city. For a long time he had been driven into a certain measure of isolation by the unfortunate system of privileges and insignia which had been bestowed on him by the secular order and by the court ceremonial which went with this. And now the faithful felt that he was so far above the parishes and their clergy that he had almost developed into an outsider whom they couldn't approach, a stranger in fact to the people whose leader he used to be. It is doubtful whether this difficult situation would have been overcome in our own day.

But we must return, after this, to the new liturgical compositions of the Frankish clergy, which held their ground because they marked a definite step forward.

In more recent times, people have been inclined to attribute the magnificent liturgy of Palm Sunday, Holy Week, and the Easter Vigil to the work of the pre-Gregorian Roman bishops. But, thanks to the investigations of Baumstark, Capelle, and Andrieu, we know today that all the imaginative and dramatic elements of these solemnities were introduced into the Roman liturgy by the Gallo-Frankish reformers. This is especially true of the procession of palms on the Sunday before Easter, itself an imitation of an ancient custom at Jerusalem which has acquired a fresh note of triumph from the hymn 'Gloria laus et honor', composed by Bishop Theodulf of Orleans. The same applies to the impressive ceremony of the gradual extinguishing of lighted candles at solemn Matins in Holy Week, and to the ceremony of the foot-washing on Maundy Thursday. It applies also in particular to the impressive present-day form of the Veneration of the Cross on Good Friday together with the chants which are sung on this occasion, i.e. the 'Reproaches' ('Improperia'), the acclamation 'Agios o Theos', sung in two languages, and the threefold 'Ecce lignum crucis'; in all these there are clearly traces of eastern prototypes, especially of those from Jerusalem. The same, finally, can be said of the numerous Easter Vigil rites which have such profound significance, i.e. the Blessing of the New Fire, the greeting of the 'Lumen Christi' with acclamations, the ceremony of the Blessing of the Paschal Candle and the hymn 'Exultet', and finally almost the entirety of the rich ceremonial of the blessing of the baptismal water.

Scholars were at one time of the opinion that the solemn anointings of the head and hands of the new bishop and of the hands of the new presbyters in the rite of ordination were a part of the ancient, pre-Gregorian rite. This theory has now been shown to be mistaken. The anointing of bishops and priests was first introduced by the Franco-German clergy sometime during the eighth century, who copied, perhaps, the example of the British Celtic Church and made this practice a part of their own liturgy. This innovation which was not confined to the sphere of ordination ceremonies, was no doubt fostered by the Old Testament. In the Book of Exodus we read that 'Thou shalt anoint Aaron and his sons and consecrate them in this way that they may minister to Me in the priesthood'. It is also worth noting that at approximately the same time, there developed in France and elsewhere the practice of anointing the king, in which custom they were quite clearly again following a biblical precedent. These two innovations and others made at this time leads us to draw an important conclusion, namely that for the clergy of France and their like-minded colleagues in neighbouring countries the Holy Scriptures of the Old Testament became the great source-book from which again and again they produced suggestions and instructions for the development of the liturgy.

Scholars had also at one time accepted the theory that the many forms of the impressive ritual that is used today for the consecration of churches were something that had been inherited from local Roman customs. Today, however, we know that the only genuinely pre-Gregorian elements in this rite are the sprinkling of the new church and the practice of stocking it up with relics (and perhaps also the Eucharisteia, i.e. the consecratory prayer in this rite). Everything else was devised for the first time by the Franco-German clergy and introduced by them into the liturgy. We owe to them, therefore, the ingenious and meaningful ceremony in which the bishop takes possession of the new building and also the washing and anointing of the altar and walls of the church (which is in fact an imitation of baptism). These enlargements of the liturgy for the consecration of churches were partly inspired by eastern precedent; partly, once more, by the Old Testament (cf. Exodus 40.10); and partly by the cultural life of the time, in particular by the geodetical practices of the land surveyors.

As we have seen, the primitive Roman liturgy was on the whole almost puritanical in its severity and brevity. Whereas the bishops of the East and those from Spain and Gaul had been very much taken by the rites of Holy Week, which they had experienced personally as pilgrims to Jerusalem, and were much concerned to imitate these in their own dioceses, the Roman bishops had not shown themselves to be exactly kindly disposed towards such ceremonies, especially as certainly none of them had visited the Holy Places as a pilgrim. Paul VI was the first to go. Nor did the Popes feel any great need to imitate emotional Greek and Latin liturgical poetry, and to adopt it into their worship at Rome.

The *hymnus angelicus* or 'Gloria', which comes originally from the Greek and which today is one of the principal adornments of our Service of the Word must have existed in a Latin translation in Rome well before the year 500, but the Roman bishop alone was allowed to intone it, and then the rest of it was sung by the people. But this was done only on high festivals, especially at Christmas and Easter; and one gets the impression that the lively swing of this certainly very popular hymn did not seem quite suitable to the celebrants who were responsible for the services, for it did not conform in any way to their ideas of what constituted a dignified liturgy. Hence not until the eleventh century could the 'Hymn of the Angels' become a normal part of the mass on every feast-day irrespective of the hierarchical standing of the celebrant. For the same reason, the growth of Latin liturgical poetry, in whose composition and introduction in places outside Rome even such as Ambrose had taken part, met with strong opposition. Not until the eleventh century did Saint Benedict of Nursia's happy idea of adding the *ambrosiani*, i.e. hymns in the style of those composed by Saint Ambrose, to his order of divine service finally bring about, in a roundabout way, the singing of hymns at the divine office in Rome itself. An exception was made only in the case of the hymn 'Agnus Dei' which came from the Greek church. But it was Sergius, a Pope of Sicilian and Syrian ancestry who in the seventh century made this hymn an integral part of the preparation for communion in the Roman mass. As we can see, the delight taken by Saint Paul in composing and singing hymns (Eph. 5.19; Col. 3.16) was not shared by the bishops of Rome, with the exception of Sergius. From the beginning, it is true, the hymn was the form of expression of the charismatics, and indeed continued to be so. The ground in Rome, however, was not suitably prepared for charismatic enthusiasm; hence, in view of these exhortations given by Saint Paul about hymns in worship, it must not be overlooked that however much Rome claimed the Apostle for its own, in so far as his theological ideas were concerned, he had not been fully *persona grata* in the Eternal City for a long time. (See App. III for examples of these hymns.)

If, then, during the eighth and ninth centuries the Roman liturgy was enriched by a series of prayers which were both less austere in their ideas and less reserved in their language, and by a series of liturgical hymns, and if its liturgical year and its sacramental rites were interspersed with a whole host of spectacular and impressive ceremonies, then she owes this, historically speaking, to the clergy of Celtic and Germanic origin of the Carolingian Empire. It was in fact the Roman liturgy as it had been developed by them which in years to come was handed down to the Romano-German world of the Middle Ages, and which both satisfied the religious needs of the people and provided them with spiritual nourishment.

It was ultimately the clergy of Mainz (so Michel Andrieu informs us) who took the ancient and modern ceremonies of the liturgy of the sacraments out of the sacramentaries and bound them together in an especially neatly put-together collection of their own, together with the appropriate directives from the Ordines. The collection lives on in our Pontificale and Rituale; and, together with the enriched Gregorian 'Missal' (now it really deserves such a title because it only contains the prayers for the celebration of the eucharist), it conquered the whole of the western world, Rome in particular. There is no need for us to say what the potential significance of these insights for our personal relationship with the Roman liturgy is. Our liturgy is Roman to the core; but in certain important parts of the liturgy of the sacraments and sacramentals, as in the ceremonies of Holy Week and the Easter Vigil, it owes its present form to the Franco-German Church. The liturgy which is performed by us today is, therefore, truly Roman, but it is at the same time also our own. Our forbears too made it spiritually their own and completed it in its final form.

vii. THE CALENDAR

I drew attention to the fact in passing that in Rome, during the seventh and eighth centuries at least, something, if not very much, was being done to develop the liturgy. In this connection I also mentioned something about a measure of enrichment of the calendar; and the manner in which this developed in the period I have mentioned has been explained principally by means of some recent research on the *capitulare evangeliorum*, (i.e. the list of portions from the four gospels to be read on each liturgical day, arranged in chronological order). We know today that in Rome between the years 600 and 800, apart from about twenty feasts of the saints and four feasts of the dedication of churches, two more feasts of Our Lord, two feasts of Our Lady, and one feast of the Holy Cross were introduced into the liturgical calendar. In order then to provide ourselves with a foundation upon which to make a proper evaluation of these innovations, we must begin by making a survey of the earlier history of the Roman liturgical year; till now we have dealt with this subject only in very general terms.

The history of the liturgical year begins with the early Church, probably with the simple fact of the primitive Christian community's making the day of the Resurrection, the 'Day of the Lord' (i.e. our Sunday), a day of assembly for worship and a feast-day (cf. John 20.26). On this day they celebrated the eucharistic meal, the 'Supper of the Lord'. Possibly the opinion that the return of the Lord, the 'Parousia', would happen on this day incited them to mark out Sunday as a special day. On the other hand it is scarcely likely that the desire to create a Christian counterpart to the Jewish Sabbath led to the institution of the Christian Sunday. For the Sabbath constituted a remembering of the Creator's resting on the seventh day and was, therefore, first and foremost a day of rest and not a day for worship. The Christian Sunday was not made a day of rest until the Emperor Constantine made it so in the year 321. The Sabbath was by no means waived or dispensed with by the early Church, but gradually fell into oblivion in those communities which were not governed by Jewish Christians. (This is particularly true of western congregations.)

The Jewish Passover feast which was fixed on the 14th Nisan, and could, therefore, fall on any day of the week, probably continued to be celebrated at the same time by the primitive Church, though almost certainly it was looked upon as a day of memorial of the slaying of the true Passover Lamb, i.e. of the Passion of Our Lord. But since the triumphal conclusion to the Passion, the Resurrection, had immediately acquired a pre-eminent position in the minds of Christian communities, it was inevitable that they should transfer the Passover celebrations to a Sunday, and together with this begin to cut loose from the Jewish Paschal feast. In the West, this cutting loose had been already completed in the second half of the second century. In the East the process took rather longer and led, in the so-called Paschal controversy, to serious divisions between the conservative and progressive wings of the Church.

The early Church continued to keep with the Jews the fifty days festal season following the Paschal festival. But in doing this it by no means immediately prescribed special days within this festal season to commemorate the events of the Ascension of Jesus and the coming of the Holy Ghost, both of which belong to the history of our salvation. In many places the Ascension of Our Lord and the outpouring of the Holy Spirit on the fiftieth day (our Whitsun festival) were not celebrated until some little time later; and on account of the transferring we have just mentioned of the Paschal feast to a Sunday (how and why they came to choose the Sunday after the first full moon in Spring has not yet been explained), the fifty days of the festive season culminating in the feast of Pentecost understandably also became detached from the corresponding Jewish season. A special feast of the Ascension on the fortieth day after Easter was instituted probably for the first time in the fourth century.

In the West, around the year 250, a new group of feast-days was added to the original nucleus of liturgical days we have just been talking about. These were the days for the commemoration of the martyrs. As with the Jewish martyrs, the celebration of these feasts was linked closely with the day of the martyr's death and with the place of his burial, which means that they had to be observed in a certain fixed place. After some time, the increase in the number of these memorials made it necessary to construct a calendar by means of which people could be informed as to the day and place of the festivals. The oldest Roman calendar of this kind is set out for us to this day in copies of a *de luxe* edition of the State Handbook for the year 354.

In the fourth century, side by side with the Easter festival and its weekly repetition, i.e. Sunday, a new kind of feast of Our Lord was introduced which was no longer concerned with the end of Jesus's redeeming activity, but with its beginning at the Incarnation. This was the feast of the Nativity. Its purpose was to put right out of Christians' minds a major heathen festival, which was celebrated on the same day, namely the 'Birthday of the Invincible Sun God', the principal deity in the imperial religion of late antiquity. Similar considerations caused the Eastern churches to institute, somewhat earlier, a Christian festival in opposition to a popular pagan 'Feast of the Epiphany' (of the Sun God, Aion-Osiris) which was kept on 6 January and which was intended to honour the 'Epiphany' of the Son of God, i.e. his manifestation to the world. Although both of these festivals (the Eastern one on 6 January and the Roman on 25 December) were closely related, during this same fourth century the Roman Church incorporated into its calendar in addition the festival of 6 January, though it is true that the meaning of this feast was slightly altered. At Rome it was made to refer concretely to the first historical revelations of the divinity of Christ, closely associated as these were with the coming of the Magi, the baptism in the Jordan, and the marriage feast of Cana. Quite clearly, after the feasts of Christmas and the Epiphany had come into being, sooner or later the idea was bound to occur of filling in the period between these festivals and Easter with more feast-days, so that by this process the life of Our Lord could be reflected in the liturgical year. In Rome, however, as we shall see, it was only with some hesitation and indeed rather late that this idea was gradually put into practice.

As the bishops of Rome became increasingly conscious of the authority they exercised, a feeling enhanced by the State's having conferred upon them some magnificent titles—this led eventually in the fourth century to the day of the bishop's taking office being counted as equal in importance to that of the emperor himself. This day was incorporated into the liturgical calendar, and called the *natale papae*. In connection with this new development, an earlier feast of Saint Peter, the feast of Saint Peter's Chair (kept on 22 February) which originally must have been a somewhat more private act of commemoration of the departed, held at one of the two supposed burial places of Saint Peter, had its meaning completely altered. From now on, the feast of the *cathedra* was understood to be the feast of Saint Peter's 'enthronement' as bishop.

The institution of the feast of the *Pascha annotina* is also probably fourth-century in origin. It owes its beginnings to the natural tendency to have a special celebration on the first anniversary of an event, in this case the recurrence of the previous year's Easter festival and the baptismal ceremonies held on that occasion. The feast, therefore, was intended first and foremost to remind the previous year's newly baptized of their reception of the grace of baptism. We should remember also the fact that the fourth century was the century of mass conversions.

Almost from the very beginning, the Christian community seems to have taken part in the exercises of prayer and fasting which the candidates for baptism performed during the period before Easter (Didache 7.4; Justin *Apology* 61). From this practice there developed the forty days (*quadragesima*) of the season of preparation for Easter, which brought the faithful together for an almost daily celebration of the eucharist, and only Thursdays remained, curiously enough, free from any liturgical celebration until the eighth century. With the introduction of an almost daily celebration during the forty days before Easter, an important stage was reached in the development of the liturgical life of the community. Whereas at first the eucharist had been celebrated only on Sundays, now it gradually began to be held more frequently.

The Ember Days, which had perhaps developed somewhat earlier, provided further reasons for doing penance and for holding services. These were the Wednesdays, Fridays, and Saturdays that came first at the beginning of three seasons in the year and then at the beginning of each of the four seasons. Like the great Roman Rogation Service, which was later instituted on 25 April, they took the place of the corresponding pagan cultic ceremonies, designed to ask God's help for the harvest at that particular stage of the year. A later generation preferred to see the origins of the Ember Days in the prescriptions of the Old Testament.

Between the fourth and sixth centuries little was added in Rome to the framework of the liturgical year. Whereas the martyr-bishop Cyprian of Carthage acquired a place in the Roman calendar on 14 September, probably on account of the fact that secondary relics from his tomb in Carthage had been deposited in Rome, the great ascetic Martin of Tours was the first non-martyr to be incorporated into the calendar, only perhaps on account of his immense popularity. Popular devotion too secured a place in the Roman list of saints for the 'Holy Innocents', the chief of the martyrs, Stephen, the two Saint Johns, and Michael the Archangel.

In the sixth century it was considered necessary to have a season of preparation before Christmas as well as before Easter. In this way the season of Advent gradually developed, which, as we have already heard, was perhaps intended to form the beginning of the process of dividing up the time between Pentecost and Christmas, to give a more complete picture of the history of our salvation.

Against the background of this picture of the development of the liturgical year, five of the new feasts introduced during the seventh and eighth centuries merit a certain amount of attention. These are the two feasts of Our Lord, two feasts of Our Lady, and the feast of the Exaltation of the Holy Cross instituted by Sergius (687–701). It is worth our while to spend a little time on the subject of these new festivals.

One of the two new feasts of Our Lord, that of the 'Meeting

of the Lord with Simeon', kept on 2 February, which until recently has been understood as being a feast of Our Lady, clearly owes its origins to the attempt made, especially in the East and then in Rome too, to make the succession of feasts follow the events of the life of Jesus. The customary procession of candles on this day, which is a christianizing of a heathen procession (*amburbale*) must on the other hand have been the custom at a considerably earlier period in Rome. The other new feast of Our Lord, 'The Annunciation of Our Lord', kept on 25 March, has had its meaning altered in the same way, and is today regarded as a feast of Our Lady. This is simply the logical consequence of the accepted fact that 25 December was the historical birthday of Our Lord. The Syrian Pope Sergius, by instituting these two feasts, made way in the Roman calendar for two festivals which had been kept for a long time in the East. The Liber Pontificalis tells us about the introduction of these feasts in the biography of this Pope (Duchesne 1,376).

The same holds good for both of the feasts of Our Lady, the 'Assumption of Our Lady' on 15 August and 'The Nativity of Our Lady' on 8 September. Under the influence of the Council of Ephesus (431) an already existing church in Rome, the Basilica Liberiana, known today as Santa Maria Maggiore, was placed under the patronage of the 'Mother of God'. At the beginning of the seventh century the same thing happened to the Pantheon, which had been transformed into a church. At the end of the sixth century a rather feeble attempt had been made to celebrate 1 January as a feast of Our Lady. But the Syrian Sergius was the first to succeed in giving Our Lady, who for a long time had had a place in the Eastern calendar, an established place in the Roman list of feasts. It was the same Pope who succeeded in the end in introducing into the Roman calendar the festival which was so popular in the East of the Exaltation of the Holy Cross, a reminder of the triumphal return of the newly recovered relics of the Cross back to Jerusalem (629). (This information can also be found in the 'Vita Sergii' in the Book of the Popes, 1,374 D.)

In all these innovations can be seen quite clearly the attempt of an Oriental to overcome the age-old reserve of the Roman Church towards the liturgical innovations of Eastern Christendom, and to bridge the gap which had developed between the Roman and Eastern Churches as a result of Rome's conservatism in these matters.

The account we have just given of the development of the Roman liturgical calendar is bound to raise some questions in the minds of those who have read it carefully. They will ask themselves whether the ordering of the liturgical year ought to have been left entirely to the changing interests and tendencies of each century and each pope. If this was so, then its growth was to a large extent dependent on pure chance. But surely (they will ask) were there not at least some rules and regulations on which each century and each pope could rely to ensure that he would not disturb or upset the liturgical year by his innovations?

The answer to this last question can be deduced from the account we have just given. The Easter festival and its weekly repetition, Sunday, is not only much older than every other festival of the Church's year; it is concerned directly with the central mystery of the faith of the Church, the redemptive work of Christ which reaches its climax in the Resurrection and whose actualization in history right through the centuries determines the sense of the liturgy. The Easter festival forms, therefore, together with the Sundays, the framework which supports the whole of the liturgical year. This pre-eminent significance of Easter and of the Sundays can, therefore, in no way become obscured or crowded out by anyone's arbitrary choice, nor by any innovation, however popular this may be.

This precedence of Easter and the Sundays has been principally lessened by the fact that too many other feasts of Our Lord, too many feasts of the Saints, and other festivals have accumulated in the calendar. Each new festival to some extent robs those already in existence of some of their importance, especially the Sundays, as together with Easter they are the important elements in the framework of the whole system. One has the impression that the Roman liturgical calendar was already lavishly filled with feasts around the year 800; and this moreover even before the onslaught of the innovations of the Middle Ages had begun.

A responsible reform of the liturgy will, therefore, be faced with three tasks. The Sundays must once more regain their dominant position without any qualifications as a weekly renewal of the Easter festival. The excess of secondary feasts of all kinds must be curtailed; and the impulse in many circles to keep on inventing and instituting new festivals must be seriously brought to a halt by means of education and legislation.

THE DONATION OF CONSTANTINE

(Abbreviated extracts from the Donation of Constantine, forged
c. 750 at Rome.)

1. The Emperor Constantine wishes Silvester, Bishop of the city of Rome and Pope, and all his successors, together with all the most eminent catholic bishops, grace, peace, love, joy . . .

2. Since Peter has been set up as the representative of God's Son, we have considered it fitting that the bishops who act on behalf of the prince of the apostles should be provided with that same princely power which belongs to our imperial majesty, but in a higher measure. We, therefore, give the Roman Church of Saint Peter and his most holy See a status higher than that of our imperial throne, while at the same time granting him imperial power and dignity.

12. We decree that the Roman See shall enjoy a primacy of rank over the four principal sees—Antioch, Alexandria, Constantinople, and Jerusalem—and moreover over all the churches in the world.

13. We make known to all that we have for the Redeemer a church and a baptistry in our own Lateran palace; and we decree that this church shall be recognized and honoured as chief and supreme among all churches in all the world.

14. To Saint Peter and Saint Paul and for their sakes to Saint Sylvester and all his episcopal followers we grant by this gift our imperial palace of the Lateran, which excels over all palaces, and further, we grant them the diadem, namely the crown upon our head, as also the Phrygium [i.e. the imperial head-dress], the

humeral cloth, the Lorum which is hung round the neck of the emperor [*pallium*], and also the purple cloak and the scarlet tunic, in fact all the imperial vestments. We grant them also, moreover, the imperial sceptres and standards and the usual imperial insignia and everything else besides which belongs to the solemn pageantry of the imperial majesty.

15. To the most eminent clergy of the Roman Church, we concede those privileges of position as are possessed by our noble Senate. The clergy shall be raised to the rank of Patricians and Consuls and given the usual dignities of the empire. If they ride on horseback, they are entitled to the privilege of having a white caparison. And they shall also have the same footgear as our senators.

16. We decree, moreover, that our most honourable and worthy father Sylvester and his successors may wear the diadem we have granted them, worked in the purest gold and precious jewels. Since, however, the Pope could not agree to wearing a golden crown over his clerical crown [i.e. the tonsure], we have with our own hand set upon his head a white Phrygium (white on account of the resurrection of Our Lord). Moreover, out of respect for Saint Peter, we have held the bridle of his horse, and thus rendered to him the service of a stable boy.

17. In order that the highest episcopal office may not fall below the dignity of the secular office of the emperor, we have given over to our Father Sylvester and his successors in addition to our own palace, all the provinces of Italy and the West, together with all districts and towns.

18. We deemed it, therefore, also fitting to transfer our imperial power to the East . . .

19. Whoever shall transgress these provisions which hold good for all time, shall burn in hell with the devil and all the ungodly.

20. This, our imperial decree, we have with our own hand laid upon the tomb of Saint Peter.

Given at Rome on 29 March, when Constantine, together with Gallicanus, for the fourth time was First Consul (317).

III

Dissolution, Elaboration, Reinterpretation and Misinterpretation: From Gregory VII to the Council of Trent

i. OUTLINE OF THE PERIOD

We have agreed that the third period of the history of the western liturgy should be reckoned as lasting from 1073 to 1545; this period may perhaps be outlined roughly as follows.

From Gregory VII (1073–85) onwards, the popes took firmly into their own hands once more that task of leadership in the realm of the Roman liturgy which for almost three hundred years they had left to rulers and bishops on the northern side of the Alps. Gregory himself attacked the preceding period in which 'the government of the Roman Church had been handed over to the Teutons' and criticized the Teutons for having shortened the liturgical day hours out of a consideration for the lazy and negligent. Hence he himself felt obliged to rediscover and restore once more the original Roman Ordo. Such a plan of campaign, however, seems to have endangered the entire shape of the Romano-Frankish liturgy now firmly established at Rome. All the evidence, however, points to the fact that Gregory's reform was of necessity confined to details of little importance, such as the number of psalms and lections to be read. It was now already impossible to 'wind back' the Roman liturgy to ancient Roman usage (*ordinem romanum et antiquum morem*). Nevertheless, the Pope now demanded that the episcopal sees of the western Church should follow exclusively the liturgical customs of the

Roman see and rigidly obey all liturgical prescriptions issuing from this source. The liturgies of Milan and Spain which did not conform to Roman usage were, therefore, from this time onwards, a permanent scandal to the newly awakened centralizing tendencies in liturgical matters at Rome.

The demand for conformity to Roman practice would have remained largely theoretical even in places other than Milan or Spain, had the new Order of Saint Francis of Assisi, whose efforts since the 1320s had been wholly concentrated on an itinerant pastoral ministry, not become, without meaning to be, the apostle of a quite distinct form of the Roman liturgy. It was only practical considerations that made the Order adopt the convenient and relatively easily carried liturgical books which were in use at the papal court. The Roman liturgy that was contained in these books had been relieved of many of the accretions that had developed in more recent years, primarily out of consideration for the Pope who quite often had to travel. Through the agency of the Franciscan itinerant preachers, these serviceable editions, principally the 'Missale' and the 'Breviarium of the Roman Curia' became well known, were received with respect, and as is only natural, were copied everywhere in the world of that time. Thanks to the disciples of Saint Francis, therefore, the western liturgy achieved a measure of unification which was not merely a theoretical or legislative unification, but one which was carried out in practice. To a great extent it was thanks to the Franciscan Order that the western world was prepared in the age of printing for a short codified form of the Roman liturgy which was to be binding on all, a liturgy moreover which on the whole was readily accepted. From the factual point of view, an especially notable factor in the liturgical development of this period was that almost every day of the year was now the feast of a saint, and a yet more closely woven network of feasts of Our Lord and of Our Lady was spread over the entire liturgical year. In an age in which the Roman liturgy was becoming more universally current, the Roman Church's early inclination to multiply the number of feasts continued to develop and now reached a pitch which has scarcely ever been surpassed since.

The liturgy of the day hours which (as we know already) had been developed especially in the monasteries was now expanded to an unbearable degree, primarily in the monasteries of Cluny. It was prescribed that at least on certain weekdays special offices in honour of Our Lady or of the Commemoration of the Departed should be recited in addition to the normal offices. The monks also said the penitential and the gradual psalms and constructed 'Suffrages' and 'Preces'. Of course those who did not have any heavy work to do and did not need much time for pastoral duties, could tolerate this task now swollen beyond all proportions; in other places, however, they groaned under the burden. Small wonder then that strife developed between the Cluniacs and the followers of Saint Francis and that the latter adopted a shorter version of the day hours which was afterwards adopted by the secular clergy. A learned Franciscan of our own day, looking back on the attitude taken by the fathers of his Order towards the liturgy, once said: 'Saint Francis discovered that Christ did not found a monastery but a Church.'

But there was something else which was to prove of yet more consequence than the increase in the number of festivals and the lengthening of the hours of prayer. The practice of priests saying private masses which had developed in the monasteries during the preceding period, now spread and triumphed over the whole of the Christian world. During this period, in places where there was a surplus of priests, in almost every church, besides the mass for the people, many masses were celebrated with no congregation at all. At the same time, the giving of communion from the chalice was abandoned and the meal-like form of the eucharistic rite, in so far as it still existed, was thereby reduced yet further. So, too, an understanding of the actual meaning of the eucharist and of the essential connection between the sacrifice and the sacrificial meal dwindled more and more during this period. The devotion of the faithful centred, even during the celebration of mass, on the Sacred Humanity of Our Lord, especially on his Passion. And in this devotion to the Passion the degree to which people immersed themselves in the painful details of the events of the crucifixion is shown by Matthias Grünewald's altar-piece in the Antonite Monastery at Isenheim. During this same period a growing religious individualism sought to satisfy its devotional needs to an increasing extent in extra-liturgical devotions, for example in devotions of many kinds practised by the fraternities.

Investigations of more recent years, however, have not demanded that we should add any entirely new details to this (from the liturgical point of view) somewhat sorry picture, which in no way measures up to the romantic idealization of the Middle Ages which prevailed a few decades ago. It has been possible, however, to delineate more clearly the most important outlines and in the process, it has become ever clearer that the most important feature of this period is not that the old and new episcopal sees of the West began to follow the Roman liturgy, nor the fact that in this process there came an increasing measure of liturgical uniformity. Of at least equal importance though of much greater consequence is the fact now long observed, namely of a change in the relationship of the people to the liturgy. For the liturgy, which was once and always should be the common act of priest and people, became now exclusively a priestly duty. The people were still present, but they devoted themselves during the sacred action to non-liturgical, subjective, pious exercises. Recent research has placed us in a better position to understand this transformation; and it is with this that we shall be primarily concerned in what follows.

ii. THE DISSOLUTION OF THE LITURGICAL COMMUNITY

In the ancient Church, the task of presiding over the liturgical action was of course entrusted to the bishop or to the priest who represented him and it was these who also undertook the important acts of consecrating and of administering the sacraments. On no occasion, however, did the early Church cease to give the people their full and proper part in either the prayers or the action; on the contrary, it was intended that the people should be able to follow both of these in detail, in order that they might not be just attentive spectators, but active participators in the action of the mass. For this reason, the prayers were said aloud and no exception made of the Canon and the Institution Narrative. Calling out '*Gratias agamus Domino Deo nostro*' ('Let us give thanks to the Lord Our God'), the bishop summoned the people to offer with him the great Eucharistic prayer of thanksgiving; and with a solemn 'Amen' (which survives today in the 'Amen' which directly precedes the *Paternoster*), the whole congregation gave utterance to the fact that they had heard the words of the Canon said by the bishop, and had prayed it with him, thus making it their own.

From what we have said, it will be understood that the step that was taken in changing from this practice to that of reciting the most important prayer of the rite in an inaudible whisper must have been a very significant one. For, by doing this, the link between priest and people at the very focal point of the liturgy was severed and the most important part of the rite became the exclusive concern of the bishop and the priest, the people being thus forced into playing the part of passive onlookers. Moreover, if they were to be excluded from this part of the liturgy, why indeed should not their often cumbersome efforts at taking part in the non-consecratory parts of the liturgy, which did nothing but hold up the course of the liturgical action, be curtailed or even allowed to vanish altogether? As we can see, a beginning had been made which was to have serious consequences; and later developments reveal that the path that had been taken was subsequently trodden to its inevitable conclusion.

But when, we may ask, was that decisive step first taken? We might well presume that this first occurred at a time when the influx of former members of the ancient mystery cults brought about a widespread acceptance of the ideas and rites of these cults, and that, therefore, this happened in the fourth century when the so-called *disciplina arcani* (i.e. the duty of observing secrecy concerning important liturgical forms and actions as well as about the terminology used in the mysteries, namely the names current in the ancient mysteries for the sacred rites) became part and parcel of the Church's life. By researching somewhat more closely into this matter, however, Jungmann has shown that this hypothesis is to a certain extent not so very far removed from reality so far as the East is concerned; but that the more conservative Roman Church, which was less inclined to accept all the ideas of the mystery religions, clung to the old practice of saying the Canon aloud right up to the end of the Classical age. The change-over to the silent Canon was carried out first in those places where (probably in the eighth century) the Roman liturgy encountered the influence of the East, i.e. on Gallican territory.

The idea had become widespread in these parts during this period (as it had somewhat earlier in the East) that the consecration of the eucharistic gifts was indeed something that had been commanded by the Lord at the Last Supper, and that this very action ought, therefore, to inspire both awe and reverence. On account of this (so people thought), the words of the Canon which were so powerful in their effect were extremely sacred (for in those days they still thought the whole Canon had the power to consecrate and not just the words of institution.) Thus to say them aloud was to show lack of respect; and the sacred action, therefore, had to be performed in the most profound silence, and was moreover the exclusive concern of the ordained bishop or priest.

Under Frankish influence, therefore, Rome too, at the latest *c.* 1000, changed both its ideas and its practice. Here, too, it now became obligatory to recite the Canon softly in a whisper, and from this time onwards, the whole of the western Church was bound to this practice. The Canon recited silently by the celebrant and the ideas which lay behind this custom, left their mark both on the outward appearance and on the inner spirit of the liturgy through the whole of the Middle Ages and their influence extended right into the period beyond.

Originally, of course, the people were able to hear every word of the Canon, they could say it to themselves while it was going on and they could see that they were taking a full part in this most sacred action of the eucharistic celebration. However, after the practice of reciting the Canon inaudibly had become widespread, the people were relegated to merely watching what went on. At almost the same time people living away from Rome had even more taken away from them, for they now lost the chance of even seeing what happened on the altar, because its position had been changed.

It is well known that the altar in the early Christian basilicas of Rome was situated (as is the altar in the church of the Lateran and in Saint Peter's today) in such a way that people could walk right round it, allowing the celebrant to face the people. Moreover, the altar of the early Roman basilica had no gradine for candles, still less a reredos adorned with pictures, a retable, or a tabernacle. The altar of the primitive period was a simple table, made of wood to begin with, later becoming a massive stone structure, having at first a horseshoe shape or round top, which still later became rectangular. As is, for example, revealed by the paintings in the lower church of San Clemente which dates from the end of the eleventh century, even after the year 1000 there were in Rome no lights standing on the altar such as are prescribed today, nor was there a crucifix (which again is obligatory today). There was, moreover, nothing on the surface of the table but the cloths, the sacred vessels (i.e. the chalice and paten), the missal and (up to the second lection), the book of the gospels. There was, therefore, nothing that could distract the eyes of the faithful from its essential function, namely the offering of the Holy Sacrifice, nothing in fact to obstruct the view of the people as they followed the eucharistic action. This took place freely and openly before the eyes of all present.

People have often wrestled with the question of when in fact the decisive change was introduced which finally led to the present arrangements in places other than Rome, whereby the priest was transferred from behind to in front of the altar, the altar itself placed against the wall of the apse, the retable introduced, and lastly a cross and a row of candles placed on the table. For some years now we have been kept informed on this point by the remarkably learned investigations of Joseph Braun, whose researches have been taken an important stage further by Otto Nussbaum. We now know today that the placing of altars against the rear wall of parish churches was a practice introduced with increasing frequency from the sixth century onwards, probably under the influence of the practice of celebrating mass for a small circle of people in side chapels; but we know also that it was from about the year 1000 onwards that outside Rome the practice of celebrating mass with the priest's back to the congregation became the general rule. Roughly at the same time, the altars acquired a retable. Candles, on the other hand, were not generally placed on the altar until *c.* 1100, the cross only for the most part at the beginning of the era of devotional emphasis on the Passion, i.e. in the thirteenth century.

From all this it follows that the new additions to the altar probably came in just at the time that the mass was beginning to be regarded as a more or less exclusively priestly action; and it is also certain that, vice versa, these changes concerning the altar (which on the whole are to be regretted) were fundamental in altering people's interpretation of the rite.

Happily, in recent decades, there has everywhere been a general growth in people's understanding of the special function of the altar. In new churches it is once more given the dominant place which belongs to it by right. Its character as a table is stressed and it is disencumbered from the often trivial and distracting ornaments and auxiliary structures and the lace hangings introduced during Rococo period. One may hope that a return to the original free-standing position of the altar and, as a result, the disappearance of this unfortunate business of the priest having to turn round at the 'Dominus vobiscum' will soon become a reality.

iii. THE DEVELOPMENT OF THE PRIVATE MASS AND ITS CONSEQUENCES

It has always been supposed that the changeover to the practice of reciting the Canon silently and of celebrating the liturgy with the priest's back to the people had necessarily some connection with the growth of the private mass. Since, however, we had not previously acquired any more precise information about the history of the private mass, we were unable to say anything more conclusive of this association. Recently, however, all this has been changed, for we now know, thanks mainly to Otto Nussbaum's research, how the private mass originated, and how it developed up to about the year 1100.

We ought here to make special mention of the fact that the private mass is in no way to be confused with the 'celebration of the eucharist in small groups' (*Eucharistiefeier im kleinen Kreis*; a subject dealt with by Johannes Wagner), for the latter was already in existence in the primitive period of the Christian religion. Celebrations of the mass of this kind differed in many respects from the normal Sunday and feast-day celebrations, especially on account of the fact that they could be held on every day of the week, and that not all the people took part, but only a relatively small group of them. The rite for such masses, for which it was not compulsory to have the full complement of clerical assistants required for the usual celebrations, was essentially simplified. As a rule, ordinary rooms served as makeshift accommodation for these celebrations, and if people were fortunate they had a chapel. Such masses for small groups were held at burials, in prisons, and on occasions also in private houses. When the practice was begun of allowing masses to be held on weekdays for a particular personal intention (called 'votive masses' from *votum*, meaning oath, wish, desire), the number of these masses for small groups had to be increased considerably.

The 'private mass', however, is something quite different from these masses for small groups. At a private mass there is no congregation whatsoever and, apart from the server, the priest is quite alone when he celebrates.

The place of origin of this third type of eucharistic celebration is the monastery (as Otto Nussbaum was the first to show from a large assembly of proof texts). The most ancient monasteries, it is true, were unfamiliar with the idea of having priests as monks; they were entirely lay communities. For a long time, the monks had had doubts about accepting priests who attempted to enter their monastery, for the disciplinary difficulties which resulted from their priestly standing seemed insuperable to superiors. On the other hand, they naturally wanted a priest near enough to be easily accessible, especially if the monastery were situated in an isolated position. Saint Benedict of Nursia discovered a satisfactory solution, for he allowed, if necessary, a monk who had proved himself obedient to be ordained priest. But when he was not officiating at divine service, he was not allowed to claim any special favours (Regula 62). Only when under Gregory the Great the monasteries began to be drawn into missionary work among the heathen was there introduced a fundamental change in this situation. Missionary work could not be carried out without priests; and now, therefore, the number of monks who were also priests gradually increased. In the middle of the seventh century, the monastery at Melrose had only four priest-monks, but in the year 784 the monastery of Saint Peter in Salzburg numbered already twenty-two priests among its ninety-seven monks. In the tenth century, however, there were monasteries with a hundred and more priests.

The priest-monks naturally felt the need to exercise the office for which they had been ordained. In monasteries with a larger number of priests the desire of each to celebrate himself could no longer be satisfied fully, merely by the fact that it was possible for each in turn to celebrate the liturgy for the monastic community. Approximately at the same time there arose another influence which made the existing situation completely untenable; the idea became widespread that the more one made use of the means of grace of the Church, especially by celebrating a mass or arranging for it to be said, the more one could ensure one's personal salvation and the salvation of the departed.

The situations and tendencies we have just described led of necessity to the creation of the daily private mass. First of all it was the priests in the monasteries who practised this new form of the eucharist. Among these the daily private mass was probably by the eighth century almost the general rule. A little while later, the secular priests followed their example.

The daily private mass led inevitably to far-reaching divergences from the ceremonial that had been in use hitherto. Because the server (who when this practice started was quite often not there) was for the most part unskilled in reading or even reading aloud, the priest himself had to read the appointed *pericopes* from the epistle and the gospel. Since also there was no choir to take over those parts which were meant to be sung, the priest himself was obliged to perform this part of the liturgy himself; and he contented himself with simply reciting those parts of the mass which were normally sung. Since also the space at the 'side altars' was as a rule extremely limited, the priest could not think of going to some special place away from the altar to read the epistle or the gospel; and why indeed should he, since the people to whom he was supposed to read the lection from this place were not there at all. Therefore the priest contented himself by 'marking' this change in position between the lections at the altar itself. He read the epistle on the right side (the 'epistle side') and the passages from the gospel on the other side (the 'gospel' side). Since, however, the lection was in fact supposed to be read to the people, the general direction at least in which the gospel was to be read was still indicated by placing the book at an angle on the altar, a practice which later gave rise to many interpretations which though profound in meaning were wholly unhistorical. Whereas, too, at the normal service the offertory procession still continued to constitute an important element, this had to be rejected altogether at the private mass. The *oblatio*, however, still continued to be marked, but was shrunk into a procession of the priest from the middle to the right hand side of the altar, where the server stood ready, not, it is true with the hosts, but with the wine. The *lavabo* which had become superfluous on account of the disappearance of the offertory procession and the custom of sorting out the offertory gifts was still retained.

We have not, however, been given a full explanation of the question as to when and where the rules for the celebration of private mass underwent a definitive codification, nor, therefore, whence the then standard 'Ordo Missae Privatae' originated, the forerunner of the edition published by the papal Master of Ceremonies, Johannes Burckard, from Strasbourg in 1502, which in turn became the basis for the account of the ritual of the mass in the introduction to our 'Missale Romanum'. The investigations of the Praemonstratensian Luykx and of the Franciscan Van

Dijk, however, seem to have brought us near to a conclusive solution to this problem. It is certain that by the ninth and tenth centuries attempts were made in large monasteries, particularly in Mainz and St. Gallen to construct an elaborate Ordo for the private mass, and our attention has been drawn to several versions of this kind. In the year 1243, however, the General of the Franciscans, Haymo of Faversham, submitted to the headquarters of his order at Bologna, a very much earlier edition of the Ordo, the Ordo 'Indutus planeta', which was to be of great importance for the history of the liturgy. The copy on which this Ordo was based has till now been untraced, but everything points to the fact that since it belonged to the Franciscans it must have been an Ordo used by the papal Curia; but so far as we can tell the Curia, surprisingly enough, did not evolve any prescriptions for the rite of private mass. Notwithstanding, the Ordo 'Indutus planeta', together with the Missal used by the Curia, was spread far and wide by the followers of Saint Francis and finally thrust into the background all other versions in circulation at that time, with the exception of those used by the religious orders. Burckard's Ordo (which fortunately has been made accessible to us by John Wickham Legge in Volume 27 of the Henry Bradshaw Society 1904), must, it would appear, in the last resort have been based on this Ordo.

At ordinary services, people in the Middle Ages (as indeed in earlier times) had special books for each section of the liturgy of the mass; the chants were continued in the 'Antiphonale', the portions of Scripture for the Epistle in the 'Apostolus', and the corresponding portions for the gospel in the 'Evangeliarium', the book containing the four gospels. The actual prayers of the mass were collected together in the 'Sacramentarium'. To have such a collection of books at a private mass, however, made matters very uncomfortable; hence the requisites of the private mass led to the construction of a 'full Missal', which contained all the texts that the priest celebrating privately might require and in which was also to be found the Ordo, in the form of directives written in red ('rubrics'). After the thirteenth century this 'full Missal' became more or less widespread everywhere.

Since it frequently happened that several private masses were held simultaneously, often at the same time as the conventual mass in the centre nave, priests at the side altars had to recite their prayers and texts as quietly as possible; hence their mass became a 'silent mass' or a 'said mass'. In places where people had not already on other grounds made the change to saying the eucharistic Canon silently, the private mass now brought this practice into general use.

It is true that, as far as we can see, there were at this time no theologians who would have challenged the fundamental feasability of the private mass; there was, however, no lack of those who spoke against and resisted its increasing prevalence. In many circles people still remembered the warning of Saint Ignatius of Antioch: 'Take care to celebrate only one eucharist; for there is only one Flesh of Our Lord Jesus Christ, and only one Chalice of unity in His blood, therefore there is only one altar as there is only one bishop together with the presbyters and deacons' (Philad. 4). This requirement of Ignatius, which had been practised for so many centuries, that the Christian community should be exclusive and gathered round a single eucharistic table, round the pastor of the congregation who presided over them, was undoubtedly yet further endangered by the private mass as it was equally by the 'mass in small groups' which on the whole was celebrated less frequently, We understand that among the Carthusians at the end of the twelfth century it was still only seldom that a member of a community of the order was allowed to celebrate daily, and that a synod at Ravenna forbade the celebration of private masses during the normal conventual mass. Saint Francis of Assisi wanted only a single daily celebration of the eucharist in his monasteries, even if more priests were available. But the stream of this development could not be checked; and those in positions of authority had to be content with preventing the over-zealous at least from celebrating more than one private mass per day or at least limiting the repetition of the private mass to a few days in the year.

The private mass had become in this third period of the history of the Western liturgy so much the role in monasteries, and then for the secular clergy, that its rite came to influence more and more the rite of the normal public service. This development began at the latest in the thirteenth century.

Even at high mass the celebrant now began to read to himself the *pericopes* and chants sung by the choir and read by the subdeacon and deacon instead of merely listening to them. The result of this was that the Missal was carried even at high mass from the epistle to the gospel side just as at a private mass.

But the influence of the private mass extends even further. Probably priests had always been in the habit of saying prayers of preparation privately in the sacristy and on their way to the altar, and it is certain that from an early time Psalm 42 and a confession of sins formed a part of such preparations. Since, moreover, the priest who celebrated privately did not put on his vestments until he was at the altar, the preparatory prayers were not said until he had reached the altar (if we may be permitted to make such a reconstruction of this development); in this way they became the 'prayers at the foot of the altar'. For this reason the Introit, the text which used to be sung at the entrance of the celebrant was not read at private mass until the preparation had been said. And the nonsensical situation was eventually reached (which still persists today) whereby as a result of people adapting the ritual of the private mass to the normal type of service (i.e. the solemn mass) the Introit chant no longer accompanied the procession at the entrance of the celebrant and his assistants, but rather the preparatory prayers at the foot of the altar.

It seems probable that already for some time, the celebrant and his assistants had said private prayers silently to themselves during the offertory procession which as a rule took a great deal of time. A confession of sins, a preliminary offering of the gifts, and intercessions probably formed the main themes of such prayers. These kinds of prayers which, by contrast to the prayers of the liturgy were spoken in the first person, were used by priests celebrating privately to fill the gap that had developed as a result of the disappearance of the offertory procession between the recitation of the offertory sentence and the 'Oratio super oblata'. This complex of prayers too made its way into the solemn mass, all the more easily in fact because the offertory procession in this service died out quickly. We may conclude from the evidence Jungmann has adduced that the prayers for this part in the mass (for which there is evidence in the sources of the early Middle Ages) were taken at least in part from the old Gallican liturgy. Like Jungmann, however, we shall not find it easy to consider this conglomeration of prayers (among which the 'Apologiae', i.e. prayers of self-accusation in the first person, are very prominent) to be a valuable or even tolerable part of the eucharistic liturgy as a whole.

The same is probably true of the origin of the silent, subjective prayers with which the celebrant today is directed to prepare himself for his own communion. These two prayers, originating also in the old Gallican liturgy, have become integral to the structure of the private mass and because of the influence of the private mass have become part and parcel of the solemn mass. In short, those parts of the body of the rite which had remained at least partly healthy were now made thoroughly sick through contact with the overpowering and unhealthy influence of the private mass.

Probably towards the end of the Middle Ages at the latest, the conviction had become almost universal that to celebrate mass personally was the duty of every priest who took his work seriously and that to celebrate personally was of greater value than taking part·in the worship of the community. From this time onwards, it was considered that every priest ought to celebrate privately either before or after the community service.

The modern practice, therefore, of priests at conferences giving up their right to celebrate privately and taking part in a mass celebrated by one of their fellow priests signifies a notable loosening up in the custom which has held good since the end of the Middle Ages. A return, however, to the custom of the ancient Christian period whereby the celebration of the eucharist was limited to Sundays and feast-days is neither considered nor supported by modern theology. This has been shown clearly in the much-discussed study by Karl Rahner, entitled 'The Many Masses and the One Sacrifice'.

iv. THE DECLINE OF THE OFFERTORY PROCESSION

A further phenomenon which is causally connected with the institution of the daily private mass is one which must not be overlooked in any account of the liturgy of the Middle Ages, namely the decline of the so-called offertory procession. In Christian antiquity, it had been the custom for the faithful to lay an 'offering' on the altar or to hand it over at the altar rails at each celebration of the eucharist (cf. p. 65). In part these were gifts, such as bread, wine, oil, and wax, which were found of use in making preparations for the eucharist or for the other sacramental actions. Partly, also, these were gifts to help towards the support of the clergy or the charitable work of the congregation. We should not be surprised, therefore, if the sources for our knowledge of the offertory procession in the early centuries mention cheese, poultry, and other gifts in kind. All of these gifts (those used specifically at the celebration of the eucharist, as well as those destined for the support of the clergy and for the works of charity of the congregation) were looked upon as being a contribution to the sacrifice; and in the offering of these gifts one could see how each member of the congregation expressed concretely his intention of taking an active part in the sacrifice, and of making an offering of his very self. The fact that most of the oblations, in an age which was accustomed to trade in kind, were products of the labours of people's own hands served to enhance the symbolism of the offertory gift in the mind of the individual worshipper. For in his gift at the offertory, he gave something of his own substance, something fundamental to his very existence and by doing this represented the giving of himself. The practical effect of such oblations was at one and the same time to provide an economic foundation for the existence of the clergy and of the church's work of charity; the clergy, like the poor, lived so to speak 'from the altar'; and the eucharistic sacrifice was at the same time the very source of the charitable activity of Christians.

This obligation to take part in the offertory procession was enforced by many synods right up into the eleventh century; then the bishop's admonitions gradually ceased, a clear sign that this institution was nearing its total eclipse. Its inability to survive is understandably connected to a certain extent with the fact that since the ninth century, primarily (we presume) under the influence of Old Testament texts, the use of unleavened bread at the celebration of the eucharist in the West became the general custom; the most important contribution to the sacrifice made by the faithful, the bread that they baked at home, became from this period onwards no longer usable as bread for the eucharist. Even more important, however, was the fact that the faithful could now no longer take a personal part in the private mass, now far and away the most widespread form of the eucharist service. In place of the gifts which they had formerly presented as offerings at the mass, there was gradually substituted the 'mass stipend' which to begin with understandably consisted of gifts 'in kind', but later simply money, by means of which the faithful claimed the right to have a mass celebrated privately for themselves and for their own personal intentions.

In this case, too, customs which through the development of the private mass had become so cumbersome gradually secured themselves a place in the ordinary parochial mass. At one time, the offertory procession had consisted of a formal procession of the whole congregation to the sanctuary, and the celebrant with his assistant ministers had there received the gifts of the faithful (as is shown by a miniature in a tenth-century document from Gaeta). Now, however, this time-consuming procession together with the business of sorting out the offerings at the end fell more and more into disuse. The papal mass *c.* 700 represents (as we have seen) a midway point in this development. Today, however, a verger collects the gifts from the congregation in offertory plate, basket, or bag (with a bell), a practice which still continues to be looked upon as an indispensable means of expressing the fact that one is taking part in the service. The celebrant, however, no longer takes any notice of this collection and carries on with his service at the altar without interruption. More recent investigations (which, however, need to be completed and taken further) have been able to show that this situation which prevails up to the present day was reached in most places around the year 1200. Only in the rite of the consecration of a bishop, and in the similarly constructed rite for the consecration of an abbot, has the shortened form of the solemn offertory procession survived in the offertory procession of the candidates who are to be consecrated.

It is yet more remarkable that at the end of the fourteenth century, at the canonization of Saint Brigitta of Sweden, to be specific, performed by Pope Boniface IX in the year 1391, the procession of offertory gifts, unabbreviated and in all the splendour which must have characterized it in the early Christian period, succeeded in being revived again within the framework of the papal mass. According to an eyewitness report, after the chant at the offertory three cardinals and six other dignitaries processed with the oblations to the papal altar. The first of the cardinals carried two candles, the second two loaves, and the third two small vessels of wine. Each of the others who took part waited with a candle and a cage containing doves. This rite for which the earliest evidence is this canonization of the year 1391 has survived ever since in later ceremonies of canonization.

How then can we explain that such an ancient form of the offertory procession should make its reappearance exactly at the moment of the canonization of Saint Brigitta? Was perhaps the old form of the offertory procession still so much alive in the home country of the new saint, Sweden, that in deference to the Swedish pilgrims it could not be left out at the Roman ceremony? Or did, on the other hand, a developed form of the offertory procession, based on the rite of the consecration of a bishop, appear to the papal masters of ceremonies to be a means of giving greater splendour to the rite of canonization. Alternatively: were the originators of this innovation perhaps people who had an affection for the history of the liturgy, who felt the need to revive once more by means of this solemn occasion an element in the liturgy which they considered precious and which formerly had been preserved only in the consecration of bishops, the consecration of abbots, and the consecration of kings and emperors?

None of this is true. The historian will know that the four-teenth and fifteenth centuries had an especial love of dabbling in allegory; and he will immediately, therefore, presume that the roots of this innovation lie in this and not in the possibility of a newly awakened feeling for the profound symbolism of the offer-tory procession. He will also perhaps recall that the lighted candles may have been intended to represent faith, the bread hope, wine love, and the doves the innocence of the new saints. Now the truth of this conjecture, which has been made merely on the basis of the history of the times, becomes extremely probable if we examine it more closely. On the occasion of subsequent canonizations, the doves in the cages were surrounded in addition by gaily coloured birds. What indeed could this addition have meant but that the people wanted to show allegorically the variety and splendour of the moral virtues of the newly canonized saints.

The high degree of probability of the truth of this conclusion is supported in particular by an interesting parallel to which Henri Chirat has drawn our attention. On the occasion of the requiem mass for the deceased Connetable, Bertrand du Guescelin, held in the church of Saint Denis on 4 May 1383 (i.e. two years before the canonization of Saint Brigitta), there was a similar offertory procession, whose allegorical meaning is clearly brought out by a chronicler of the time. The procession of those bringing gifts was begun by four knights on foot, wearing the armour of the dead Connetable, and in so doing representing, so to speak, the person of the departed. They were followed by four other knights on horseback carrying the weapons and the standard of the deceased. Then came the new Connetable with two marshals, accompanied by eight cavaliers, carrying a shield face downwards with lighted candles set on the reverse side; according to the chronicles, this was supposed to show that the dead man had now lost his high rank on earth. After these noblemen, there appeared four royal princes, each carrying an unsheathed sword; and the chronicler suggests that they brought their swords as a thanks-giving for the victories won by the deceased, as the nobles who preceded them with his arms and his standard had done. The procession ended with an even larger number of other knights, who probably represented the house of Guescelin in the offertory procession. Since the chronicler expressly observes that offertory processions of this kind were the custom at the obsequies of barons and princes, it is clear that this particular one is in no way an isolated precedent.

We may well doubt whether offertory processions wrapped up in allegorical meanings (as we have just described them) have much to say to us today. The offertory procession in its simplest form, however, as it is now again being practised, is quite a different matter. Each person who takes part in the eucharist places beforehand, or possibly not until the offertory, his own host on the paten or in the ciborium. The idea that the sacrifice of the altar is not just the sacrifice of the celebrant, but the sacrifice of everyone present can by means of this ceremony be brought much more expressively to the forefront of people's minds than by means of a simple instruction. It is on account of this very fact that many enthusiastic parish clergy are unwilling to forsake this simple way of making the essence of the ancient Christian offertory procession live once more today.

v. THE MEANING OF GENUFLEXION

After having shown the dire effects on the liturgy of the private mass, I must here say something in conclusion about a development which drew to its close in the Middle Ages but which is still having its effects today, and which concerns an important ritual gesture, the act of genuflexion.

Throughout the whole of the ancient world, the act of bowing the knee had already acquired a variety of meanings. The penitent slave who had committed some fault threw himself on his knees; hence this gesture was an act of penitence. The prisoner of war, too, threw himself on his knees if he wished to petition the victor to spare his life, and so did the religious man when he besought the gods with especial fervour; hence genuflexion was also a gesture used in requests. At the same time it became (especially in its exaggerated form of prostration, i.e. throwing of oneself full length on the ground) an expression of homage and even of adoration. For this reason, the religious man knelt in front of the statues of the gods, the subject knelt down, too, in front of his ruler whom he looked upon as a god, or in front of his picture. Since genuflexion was in this case an expression of adoration, the Christians in the age of persecution had, besides refusing to offer sacrifice, also to refuse to genuflect to images of the gods and the emperors.

About the middle of the third century, however, the gesture of kneeling had fallen so much into disuse and lost its value, that in many circles in Rome it was no longer felt to be a sign of adoration in the worship of the gods and the emperor. As a result of this, in the year 257 the Roman State declared officially that genuflexion to images of the gods of the State and of the emperor no longer constituted an essential element in heathen religion, nor indeed did the offering of incense to these same images. Both, they said, were only ways of expressing one's loyalty as a citizen of the State, they were but *Romanae caeremoniae*. The Church of the third century, however, did not draw any particular conclusions from this change in the situation; for well thought-out reasons she made no use of this way of escape that the State had opened up in the dilemma that obtained between state ritual and Christian monotheism.

Things were different, however, under Constantine. The Church now had no more scruples about permitting the person or the image of the emperor to be honoured by the act of genuflexion. She even encouraged her faithful to use this same gesture to honour objects which indeed were holy yet not deserving of adoration, such as the altar, relics, and the images of the saints. She even tolerated the fact that imperial privileges granted the bishop the right to be greeted by people genuflecting to him, and that bishops could claim their right to these privileges granted to them by the State, even in the house of God. From this time onwards, genuflexion in the liturgy of the West became no longer merely a gesture of penitence and supplication, but also an act of veneration, normally performed to the altar, to relics (especially relics of the Holy Cross), to the bishop, and finally even to the crucifix.

This being so, we ought to realize that no small burden is laid on those responsible today for instructing the faithful. The performance of eucharistic worship has accustomed the faithful from their childhood upwards to understand the act of genuflexion as a symbol of adoration and (perhaps when confessing their sins) of their humbling themselves before God. It is going to be very difficult to make these same faithful understand that genuflecting to an altar with no tabernacle or to the bishop must be understood in quite another sense, i.e. to make them see that such genuflexions are simply a token of respect.

Romano Guardini once said during a lecture that one of the most important tasks before us in liturgical renewal today is to restore a new fullness of meaning to all words and gestures used in worship. There must be no more formulas which do not have to be taken seriously–as for example, the 'Ite missa est'—for up till very recently the priest saying it had no intention whatsoever of telling the people to depart. Nor must there be any acts or gestures which waver about uncertainly between two different meanings. One of the basic demands that is made on the liturgy is, therefore, that it should be wholly and truly genuine. We should remember the words of Jesus in John 4.23: 'The true worshippers will worship the Father in Spirit and in Truth.' Let us, therefore, remember also that in ancient times, the bowing of the head and the standing with one's head bowed were primarily ritual gestures of respect and honour; so much has been made clear in our description of the papal mass *c.* 700. It follows, therefore, that between 700 and the eleventh century, a change crept in; genuflexion was introduced via the court ceremonial as a gesture of honour to be used in churches, and from that time onwards the more ancient rite of bowing and standing with one's head bowed was forced into the background until finally genuflexion became almost the only important gesture at the eucharist. Any reform in the liturgy, therefore, would have to cover ritual gestures as well and restore a little order in this sphere. First and foremost, genuflexion would have to be severely limited. Many bishops have fortunately already begun to deprecate from the bottom of their hearts their being greeted with genuflexions (except during the liturgy) and their hand being kissed (the fact that nowadays it is the ring that is kissed and not the hand does not in fact make any essential difference). But it is just as important that we should restrict the use of genuflexions in the liturgy itself, especially in eucharistic worship. The other ritual gestures, too, should be reconsidered and be made more comprehensible than before to the congregation (in so far as such gestures deserve to be understood). The people ought to know the meaning of the crossing of oneself, of signs of the cross, of the striking of the breast, the kissing of the altar and the gospel book, why the priest stands with hands extended, why he folds his hands and raises his eyes. A better understanding of these and other gestures could lead to a spirited and not merely mechanical performance of them. It is a long time now since Romano Guardini presented us with his observations on the most important of these ritual gestures. It is to be hoped that these observations will once more be studied and read in the interests of a genuine and thorough reform of the liturgy.

IV

Rigid Unification in the Liturgy and Rubricism:
From the Council of Trent to the Second Vatican Council

i. OUTLINE OF THE PERIOD

The fourth and last section of this history of the Western liturgy begins at the Council of Trent in the year 1545, and takes us down to the beginning of the Council next but one, the Second Vatican Council in 1962. This period may be sketched roughly as follows.

As a result of the attacks made by Luther and Zwingli on the mass, but equally, however, as a consequence of the generally widespread discontent on the part of Catholics with the discordant, one might even say, chaotic state of liturgical practice and the similar condition of the liturgical books, the Council of Trent, viewing the immense number of abuses and perceiving that the bishops would never deal with the problem of reformation if left to themselves felt bound to keep a watchful eye on the process of reforming the books used for the eucharist and the hours of prayer, and at the same time to watch over (as is only natural) the reform of the liturgical practices codified in these books. In the year 1546, as a result of Bishop Tommasso Campegio's shrewdness in drawing people's attention to the fact that the Church possessed a uniform Latin text of the Bible, i.e. the Vulgate, people for the first time thought concretely about making radically revised editions of these liturgical texts which should be binding on the Church everywhere and which would also ensure a uniformity in the liturgy that allowed for no loop-holes. It was not until the Council was nearing its end, however, that it became possible to implement this idea in the face of those who rallied to the defence of the Bishop's prerogatives. Since, however, it was not possible for the new editions of the Missal and Breviary to be produced by the Council itself, the Council Fathers at their twenty-fifth session in the year 1563 had to be content with entrusting the continuation of this task to the Pope.

As a result of this decree the Council gave the Curia the chance, which they (the Curia) welcomed gladly, of availing themselves of the claim which had been theirs since the time of Pope Gregory VII, namely to the exclusive right of jurisdiction in liturgical matters without risk of encountering any stronger opposition and of proving to the whole world by the documents they produced that this claim was really authentic. The period of episcopal independence in liturgical matters which stretches right back to the early Church was thereby first in principle and then also in practice brought to an end.

The commissions instituted by Pope Pius IV for the implementation of the Council's decisions which were later ratified by Pius V carried out their work with relative swiftness, first with the assistance of and later under the presidency of scholarly Cardinal Guglielmo Sirleto. By 1568 it was possible for Pius V to publish the 'Breviarium Romanum', the new compilation of the hours of prayer, and in 1570 the corresponding collection of mass for-mulas, the 'Missale Romanum'. The titles given to these new books with the emphasis on the 'Romanum' epitomized the situ-ation. The papal regulations which were added prescribed that except in those sees which had had their own peculiar liturgy for more than two hundred years, these two books should everywhere form the basis of all worship; further additions and alterations in them were to be exclusively the concern of the Holy See.

This act confirmed the process of liturgical centralization, which was further supported by the institution in the reign of Pope Sixtus V of a senior Roman authority for liturgical matters, the so-called Congregation of Rites. To this was appointed the

task of giving an authoritative interpretation to the ritual directives of the new liturgical books and for seeing that they were
carried out. With this development, the 'rubricist' (i.e. a person
skilled in liturgical law) began to play an important part in the
liturgical life of the Church. In this fourth period of the liturgy,
the effect of such men was so telling, that we have very cogent
reasons for entitling this fourth period of history of the liturgy
the 'epoch of rubricism'.

The Council of Trent had officially only provided for the
issuing of a revised edition of the Missal and Breviary. The
Roman Curia, however, felt duty bound to produce authoritative
editions to cover the remaining departments of the liturgy. Hence
in 1596 in the reign of Clement VIII, there was published the
'Pontificale Romanum', which contained the formulas for the
sacraments and sacramentals reserved to the bishop; and in the
year 1614, there followed (in the reign of Paul V) the 'Rituale
Romanum', the book containing the forms for the administration
of all those sacraments and sacramentals which were not the
exclusive preserve of the bishop.

The Frankish Church, which in past centuries had been a prime
opponent of all such claims made by Rome, had also joined in the
work of implementing this process of liturgical centralization
begun by the Roman Curia on the basis of the authorization given
them by the Council. Since many a Frankish bishop did not need
to introduce the new books into his diocese, as he could appeal
to the fact that he had an ancient local 'Gallican' tradition of the
liturgy which went back more than two hundred years, in France
this radical break with the past was not everywhere felt so strongly.
Not until the 1730s, when people were thinking once more
'about Gallican freedom', was there a reawakening of this opposition to the uniform liturgy of Rome and of the demand that
bishops should one more be granted their rights of jurisdiction
in liturgical matters. Up to the outbreak of the French Revolution
(as Prosper Guéranger has established), out of 130 bishoprics,
80 had turned their backs on the Roman liturgy and had recourse
once more to the pre-Tridentine national traditions. Such tendencies spread to the Tuscan episcopate, which in 1786 at a synod

in Pistoia demanded a return to the primitive Church and the abolition of the private mass and all side altars, but the Roman Curia with the help of an Italian national synod was able to nip these tendencies in the bud.

Even in the previous period, the devotional life of the faithful was only to a relatively small extent conditioned by the liturgy (we must not exaggerate the value of the distribution and influence of mass-books in the vernacular and of vernacular explanations of the mass which have only recently come up for consideration, thanks primarily to the labours of Theodor Bogler). Nothing was altered during this new period. The devotion to the Son of God, present in the tabernacle on the altars, to his most Sacred Heart, and to His Passion, and equally the almost infinite number of forms of devotion to Our Lady— all these were more congenial to the pious than the existing forms of the liturgy which for the most part were not properly understandable, especially as the liturgy from Middle Ages onwards was looked upon as the exclusive concern of the priest. Hence while the celebrant 'read' the mass at the altar with his back to the people, the faithful were busy with other devotional exercises, mostly of a subjective nature. They sang hymns in the vernacular, whose content had little or even nothing at all to do with the liturgy; they read, wrapped up in themselves, a 'mass devotion' or prayed the Rosary silently to themselves. Only at the three main parts of the eucharist: the offertory, the consecration, and the communion did the faithful, raised by the server's bell, turn their attention briefly to the sacred action that was being performed at the altar, in order that they might make certain recommended 'affections'. Seldom indeed was it the custom for them to take any active part in the sacrifice of the mass by making an inward offering of themselves or by actually making their communion.

Since communion was given preferably before or after the mass or quite apart from the mass, it was not clear to the faithful during this period how this stood in relation to the eucharistic celebration, i.e. they could not see that their communion was the food of the sacrifice, and its necessary conclusion. First and foremost, communion was the 'receiving of the sacrament of the altar'. Only rarely did people communicate because the rigorous pastoral theology which prevailed at that time considered it necessary for people to make their confession before communion. When, however, people went to the 'table of the Lord' they gladly 'offered' their communion 'for specific intentions'. And instead of actual communion they were often earnestly exhorted to make an act of spiritual communion.

It is only right and proper that we should confirm that it was the movements of Jansenism, Gallicanism, and the Enlightenment, disapproved of as they were by the Church and for the most part condemned as a body for being deviationary, which, just like the Reformation in the sixteenth century, detected some fundamental weaknesses in liturgical practice and were concerned to eliminate them. From a diversity of motives, they proposed that the liturgy should be simplified and that its main ideas should be better worked out. In a variety of ways, they attempted also to bring the faithful to participate intelligently in its celebration. We shall indeed have to take into account the remote and hidden influence of such attempts at reform if we are to expose clearly the main impulses behind the development which took place in the ensuing period.

The next stage in the intellectual history of Europe, Romanticism, was also to prove beneficial to the liturgy. It was Romanticism which awoke people's sense of history and led many clergy and faithful Christians to inquire into the origin and meaning of liturgical gestures, vestments, vessels, rites, and feasts. From the middle of the nineteenth century onwards these stirrings were expressed in a particularly lively manner in French Benedictine monasteries (Solesmes), and then also in some abbeys in Germany (Beuron) and Belgium (Maredsous). Out of this there grew, quite gradually, but in ever-widening circles, the desire for a renewal of liturgical life. The revolutionary decretals on the subject of communion of Pius X in the years 1905 and 1910 (Denzinger, Ench. No. 1981 ff.; 2137 ff.) which, contrary to the practice widespread since the Middle Ages, recommended frequent communion and the communion of children at an early age, together with the efforts of the same Pope to cultivate to a greater extent the singing of Gregorian chant (especially in the form of community singing) gave such tendencies a powerful impetus in the first decade of the twentieth century.

After the end of the First World War, the newly awakened interest in liturgy faced expression on the one hand in an ever-increasing demand for more research into the history of the liturgy, and on the other hand in the desire of the faithful to be instructed in liturgical matters. It so happened that for both of these purposes, the right people were found at the right centres and at the right time. The Benedictine Abbeys of Maria Laach (headed at that time by that notable abbot, Ildefons Herwegen, who died in 1946) and of Mont César at Louvain in particular concerned themselves with the history of the liturgy; and it was these monasteries which produced such leading scholars as Odo Casel (d. 1948), Bernard Cappelle (d. 1961), and Kunibert Mohlberg (d. 1963). In German-speaking areas the 'Jugendburg' at Rothenfels on the Main and the Austrian 'Stift' at Klosterneu-burg served as centres for the apostolate of the liturgy. The achievement of Pius Parsch (d. 1954), who worked from his base at Klosterneuburg, for the more general run of the church people was matched by what was done for students at Rothenfels under the influence of Romano Guardini, while in Berlin Father Johannes Pinsk (d. 1957) claimed the attention of the educated of every age group with his uncompromising periodical *Life and Liturgy*. In French-speaking circles, the influence of the Bene-dictine Dom Lambert Beauduin in propagating liturgical ideas began early and has lasted for a long time. In a now famous speech to the convention of Catholics at Malines in the year 1909, this extraordinary man appealed courageously for a renewal of the liturgical life of the Church in a speech which made him the founder of a new and powerful movement.

After the Second World War the fact could no longer be over-looked that a world-wide, comprehensive movement of ecclesias-tical reform had been set in motion by these reforms of the liturgy. The Encyclical 'Mediator Dei', promulgated by Pope Pius XII on 20 November 1947, gave special praise to those who had pledged themselves to a renewal of liturgical life, but at the same time issued a warning that many of them were too anxious for innovations and for this reason raised a series of warning signals. All the same, in 1951 and in 1952 devotees of the liturgy had one of their most pressing aspirations fulfilled when the liturgy of the Easter Vigil which for centuries had nonsensically been transferred to the morning of Holy Saturday was once more restored to its proper place in the evening. On the other hand, permission to hold evening masses which was first given in 1953 and then freed from all restrictions in 1958, a practice, which it is true goes right back to the primitive Church, was not primarily designed to satisfy a liturgical *desideratum*; in this case, it was rather pastoral points of view which decided the issue. The Church, taking note of modern working conditions, ensured that men of today who had many heavy strains put upon them should have an extra long night's rest at the week-end.

A few years later, the International Congress for Pastoral Liturgy which met in the year 1956 at Assisi, and the Conference for Liturgy and Missions held in 1959 at Nijmegen made it clear that the time was ripe for making a radical decision. The Church could no longer stand aloof and remote from the movement of liturgical renewal; it was essential that she should unreservedly embrace this movement and make it her own. That Pope John XXIII summoned the bishops of the world to assist the process of the reform of Christian life by means of these newly acquired perspectives marks the inevitable conclusion of a centuries-long period of ever-accelerating development. One of the fruits of the first session of the Council was the 'Constitution on the Sacred Liturgy' promulgated by Pope Paul VI on 4 December 1963.[1]

With the Second Vatican Council and its constitutions, a new period in the history of the western liturgy had made a most promising start.

---

[1] See Appendix I, p. 153.

ii. THE GUIDING PRINCIPLES OF THE TRIDENTINE COMMISSIONS FOR THE REFORM OF THE LITURGY

It would certainly be very useful for future liturgical reforms if we had some knowledge of the proceedings of the commissions appointed by Pius IV and Pius V to produce the two books requested by the Council. We would then know what proposals for reform were submitted to them other than those which had already been suggested during the Council, what discussions these had provoked during the sessions, and what principles had been established with regard to the editing of the calendar, the Ordo, and the various prayers of the Breviary and Missal. If we knew these details, we could learn much to help us in the reforms incumbent on our own generation and would probably also receive many a warning. Unfortunately, however, so far none of the acts dealing with the work of the Commission have come to light; and the monograph dealing with this by Cardinal Sirleto, President of both Commissions during their final sessions, has unfortunately not helped to bring to light much substantial information.

In order to rectify as far as is possible this sadly-felt omission the author himself, in conjunction with the members of the seminar he was conducting at that time at the University of Bonn, carried out an investigation twenty-five years ago. The object of the exercise was to bring into relief the special interests of the Commissions charged with the preparation of the Breviary and Missal by comparing the calendar of the two books with the evidence known to us already from the history of the Roman liturgical year. The investigation proved worth while. It was possible to establish some important points which a possible discovery of the acts of the Commission could not possibly have refuted or corrected, but could at most have complemented or made more precise. Fortunately two gifted and energetic members of this seminar, Ernst Focke (who, sad to say, was killed in the Second World War) and Hans Heinrichs, pursued the discoveries we had succeeded in making together yet further, and published them in an excellent and scholarly article.

Before this appeared, we knew only that the Roman Church had been continually adding new feasts to its calendar, especially after the year 800. Now at last we have been provided with a more exact account of this process. Between 800 and 1100, about forty new feasts were added, between 1100 and 1200 about fifty, and between 1200 and 1558 about 200. At the end of this development, practically every day was taken up with a feast, and many days had several. The comparative study of the calendars revealed no trace of any attempt to make a reduction in the number of feasts which means that the growth in this series of feasts was not restrained by any of the Popes between the years 800 and 1568.

It was the calendar of 1568 and 1570 which for the first time called a halt to this development. The two Commissions did not introduce a single new feast, despite loudly expressed hopes that they would. On the other hand, the new calendar was thoroughly purged by its makers, and now no less than 157 days are completely free of any festivals. They were particularly firm in reducing the number of feasts in the months of March and April; clearly the Commissions wished to keep Lent as free as possible from festivals in order to accord with the spirit of this season. There can, therefore, be no doubt that the Commissions objected to the large number of feasts which had up to that time filled the liturgical year, and made very serious efforts to make do with considerably less.

We get the most important insights into this question, however, if we investigate what kind, from which period, and what are the origins of the various feasts which the Commissions allowed to remain in the calendar. For indeed we find among them festivals from every century, but the feasts from the earlier period are quite clearly given priority of status. No less than 85 per cent of the saints provided for in the new calendar belong to the first four centuries. On the same grounds, the number of martyrs is also very high and these constitute no less than 50 per cent of the whole. To these feasts of the martyrs must be added the feasts of the apostles which alone comprise no less than 10 per cent of the total number, so too some of the feasts of the popes. These last by themselves make up (significantly) 18 per cent of the whole. The remainder of the feasts of the saints falls fairly evenly into groups of doctors, founders of religious orders, confessors, and virgins. What is also significant is that the Commissions preserved all the feasts of Our Lord and Our Lady which had come into being up to that time, and in this respect had made a single exception in excluding the Feast of the Presentation of Our Lady in the Temple (21 November). (It is noteworthy that by the reign of Sixtus V this feast, which is based on a legend, had been re-introduced, significantly at the instigation of Sirleto himself, who even during the reign of Gregory XIII had been instrumental in reintroducing the feast of Saint Anne (26 July); presumably Sirleto went back on the resolutions made by his own Commissions in the face of criticism from pious circles.)

It is also enlightening to make a survey of the saints' origins. Almost 40 per cent of the feasts were of saints from the city of Rome, a further 12 per cent of saints from Italy. The East, too, was strongly represented because the New Testament saints were all included; Spain, France, and England contributed two saints each, and Germany only one, Saint Ursula.

On the basis of this discovery, we may now (with our two experts) define the tendencies of the Commissions by saying that their purpose was fundamentally to return to the ancient calendar of the city of Rome; and that they also intended to enrich this calendar sparingly with a few more recent groups of feasts (those of the founders of religious orders, the doctors of the thirteenth century, and those venerated in the declining years of the Middle Ages as helpers in times of adversity.

What particular edition of the Roman calendar, however, did the Commissions have in front of them? There are many indications which point to the fact that it was the calendar used in the time of Gregory VII. Clearly in this Pope the Tridentine age saw the most important exponent and defender of ancient Roman tradition, standing as he did on the threshold of the period of centralization in the Western liturgy. We have, of course, already seen the extent to which the Commissions were correct or otherwise in making such a judgement.

The detailed investigations of Hubert Jedin have shown that these tendencies brought to light in the process of clarifying the new calendar undoubtedly conditioned the rest of the work undertaken by the two Commissions. Their fundamental principle may be summarized as follows: 'The nucleus of the new uniform liturgy shall be the ancient liturgy of the city of Rome as it was in the time of Gregory VII. This nucleus is only to be enlarged by a few more recent elements which, however, must be of overwhelming universal significance.' The manner in which this principle was put into practice in the purification of the formularies (for example, by the radical reduction in the number of votive masses, sequences, hymns, prefaces, etc.) has already been demonstrated in outline by Jedin. All that is left for scholars to do now is to carry out research into the details of this process.

In his attempt to make a conclusive judgement on the work of the two Commissions and at the same time to give his opinion of the activity of the Council of Trent in liturgical reform, Jedin comes to the following conclusion. The work of renewal effected in the Breviary of 1568 and the Missal of 1570 restored 'simplicity in liturgical life, created unity in ritual and gave clarity to the rubrics!' The new uniform liturgy, therefore, together with the decrees on dogma and the reformation of the Council of Trent, plus the single Latin Bible was, so to speak, a steel brace which, despite all the nationalistic and episcopalizing tendencies of this age of absolutism, held the Church together under a papacy which from the religious point of view had itself undergone a reform. Liturgical centralization was, therefore, according to Jedin, 'a historical necessity'. It demanded, however, some great sacrifices, 'the repression of the rich liturgical individuality of the peoples of the West, and the suppression of so many of the creative forces which in the Middle Ages co-operated in shaping liturgical life'. According to Jedin, therefore, the 'Tridentine' Missal like the 'Tridentine' Breviary did not strike a real balance between liturgical centralization and local liturgy. So, too, the 'liturgy of Trent' is not 'the last and only possible word from the Church concerning the Opus Dei'.

The pattern according to which the two Commissions, instituted for the purpose of creating a new Missal, carried out their work (which we have described above) reveals two extremely important ideas. One is that in their opinion the 'Roman liturgy' was not a liturgy made up of a combination of the liturgical heritage of all the provinces of the Church, but rather a liturgy essentially coterminous with the liturgical tradition of the city of Rome with its local saints and local churches. The titles 'Missale Romanum' and 'Breviarium Romanum' were, therefore, to be understood in the narrowest sense, i.e. in the local sense; and as a result of this it is only logical that the Commissions should, for example, have allowed all local Roman notices about stational services to remain, and that they should have removed from the Breviary and Missal all feasts of the saints which had not in the meanwhile become domiciled in some way in the Eternal City itself.

The second idea was that the early centuries were the golden age of liturgical development, and that all that came afterwards was a rank undergrowth which could and should be cut down.

The first of these ideas is today scarcely any longer defended in its entirety by the leaders of the Church. The age of absolute unity in the local Roman sense is over, for the Church would certainly run the risk of becoming estranged from great areas of the world, were she to want to hold on unrelentingly to this ideal. She cannot at one and the same time want to be the Church of the world and the Church of the city of Rome. This was made emphatically clear by the Congress for Liturgy and Mission at Nijmegen. So far as the instructions, which we mentioned in passing for the stational services in the Roman Missal, are concerned, the historian will no doubt continue to view them with interest and with Cardinal Sirleto and Hartmann Grisar enjoy tracing the hidden connections between the prayers and the appropriate stational church. But the liturgy would be in a sorry state if its meaning were only open to historians and experts on the city of Rome and if it could only provide a small group like this with that 'edification' (this word naturally taken in its original sense) which was so emphatically demanded by Saint Paul. We ought, therefore, in the future to omit those stational instructions so that they do not obscure the fact that the liturgy is of universal application.

However, the second idea we saw introduced by the two Commissions, namely the idea that the early centuries were of a higher standing than the later as far as the liturgy was concerned, is of fundamental significance. People have been greatly concerned with the problem as to how far we are justified in speaking of a development of errors in the history of the Church in general, and in the history of the liturgy in particular, without coming into conflict with an essential point of the Church's teaching, namely with the dogma that the Church under the guidance of the Holy Spirit cannot err. We worry sometimes that we may be overstepping the mark in urging a return to the sources, to the beginnings of the liturgy of the primitive church. The practical standpoint adopted by the two Commissions for reform offers an answer to this difficult theological problem. They were, after all, not afraid to cast off a centuries-old development in the liturgy (cf. the title we gave to the third chapter), declaring an earlier state of affairs to be the ideal one and ordering a return to it.

iii. THE CONGREGATION OF RITES AND ITS WORKING METHODS

It was the express desire of the Council of Trent that the new books should be used uniformly throughout the Latin Church. In order, however, that this new uniform liturgy should not disintegrate after a time into a number of variants, with everything becoming as chaotic as it was before, a central authority was set up in Rome to look into these matters, and called the 'Congregation of Rites'. The function of this body was to pronounce judgement on what was liturgically lawful. The main source of their legal pronouncements was the collection of liturgical books, composed in the course of implementing the decisions of the

Council in 1563, and they drew especially on the group of instructions for the performance of the sacred actions, printed in red and called 'rubrics'. Besides these, however, there were secondary sources for their legislation, namely: (a) such decisions as had been approved by the Congregation since the day of its foundation; and (b) 'custom'. So far as 'custom' was concerned, practically speaking, it was only the Roman custom that counted; and on this basis the Congregation drew conclusions as to how certain rubrics were to be interpreted in practice.

The liturgy as a whole and its parts have been shaped by the course of history. The vessels, the vestments, the gestures, the ceremonies, the formulas, the prayers, the hymns, sequences, feasts, and the chants—each and every one of these came into being at a certain moment in time and underwent for the most part a long development (sometimes lasting for centuries). Many elements in the liturgy underwent change in the course of their history, and were often altered in such a way that their original form became totally changed; with the result that the actual and original meaning can now no longer be deduced from the form in which it exists at the present day. For example, does anyone today realize that the Roman albs made of lace from the waist downwards or fiddle-back baroque chasubles were both originally just ordinary garments? Or, looking at an altar with a tabernacle, do they realize that the altar is not holy because it has a tabernacle, but because it is the table upon which the Son of God descends at the eucharist?

Since, however, the liturgy as a whole (as in all its details) has been structured by the processes of history, the Roman authorities, in making their decisions on a liturgical point, ought to have asked first 'What is (historically) correct', and only afterwards 'Are we fulfilling the demands of the law?' In other words, how could they reach the kind of decision which would ensure that the particular element in the liturgy which was actually under discussion remained in line with its original, i.e. historical, meaning?

At the time when the Congregation of Rites was founded and was developing its practice, however, humanism had already succeeded in sharpening people's sense of historical development, but this understanding had not as yet been adequately developed, nor indeed was it very widespread. Nobody at that time thought of instructing the new authority that before they asked the question as to what was commanded by liturgical law, they should first ask and then answer the question as to what was historically correct. Because they forgot to do this, the Congregation of Rites, without actually intending to, ran the risk of pushing liturgical actions and institutions in such a direction that they acquired a meaning wholly opposed to that which they originally possessed, and of using its authority to confirm for ever this warping of the original meaning. The fact that the Congregation in its dealings did not always escape this danger can be illustrated by two decisions which today have lost their purpose, but which in their time caused vehement discussion and much irritation.

The first case: On 9 December 1925, the Congregation of Rites rejected the so-called Gothic Mass vestments. They said that wherever people had such vestments manufactured, they were departing from the practice of the Roman Church, which had long since abandoned the Gothic form and only allowed the Baroque. Unless they had the special approval of the Holy See, no one was allowed to make changes in the form of vestments, just as they were not allowed to make changes in the liturgy itself.

Looked at purely from the point of view of liturgical law, this Roman decision was quite incontestable; for without doubt changes within the sphere of the liturgy of the mass since 1570 had only been permissible with the consent of the Holy See (and, therefore, of the Congregation of Rites). But the Roman decision of 1925 concerned a very delicate borderline question of style and taste. Did in fact the Congregation do right to impose this ruling by appealing to an important basic principle of liturgical law to impose on the whole Church a definite standard of style and taste? This standard had been reached in Rome as in almost all European countries around the year 1650. And in this period the chasuble had acquired the shape of a fiddle covered with gold *appliqué* work. But whereas in Rome, which had a preponderance of Baroque churches, people adhered to this style right up to the present century, in other European countries, because of the

Gothic or Romanesque style of the churches which had been preserved or newly constructed under the influence of the cult of the medieval initiated by the Romantic movement, people realized that they were bound to return to the older form of chasuble, which had never wholly fallen into disuse, especially outside Rome. A synod held in Prague in 1860 decided to keep this kind of chasuble, and their decision was even approved by the Holy See. Since that time, the handsome Gothic chasuble has enjoyed increasing popularity, especially in Belgium, Holland, and the Rhineland. All these countries felt the decree of the Congregation of Rites as an offence to their sense of taste as well as to their concern for the dignity and harmony of worship. But fortunately at the time of this decision the Gothic chasuble also had some friends in Rome. The papal Master of Ceremonies, Carlo Respighi, had come across the Gothic chasuble while abroad, and in his capacity as director of the Papal Commission for Christian Archaeology had had some vestments of this pattern made for services in the catacombs. It is probably to be attributed to his influence that the decree of 1925 was not carried out with the severity that had been applied in the initial stages.

In this case it would have been easy for the Congregation to protect itself from failing to make a proper evaluation of the situation. Today we can still admire the magnificent array of Dalmatian martyrs on the wall behind the altar of the chapel of Saint Venantius, close to the Lateran baptistry, composed by a Roman mosaicist in the seventh century. Here we can still see what the two most important liturgical altar garments, the chasuble and the dalmatic, looked like in the early period of ecclesiastical dress. At that time, they were still real, flowing garments, not stiff pieces of ornamentation as in the Roman Baroque period. The chasuble, the ritual garment of the bishop and of his representative, the priest, was a costume shaped like a bell and reached down to the feet, made of thin, usually dark-coloured material which was gathered up on both sides in order that the wearer's hands and forearm might have sufficient freedom of movement. On the other hand, the dalmatic, the liturgical dress of the deacon and of his assistant, the subdeacon, was a full, embroidered tunic with

wide sleeves, in design strikingly similar to the Benedictine or
Cistercian *cuculla*. The beauty and splendour of the chasuble and
dalmatic in their early Christian forms cannot be surpassed. They
are among the classic creations of mankind in the sphere of dress.
The chasuble, with the essentially curved shape of its flowing
folds and dark colour emphasizes the dignity of the priestly
shepherd of the congregation and befits his age, whereas the
dalmatic with its light colour, simple vertical folds, and wide
sleeves for freedom of movement underlines the youthful assistant's role of a servant.

Joseph Braun's book about liturgical vestments, which is still
a standard work on this subject tells us how in the course of
centuries the taste of each successive period succeeded in so
reducing the size of the chasuble and dalmatic until they finally
acquired their Baroque shape, a shape moreover which is now
impossible to imagine was originally that of a real garment. This
being so, was it in fact advisable for a decision from Rome to call
a sudden halt to individual periods and countries using their
sense of style in church vestments, making the norm for every
size the final stage in a development which, viewed historically,
has always been retrograde.

Another questionable decision took place on 14 January 1921,
when the Congregation of Rites decided that the final section of
the 'Sanctus', i.e. the 'Benedictus', should not be sung at high
mass until after the Consecration. In this case, too, the decision
was probably based exclusively on the customs of the city of
Rome. But a glance at the history of the liturgy will show once
more to what extent the meaning of the 'Sanctus' was misunderstood.

From the earliest times the first part of the great eucharistic
prayer (today known as the Preface) ended with a reference to the
angels praising God in heaven. At this point, the Roman bishop
(presumably from the fifth century onwards) interrupted the
eucharistic prayer in order to give the congregation a chance to
sing this hymn of the angels, the 'Trishagion'. For this purpose
the text of Isaiah 6.3, which is also found in the liturgy of morning prayer in the synagogue, was used. The bishop waited of

course until the congregation had sung the hymn of the angels to its conclusion; then he carried on, aloud, as he had begun, with the recitation of the eucharistic prayer.

As time went on, people gradually lost the feeling that the two parts of the eucharistic prayer and the 'Sanctus' belonged together. For when the practice was begun of the celebrant saying the second part of the eucharistic prayer in a low voice (we have already described how this development came about), it must have seemed meaningless to make the celebrant wait until the 'Sanctus' was over before finishing the prayer. It finally transpired that the people found this wait more and more difficult to endure, since for some time now the singing of the 'Trishagion' had been performed by a choir and had grown into a time-consuming, artistic piece of choral music. Thus the 'Sanctus' became a hymn, which now, freed from its place in the eucharistic prayer, filled in the silence between the Preface and the Consecration. When, therefore, in the Baroque period the polyphonists strove to develop the music of the 'Sanctus' yet further without regard to the sacred action at the altar, it was proposed that the second part of this hymn, the 'Benedictus', should not be sung until after the Consecration, especially since the text seemed to justify such a division. The hymn, thus extended, could not fill in the silence between the Consecration and the Paternoster. These Roman practices, which after all were the result of the tyrannical behaviour of the polyphonists, were regarded by the rubricists of the Congregation of Rites as representing the normal and ideal state of the liturgy; hence they decreed that it was not permissible to sing the 'Benedictus' before the Consecration.

Both these examples reveal that the Congregation of Rites is in need of a reformation, and not merely an administrative reform, for the Congregation of Rites was given a department for liturgical history by Pius X in 1908, and yet it was still possible for them to make decisions like those of 1921 and 1925! What in fact is needed is a new directive as to how this department of the Curia should perform its services. In the light of the conclusions we have reached, the directive that should be given is that each case should be decided according to what is historically correct; considerations of liturgical law should be relegated to second place.

iv. THE LITURGY AND THE VENERATION OF THE SACRAMENT

In our introductory survey of the fourth and last period of the history of the Western liturgy, we suggested that during this period it was not the liturgy itself but rather the devotion to the Sacrament which particularly appealed to the faithful. This rather bold statement must now be set within a wider context by taking a look at the history of the veneration of the Sacrament. Peter Browe in particular deserves much credit for the researches he has carried out on this subject.

In Christian antiquity part of the bread which had been consecrated was kept back after every mass. The faithful were allowed to take home with them a part of the bread which had been put in their hands (not in their mouth) at the communion and eat it whenever they wished. They not only used it to sustain themselves, they also carried it around as a means of protection, as was the custom of the popes of the Middle Ages who used to take the eucharist with them on their journeys. Some of the eucharistic bread was also reserved in the church itself until the next service. This supply was needed in case the *viaticum* (the food for the journey into the next world) had to be given to a dying person. The holy bread was also reserved in order that it might be dropped into the chalice at the next mass as a *fermentum* (leaven). This custom was intended to give expression to the fact that despite the interval in time, between the services the eucharist was in fact one with every other eucharist. In the church the container used for the consecrated bread (the *capsa* or *pyxis*) was probably kept first of all in a cupboard in the sacristy (*conditorium*) and later in a cupboard in the wall near the altar, or in a few places in a metal dove which hung above the altar.

The way in which the eucharistic bread was venerated in those

days is described in Ordo Romanus I. When the bishop entered
the church to celebrate mass, he bowed to the *capsa* containing
the consecrated bread (*sancta*) which had been left over from the
previous celebration. This was all that was considered necessary.

The Berengarian controversy of the eleventh century (as we
have already heard) did much to further the practice of genuflexion to the eucharistic species. In the twelfth century it became
the custom to set a lamp, known as the 'Everlasting Light', in
front of the place where the eucharist was kept; and yet another
hundred years later, the priest began to elevate the bread after the
consecration. This may perhaps have been intended to compen-
sate for the fact that on account of the change in position of the
altar and the celebrant the faithful could no longer see what was
going on. But this was not so. Édouard Dumoutet has shown that
the elevation was introduced because people thought that the
sight of the host had a special saving effect. And since the chalice
had less power to satisfy this need of the faithful to see the
sacrament, its elevation only became the custom at a later date.

When the elevation took place, the faithful (and the celebrant
too) genuflected both before and afterwards, thereby introducing
the veneration of the sacrament into the liturgy itself. At the same
time the practice was begun, out of respect for the eucharist, of
communicating only on rare occasions whereas according to the
ideas of the early Church, taking part in the liturgical celebration
meant taking part in the offertory procession and also in the
communion.

The idea of constructing a special feast of the Blessed Sacrament (Corpus Christi) in order to meet the devotional needs of
that time, began with Saint Juliana of Liège. Introduced in Liège
in 1246, the feast was prescribed for the whole Church in 1264 by
Pope Urban IV. Because Maundy Thursday was the old-estab-
lished day of the commemoration of the institution of the
eucharist, a Thursday seemed best suited for this new feast; and
hence they chose the Thursday in the week following the Octave
of Pentecost.

People's longing for a 'saving look' at the eucharistic bread,
and the delight the Middle Ages took in public processions led to

the practice of the eucharist being carried around in a triumphal procession on Corpus Christi. The sacred bread was carried at these processions in an *ostensorium*, today called a monstrance; and the high lights of the processions were the repeated blessings of the faithful with the 'Sanctissimum'.

Out of the practical circumstances of the Corpus Christi procession, there developed almost automatically the custom known as the 'Exposition of the Most Holy Sacrament'. It was necessary both before and after the procession to place the monstrance on the altar, and the next thing people did was to make it an object of veneration where it stood. It was only a relatively small step from this to the exposition of the Blessed Sacrament during the celebration of the mass itself; this was already done in the fourteenth century, especially in North Germany; and in 1456 Pope Calixuts III was still able to call it a 'German custom'.

From 'exposition' in the morning, people eventually came to 'devotions to the Blessed Sacrament' in the evening; these regularly ended with the 'benediction of the Sacrament'.

In the declining years of the Middle Ages, however, there were already some theologians who did not take part in this prevailing eucharistic cult without comment, among them was the great Nicholas of Cusa. Their criticism was developed in a more acute form by the Reformers on account of their new theology of the eucharist; for these, genuflexion to the 'Most Holy Sacrament' was tantamount to idolatry, and from this time onwards, further developments in the veneration of the Sacrament were largely influenced by the idea that to venerate the Sacrament was the sign of a warlike confession of faith. The Corpus Christi procession in particular now became to a considerable extent a demonstration that one held the correct beliefs. The introduction too of the 'forty hours devotion' and of 'perpetual prayer' is probably connected with the attacks of the Reformers and their followers. Sodalities and religious communities were founded for the same purpose of 'perpetual adoration' and for reparation for the insults which, according to widespread opinion, were continually being paid to Our Lord, hidden under the form of bread.

From the cupboard in the wall, in which as a general rule the eucharistic bread was kept in the closing years of antiquity and in the early Middle Ages, the high and late Middle Ages saw the development in many places of the richly equipped architectonic 'sacrament house'. On the other hand, it was the custom in Rome in the sixteenth century to keep the 'Most Holy' in a container on the high altar itself in churches which were then being built. From the well-known passage in the Apocalypse: *ecce tabernaculum Dei cum hominibus et habitabit cum eis* (21.3), this container was called a 'tabernacle' (tent) and was, therefore, veiled in a *conopeum*, i.e. a silk covering which was intended to give it the appearance of a real tent. By 1614 the Roman tabernacle was prescribed in the new 'Rituale Romanum' for the whole Church.

While the Jansenists were urging the Church to restrain the cult of the Blessed Sacrament, the Jesuits (and here we return to the theme of this section) were so much the more active in promoting it. In their churches, designed by gifted architects in the Baroque style, the veneration of the eucharist reached its most magnificent climax.

The reredos beneath the high altar in these Baroque churches became further developed into a magnificent framework for the 'throne of exposition (*expositorium*). The name 'throne' pointed clearly to the fact that in this period, the contemporary protocol and style of the courts of princes was adapted to the purposes of the veneration of the eucharist (an observation first made by Joseph Kramp). For the second time then in the history of the Western liturgy, court ceremonial had its effect on ecclesiastical affairs.

There developed now a careful ceremonial, prescribing the manner in which clergy and faithful should greet the Lord, enthroned under the form of bread, how clergy were to behave when moving from the centre of the altar to the epistle or gospel side, and back to the centre again, and how and where they had to stand when, during the exposition of the 'Most Holy' they received the censing or went to wash their hands. The celebration of mass *coram sanctissimo*, according to these new formulas, involved the celebrant in an increasing and almost unendurable number of genuflexions. The eucharistic Christ, here holding court, had to be treated in exactly the same way as an earthly prince.

No wonder, therefore, that the Son of God, hidden as he was under the form of bread, should in many places acquire a body-guard of courtiers. The author himself can still remember well the 'Paggi del Santissimo Sacramento' in white Spanish costumes, who, with an imitation sword at their side, were to be seen in Roman churches at high festivals. Small wonder, too, that poly-phonic and instrumental church music was now in many ways very like the music of court.

During this period the interior of the church itself became a throne-room, whose main wall was completely covered with the massive architectonic and often magnificent structure over the altar. The altar itself played only a subordinate role in the total aspect of this end of the church and had become debased to a mere detail by the tabernacle and the throne for the exposition with all their trappings. On the other hand, the throne-room character of the Baroque church interior excluded all side aisles (at least in principle). From every seat in the church people had to be able to see the bread in the monstrance, as (vice versa) the heavenly Lord had to be able to see every one of his visitors. Hence the Baroque period gave rise to a church interior which once more had the effect of gathering people together. Only the motive for making such a building was not the actual liturgy itself, but the cult of the Sacrament which had swallowed up and subordinated the liturgy to its own purposes.

Meanwhile, however, the after-effects of an unhealthy Baroque devotion to the Sacrament were to a large extent removed. The most extreme expression of this kind of piety, the misuse of the mass as a devotional exercise in front of the monstrance, was well known to the older generation. Quite rightly, the Congregation of Rites has only reluctantly tolerated the *missae coram exposito* (*sacramento*) and has suppressed it more and more over the past thirty years. Our growing understanding of the essence of the mass itself has helped us see that such celebrations involve the amalgamation of elements which are clearly incompatible.

The altar table, which in the Baroque period had been treated as something of little importance, has in our churches today regained its status as the place for the holy sacrifice and the focal point of our church interior. The retables have once more disappeared, though the tabernacle, protected by earlier decisions of the Congregation of Rites, has still been allowed to remain on the altar. We are still shy of returning to the old forms of reservation and of separating once more the altar for the sacrifice from the place where the eucharist is reserved, after the centuries for which they have been together.

The tabernacle is the one obstacle remaining in the way of our churches re-acquiring the traditional arrangement; the celebrant ought to have his place once more in the apse, i.e. behind the altar, and ought once more to be able to celebrate on the apse side of the altar, facing the people; for if the people are to celebrate the eucharistic sacrifice together with the celebrant, they ought also to be able to see and follow the offering of the sacrifice on the altar itself.

v. THE LITURGY AND CHURCH ARCHITECTURE

In the previous section we explained that the highly questionable concept of the liturgy that was developed during the Baroque period created for itself the kind of church building which best suited it. This has happened in every age, for each period has shaped its church buildings to accord with its own liturgical ideas. Unfortunately we still lack a history of church buildings viewed as buildings constructed for the liturgy (with the exception, however, of an unfinished study by the Protestant liturgist, Gerhard Kunze, interrupted by his early death). This is an important subject, for we ought to be acquainted as closely as possible with the effects of church buildings and the forms of the liturgy upon one another, so that we may be able to construct our own churches correctly. Since we of this generation are nowadays in the position of having to construct an especially large number of churches (for, as is well known, more churches are being erected than ever before) this undertaking is extremely urgent. A few short reflections on the subject seem to be called for and we shall, therefore, attempt to formulate a basic principle by examining how church buildings in the most important periods of the history of the West stood in relation to their contemporary liturgies.

We should, to begin with, be careful to point out here that the question we are asking is entirely different from that which historians of the Middle Ages are at present so fond of asking. They start from the conviction that church buildings were always meant to express certain religious or religio-political ideas; so they try to deduce these ideas from the buildings in which they are expressed. For example, the ancient Christian basilica is supposed to have been planned as a copy of the heavenly Jerusalem, and the Romanesque church is supposed, according to the intentions of its architects, to have represented pictorially the kingdom of God.

In our opinion, however, all these theories have missed the mark. Church architects in all periods were faced with an identical task, namely to construct a house for the liturgy of the people of their own time. This problem, however, could never be solved twice in the same way, because the needs of the various congregations and their ideas concerning the liturgy changed just as much as the taste of each period and the technical means available, quite apart from the artistic idiosyncracies of the master-builders themselves. The finished churches, however, i.e. those which were admired as great achievements by people living at the time, were the subject of much musing, meditation, and explanation. People read ideas into the finished churches just as much as interpreters of the liturgy such as Amalar read ideas into the liturgy when explaining liturgical actions. We must be very careful, therefore, of keeping primary purposes and subsequent interpretation well separated. Naturally it is conceivable that certain subsequent interpretations of churches were fully in accord with the general temper of the time. But then these inevitably determined and modified the liturgical concepts of the time and subsequently reappeared as liturgical ideas, as could be demonstrated in the case of the Baroque liturgy. However, congregations always gave the architects the same commission: 'Build us a church', they say, 'for the liturgy as we practice it and as we understand it!' The task, then, of the historian of church architecture is to establish the relationship that has existed between church buildings and people's understanding of the liturgy in each period of Western history. The tracing of subsequent symbolic explanations of churches is a task of quite a different sort. We should, therefore, follow the example of Joseph Sauer, and avoid drawing any direct conclusions from contemporary church architecture on the basis of symbolic ideas to which our attention may have been drawn. In between both of these, there is the liturgy of the day and the interpretation of it; and this seldom coincides with the development of symbolic ideas about it.

When we mentioned church architecture just now we meant naturally by this the substance or nucleus of the church and not its accessories. In addition, however, every church has structures and features built inside it, which are incidental to the performance of the liturgy and indeed to the place of worship itself and which, therefore, do not constitute a part of the building programme which the liturgy dictates. Such, for example, are the church porch, the pulpit, the choir-stalls, the stained-glass windows, the turrets, etc. In constructing these, the whims of each age for non-liturgical (e.g. allegorical) trends of thought can be given free and direct expression; and it would be a serious error to conclude from the idea we can deduce from a doorway or stained-glass windows, that these same ideas must, therefore, be fundamental to the whole building.

This having been said, let us now return to our main theme.

It is sad that we do not know anything definite about the average church of the first three centuries. We can only suppose that already in the year 100 there existed in large towns special houses of assembly erected by the community, whereas in small places (as at the very beginning) a room in a private house (a 'house-church') or a rented hall proved sufficient.

For as long as the room used for worship only needed to provide for the eucharist celebrated in conjunction with an ordin-

ary meal, as in the primitive period, it was a particular advantage
for this room to have a more or less rectangular shape. In it, the
tables and couches for the faithful were grouped around the
table and couch of the bishop and his assistants. However, as
soon as the celebration of the eucharist became detached from the
ordinary meal, the reclining couches became superfluous and
instead of having several tables, only one, namely the bishop's,
was required. At this table the bishop had to officiate in front of
the whole community. This could be done in a square room just
as well as in a long rectangular room. But when, however, the
Service of the Word was combined with the celebration of the
eucharist, the bishop's table had to be arranged in such a manner
that the bishop could speak to the community. Now, therefore,
the oblong shape of the room became the rule. 'The church must
be long in shape and must face east; in this way it resembles a
ship', we read in the 'Apostolic Constitutions', a church order
put together out of primitive material in the closing years of the
fourth century (2, 57, 3 F).

In this oblong room the table used as an altar probably did not
always stand against the wall opposite the entrance, but was sited
more towards the centre of the room. It was a movable, round,
horseshoe or square-shaped table, and not very big; no different,
in fact, from the tables which were in common use for meals
during this period. In front of this table stood the faithful,
arranged in strict order according to their sex, age, and so on.
Behind the table stood the bishop's chair, forming the centre
piece of a horseshoe-shaped bench (a last reminder of the times
when, at the Eucharistic meal, people lay on cushions arranged in
the form of a half circle); on the bench (*subsellia*) to the right and
to the left of the bishop sat the presbyters, and on occasions
episcopal visitors. The acoustic problems were solved by the fact
that the desk for the lections was pushed almost into the middle of
the room. If, on account of the size of the community, the need
for a larger room arose, then rows of supports would have
been used for the ceiling, with the result that the room became
divided into 'aisles'. In those assembly houses which the communities had erected for themselves and which were not taken

over ready-made, the main axis probably ran from the very beginning in an East–West direction, because it had been the custom
from time immemorial to pray facing East. And since the façade
of these assembly houses usually faced East, the congregation
had to turn towards the door when praying. Not until the middle
of the fourth century did the practice become general everywhere (probably for practical reasons) of placing the façade at
the west end. From that time onwards, only the celebrant and his
assistants had to face the East for prayer.

The Emperor Constantine, bent on making the Christian
Church, of which he had become a member, a community which
would be able to compete with pagan groups and at the same
time raise monuments to himself, was the first to build monumental churches; at first in Rome, and then elsewhere, he built
churches which did not merely attempt to do justice to the
spatial needs of a small community that had diminished in size
through being divided up. The first church constructed by him
was the Lateran basilica in Rome, an imposing building well
suited in size to the large Roman congregation, which on account
of its size had for some time now been divided up into several
districts, each of which had its own 'titular church' (i.e. district
church). The style of architecture chosen by the imperial architect, is, as we know today, nothing less than an adaptation of the
style currently used for large public buildings ('basilicas') to the
needs of a congregation in a large town for their liturgical
assemblies.

A long, rectangular room, flanked on both sides by two rows
of closely-set columns terminated at the west (the Lateran
basilica still has its façade at the east) in a semi-circular construction, raised up slightly like a stage, without windows and with a
vaulted roof (*concha*). This was the apse, against the walls of
which there was placed the bench for the presbyters (*subsellia*)
and, in the centre, the bishop's chair (*cathedra*). In front of the
apse was the altar, an altar moreover which stood under a balda-
chino, the 'Ciborium'; the canopy of which was supposed to
portray the heavens, and was intended to single out the altar,
the place where in a mystery Christ was made present. Since the

altar, which was still a small one, could not by itself take all
the offertory gifts of so great a community, seven other altars were
arranged in front of it and at the side, to be used only for the
gifts, however, and not for the consecration. The rows of
columns which flanked the interior in front of the apse supported
arches on which rested the high upper walls. This 'heightening of
the basilica' is very characteristic of this style of architecture. The
upper part of the upper walls was broken up by numerous
windows so that the interior itself was amply lit from above. Two
narrow side aisles ran parallel to it on each side, setting their light
from the central area—a fact which is sufficient to show that the
side aisles were not thought of as being a place for the congregation to stay in but rather as gangways to take the traffic of people
up and down. At divine service the clergy and people were
gathered together in the centre nave only. (In the pre-Constan-
tinian churches which had only a few supports for the ceiling this
may well have been different.) By means of the perspective
effect of the columns which were evenly and closely lined up side
by side with one another, as were the arcades, cornices, and
windows, things were so arranged that the eyes and attention of
the faithful were gently but firmly drawn towards the altar and
the sanctuary, where the eye was held captive in the semi-circle
of the apse.

In this first church to be built with everything that the architecture of antiquity had to contribute, we are clearly dealing with
a *Richtungsbau*, i.e. a building in which each and every part was
focused on the altar. The celebrant, together with his assistants
and the congregation, stood opposite one another, both facing the
altar. The side aisles were designed to facilitate the processions of
the faithful to the place of sacrifice; such processions took place
on two occasions at each eucharist, first at the end of the Service
of the World, when each of the faithful presented the oblations
he had brought with him (in the 'Sacramentarium Leonianum'
we read on one occasion: 'We have heaped gifts upon thine altar',
ed. Mohlberg, 237); and secondly at the communion, when each
received his part of the consecrated bread and wine.

Obviously, in so large a church as the Lateran basilica, the bishop now found it quite impossible to make himself heard. Even when reading desks (ambos) for the deacon and sub-deacon were moved further into the centre aisle, it was impossible to read the epistle and gospel and expect everyone to be able to understand the lections. The same applied to the words of the liturgy spoken at the altar. For, like our cathedrals, churches structured like the Lateran basilica serve primarily the purposes of the church on big ceremonial occasions. They are not the ideal place for celebrating the liturgy.

In front of the facade of the Lateran basilica, there lay a great forecourt, the atrium, lined with porticoes all round to protect the church from the secular activities of the town. Here the members of the congregation performed the customary washing of their hands before prayer; and for this purpose a *cantharus* with running water had been placed in the centre. The catechumens and penitents could remain in the atrium for such times as they were excluded from the service, and in the atrium also charity could distribute to the poor the gifts she had acquired at the altar.

At the side of the basilica stood the *baptisterium*, a round building with a circle of columns inside forming a framework round the large font (*piscina*). The *piscina* was illuminated by the light coming from the cupola while the gallery outside the columns was without windows like the side aisles of the basilica itself. An ancient ordinance prescribed 'You shall baptize in living water' (Didache 7.1.3); and hence there was always running water in the *piscina*.

The basic plans used in the kinds of church built under Constantine, i.e. basilicas and baptistries, were clearly looked upon as providing a complete solution to the problem of how churches should be built. In any case, they were copied again and again by succeeding generations, though it is understandable that only rarely were they copied preserving the same proportions. In large buildings a transept (an aisle crossing the main aisle) was often inserted between the apse and the centre aisle, which enlarged the sanctuary on each side and at the same time gave the whole church a cruciform shape. Richard Krautheimer has shown, from his collections of some earlier references, that it was not a symbolic idea, i.e. a reminder of the cross of the Redeemer, which gave the impulse to the construction of the transept, but rather the practical needs of the liturgy. There was need of a place level with the altar where the offertory gifts of the faithful could be placed, or alternatively it was necessary to give the faithful a chance of coming nearer to the memorials of the martyrs which were associated with the altar. A triumphal arch which anticipated the outline of the apse ensured that the transept did not break the connection between the centre nave and the sanctuary.

The influence of the Constantinian baptistry soon came to an end; large baptistries were no longer needed in the age of infant baptism, and a small chapel at the entrance of the church proved sufficient. On the other hand, however, the influence of the Lateran basilica has lasted to the present day, for modern architects have kept to the long rectangular outline which was chosen for that impressive Christian church, the Lateran. This is truly amazing, for, from the point of view of the liturgy, this shape has not always proved successful. The faithful ought to be as near as possible to the altar in order that they may watch the sacred action, and fully understand the words of the liturgy. On the other hand, the Western, Roman liturgy (as opposed to the Eastern) permits of no central structure for the celebration of the eucharist. The Western liturgy demands that there should be a lively to-and-fro of words and actions between the celebrant and the people, and not that each should remain lost in contemplation where they stood. The West has, therefore, to keep to these longitudinal buildings, and the question remains whether there is any way, other than the congregation becoming smaller, of overcoming the optical and acoustical difficulties of such buildings, whether in fact it is possible to make the change (by a general loosening up of the traditional outline) to diamond shapes instead of squares, to trapezia or elongated ovals. Some pleasing attempts at this sort of design have recently been made; but now we must return to our historical survey.

In the Middle Ages, the brick used in the construction of early Christian churches was abandoned in favour of quarried stone. Connected with this (though just as much with the fact that the

German clergy and laity had other feelings about the matter) was the fact that the light, cool, Classical style of the Roman basilicas was quenched by this change of material. The churches acquired heavier walls and columns or pillars. The number of windows was reduced. The apse was made lighter by small apertures to let in the light; and the sanctuary was put on a higher level on account of a crypt being made underneath it. All this already foreshadowed the divisions of both church aud liturgy into two. On the stage the clergy celebrated the liturgy and on the lower level the people celebrated the liturgy at their own altar. This division was finally effected from the twelfth century onwards by the setting up of a choir screen and in front of this an 'altar of the Holy Cross', which to all practical purposes was a second high altar. The celebrant at the altar turned his back to the people; the altar was finally pushed right up against the wall, and was given a retable or reredos. The bishop's throne had to forfeit its place in the centre of the apse and be put at the side against the left wall. The chapels in the ambulatory around the chair and in the apses at the end of the side aisles acquired altars for the celebration of private masses. Bell towers framed the façade and a bigger tower marked the intersection at the crossing. (It is possible that the tower is in fact a distant echo of buildings commemorating the shrine of a martyr.) The atrium, which remained for some time, vanished in the eleventh century, probably because its liturgical function had not been impressed with sufficient clarity on the minds of people in general, or else because it had ceased to serve the purpose for which it was originally designed. It survived for a little longer in the form of a kind of narthex or antechamber. All in all, one has the impression that church architecture began at first hesitantly and then with increasing speed to emulate the breaking up of the community and its liturgical life.

In the Gothic period, however, things were different. The architects had greater technical experience and could let more light into the interiors. Narrow spaces and thick walls were now no longer tolerated, nor low and heavy vaulting. The supports were set wide apart from one another and linked together; the outer walls were set with enormous windows which were filled with gaily coloured glass, whose colourful pictures prevented people concentrating on what was going on in the liturgy. Side chapels met the need of the increasing demand for altars for private masses, and at the same time they gave the many guilds and fraternities into which the congregation had been divided an opportunity to hold their special services. The choir in cathedral and monastic churches was extended in order to make room for the rows of stalls for the numerous clergy or monks who performed their daily office here. The influence of the mendicant orders gave increasing importance to preaching, both during the liturgy and on other occasions, and the acoustical situation compelled people to separate the preaching of the word of God from the altar and to have it performed from a pulpit near the centre of the church. This separation of the altar and the sermon both furthered and reflected the fact that the sermon was becoming thematically divorced from the liturgy. This high altar acquired heavy painted panels above the retable and the pictures on these could be changed according to the season of the year, all of which distracted people's attention from the liturgy and encouraged them to contemplate the life and suffering of Christ and of his saints. During the Gothic period the church building, therefore, is both as a whole and in its individual parts the reflection of the change in the devotional habits of the faithful and of the continuation of this process of disintegration we have already observed.

As far as we can see, church architects of the Renaissance period did not make any substantial changes in the forms of the late Gothic church (apart from details of decoration); in the Baroque period, however, as we have already seen in the previous section, all this was changed. By dispensing with the screen and by a better arrangement of the side altars, the congregation was no longer divided into two. Now a single large room without chapels brought the whole congregation together, for it was intended that the members of the congregation should be as close to one another as possible during divine service. This kind of service, however, was not the pure unadulterated liturgy, but really a devotion to the Sacrament which went under the name of liturgy.

Since the last echo of the Baroque age died away, church architects have in fact only copies what the Romanesque and Gothic periods left behind in the way of patterns; only rarely have people gone back to the early Christian basilicas (e.g. at St. Boniface in Munich). But after the disruptions of the First World War, discontent concerning the spiritless repetition of the old styles became so general, and people's understanding of the liturgy had already been so greatly increased that something quite surprising happened. Architects (like makers of liturgical vestments) ran, so to speak, ahead of developments in the liturgy; that is to say, they began to build churches which did not correspond to the actual liturgy of the day, but rather to a reformed kind of liturgy such as they hoped for in the future. They now began to construct the sacred area in such a way that the congregation celebrating the liturgy there could once more feel themselves an entity, a unity or a family. It was intended that nothing should distract from the sacred action at the altar. Hence the simplicity of the walls and ceiling; hence the disappearance of disturbing windows behind the altar; hence the sparing use of sculpture and painting; hence the many kinds of attempts, which developed during the post-Tridentine period, but which only the Baroque architects succeeded in carrying out neatly, to move the confessionals (with three partitions) into side chapels and boxes (these were developed in the post-Tridentine period and only the Baroque architects succeeded in letting them into the walls). The altar became once more the focal point for the congregation. It looked once more like a table, for the attempt to make it look like a monument had sometimes led to it looking all too much like some gigantic tomb.

Architects were also concerned to keep everything away from the altar which did not help people to understand its importance. Hence a portable cross was made and either placed behind or hung over the altar. Often one sees the candles set at the side of the altar or ranged behind it; flowers disappeared, as did the lace. The latter had crept into liturgical affairs during the age of Rococo, in which it served to decorate the altar, albs, choir dress, chalice veils, etc. Lace, however, even if it is beautifully made, is out of place in churches. In origin it always has been and still remains a part of domestic life.

Architects also took a great deal more notice of the baptistry once more. It was brought into much closer and more meaning-ful connection with the church by arranging, for example, for it to be placed inside the church at the entrance. The idea of making the 'living water' in the 'baptismal fount' water which actually flows has recurred.

Taken all in all, a great deal of valuable and instructive work has been done in the realm of church architecture. The right buildings for a reformed liturgy and a reformed congregation have already been constructed. Nevertheless it was certainly a good thing that immediately after the Second World War (in 1949) the liturgical commission summoned by the conference of bishops at Fulda laid down some guiding principles for building churches, setting both the lower and upper limits to which people could go. [These principles were also provided in England by a group of architects under the guidance of Peter Hammond. Trs.] Le Corbusier's chapel at Ronchamp (built in 1955) has shown that a delight in architectural experiment which is not sufficiently restrained and subordinated to considerations of theology and liturgical history can lead to some dangerous misunderstandings and mistakes.

A Christian church such as that built at Ronchamp could only have been built by someone who, although he has a kind of natural religious feeling, has never encountered salvation history. To understand the commission to build a Christian church as though it were a primitive cave into which frightened man could creep to hide himself from a divinity he felt to be uncanny and from the demons of this world could only happen to an architect who has still not ventured beyond the 'antechamber' of salvation history. A Christian church cannot and must not ignore the fact of salvation. The liturgy of the Church stands in the very centre of salvation history and not in empty space, a fact that has not been sufficiently taken note of by Rudolph Schwarz in his speculations concerning the basic forms of church architecture. The possibility of such misunderstandings should be obviated by the 'Guiding Principles' of 1949 which we have mentioned. These guiding principles in a revised form are presented here in Appendix II in their original wording.

APPENDIX I

THE CONSTITUTION 'ON THE SACRED LITURGY' OF THE SECOND VATICAN COUNCIL, 4 DECEMBER 1963

The leading German-speaking liturgical historian of our day, Joseph Andreas Jungmann, gave the 1963 Constitution an enthusiastic welcome. 'A great task', he wrote, 'undreamed of a few years ago, has now, we are glad to see, been brought to completion. That Spring which dawned fifty years ago has since blossomed and flowered and borne fruit in a rich harvest.' I agree with this evaluation of the situation, although with certain reservations. For so far the wishes of those people who have been clamouring for a reform of the liturgy have not been granted, and the Constitution itself has only just begun to make their fulfilment possible.

The Constitution next declares, with no reservations whatsoever, that what is needed is a fundamental and comprehensive renewal of the liturgy. The principle propagated and practised during the era in which the liturgy was governed by a central authority, namely that the sacred texts were not to be tampered with, has been abandoned altogether. The concrete form of the liturgy can henceforward differ as much according to country or culture as is possible without its departing from its basic essentials as laid down by the Founder of the Church and developed by tradition. Even the regulations affecting the celebration of the eucharist proper are not to be excluded from this process of renewal.

According to the Constitution, the object of this reform is fundamentally a pastoral one. It ought to be possible for Christian people to take as full a part in the celebration of the liturgy with all its rites and texts, as they did in early Christian times. The Constitution says that it is not sufficient for the people merely to be present and say their prayers; rather they ought, both as a congregation and as individuals, to take a conscious and active part in its celebration. The invitation 'Oremus', which the celebrant frequently pronounces, ought to mean that the congregation and the celebrant are going to pray together. And the people's 'Amen' ought to have its significance restored and become the affirmation by the people of the prayer which has been read at the altar; for by saying 'Amen' they show that they have followed the prayer inwardly for themselves and have in fact made their response to the bidding 'Oremus'. The liturgy ($\lambda\epsilon\iota\tau\text{ου}\rho\gamma\acute{\iota}\alpha$) by its very nature is the cultic activity of the whole Church of God; for the whole Church is present wherever the people of God is assembled together; and, therefore, it is only right that the liturgy should be a corporate act.

Since the people are once more to take an active part in our services, the Constitution recommends that Latin as a liturgical language should be abandoned in favour of the vernacular wherever suitable or indeed necessary, especially in the administration of the sacraments. Local conferences of bishops are to be responsible for tackling this task and finding the best way to do it. For whereas in the primitive Church and in the Middle Ages it was the individual bishop and, from the Council of Trent onwards, the Curia which made decisions on liturgical questions, as a result of the Constitution an authority mid-way between the two (which in many countries is entirely new) has been set up to deal with such eventualities. It is true that the Curia must in each case give its approval. But already permission has been given for the celebrant himself to read the lections at mass in the vernacular.

The Constitution suggests further that we have come to celebrate the eucharist in a way which in many respects is impossible for the people to understand. Since this is so, it is our duty to restore the clear outlines of the structure of the rite, which have been lost over the years, and to restore to the prayers, in particular the Canon, their original clarity which has likewise become obscured in course of time. It will be left to the experts to work out the details.

The lections prescribed in the Missal today ought also to be re-arranged so that the faithful once more have access to the full riches of Holy Scripture, in particular the New Testament. The sermon which follows the lections (and which is obligatory on Sundays) ought also to be linked thematically with the biblical lections and with the prayers of the day.

The Constitution, and I agree, deplores the disappearance of the Intercessory Prayer. It provides, therefore, that at least on Sundays and festivals such a prayer should be said in one of the approved forms after the sermon. Communion in both kinds may also be permitted once more in special circumstances. The Holy See, on the recommendation of the bishops, is going to put out some more exact prescriptions on the matter.

Concelebration, which was once the practice at masses celebrated by the bishop of Rome and is today something that monastic communities in particular are asking for, is again to be made possible. In liturgical matters in general, things done in common take precedence over those done in private; and although it is emphasized that the priest retains his right to celebrate a private mass, it may well be that when concelebrated mass is fully explained, then the last days of the private mass will have dawned. Liturgical gestures too, like the acclamations, are once more to be given their proper significance (cf. my comments above on the 'Amen'); and also within the liturgy ritual silence is once more to come into its own.

So far as the other sacraments are concerned, only baptism is dealt with in any great detail by the Constitution. They provide that if baptism is administered at times other than Easter, then, in future, baptismal water can be freshly blessed and a somewhat shorter prayer, rather like the Easter prayer for blessing the water, can be used. Moreover, the ceremonies of baptism, like those of all other sacraments, should be examined to see if they can be made more easily understood by Christian people.

The saying of the Breviary—the *Officium Divinum*—which for many years has been felt to be too heavy a burden, especially by the already overburdened parish priests, is in future no longer to be merely a duty but rather a form of prayer. Because of this, Lauds and Vespers are to be given priority as liturgical forms of morning and evening prayer, whereas Prime has been removed altogether. Of the so-called 'Little Hours', the priest himself can choose to say whichever corresponds to the time of day he happens to be saying them. Further, the number of psalms to be said each day is to be reduced. A revision is also to be made of the Breviary lections, and, in particular, more use is to be made of Holy Scripture.

On the subject of the liturgical year, the Constitution explains that Sunday is the most important of the Church's festivals. Other feastdays can take precedence over the Sunday only if they are of the very highest rank. Further, only those saints are to be commemorated by the whole Church who are of significance for the whole Church; and, wherever they coincide, the feasts of the saints must not take precedence over those feasts which concern the history of our salvation.

The use of episcopal insignia (i.e. the 'pontificals') is in future to be reserved to those priests who are actually bishops or have special jurisdiction.

Polyphonic and instrumental music is not to be excluded from the liturgy, provided it fits in with the spirit of the liturgical action. Pride of place, however, is to be given to the organ and the traditional single-line melody used by the Church, i.e. Gregorian chant, of which new editions are to be made. Care should be taken, however, to provide smaller congregations with books containing easier melodies.

The Constitution also makes clear that the Church recognizes no particular style of architecture as being exclusively its own. Splendour and pseudo-artistry must be avoided in the building of churches. Images of the saints, may, as hitherto, be set up in a church, but only so many as are suitable, and they must furthermore be arranged in proper order. Commissions of experts are to advise the bishops in supervising church architecture and church art, and academies of art are to educate artists in the requisite artistic abilities. The Church's regulations concerning the altar, tabernacle, baptistry, pictures, etc., are to be reviewed as soon as possible.

The study of the liturgy is in the future to form a part of the education of seminarians, and indeed is to be a major subject in their curriculum. Furthermore, this subject, known as 'liturgics', is not only to be studied from the point of view of dogmatic and pastoral theology but also historically. Special institutions and commissions are to be set up (where these do not already exist as in Germany, France, and Switzerland) for the development of people's abilities to teach the liturgy, and to advise bishops and conferences of bishops on liturgical matters.

As a result of looking at the liturgy in a more comprehensive way, from the theological as well as from the historical point of view, care ought to be taken in the future to develop the liturgy organically, so to speak (i.e. in close harmony with its origins), and to avoid spoiling it with clumsy appendages.

It is not without some satisfaction that historians of the liturgy note that the Constitution does not say a word about any increase in the practice of devotions to the Blessed Sacrament; this in fact receives no mention at all. Probably in the Services of the Word which, the Constitution recommends, should be held in the afternoon, the veneration of the Sacrament will be included as an addition or a conclusion. In this way, the Constitution silently corrects a tendency that has grown increasingly powerful to shift the central point of the liturgy from the eucharistic sacrifice to the veneration of the Sacrament.

The foregoing account of the Constitution reveals the extent to which the Second Vatican Council has met the wishes and demands of the 'liturgical movement' and of historians of the liturgy. So far they have only enunciated principles; hence the 'reserve' which I mentioned at the beginning of this chapter. But the decisions are yet to be made as to how these principles are to be followed and, therefore, as to what is to be the concrete form the liturgy is to acquire both in the near and in the distant future; such decisions remain in the hands of the local conferences of bishops and, in the last resort, with the Curia. Let us hope that in this final decision that they have to make, the Curia will give the last word, not to the rubricists of the old school, but to the true experts in the liturgy and its history.

THE INSTRUCTION ON IMPLEMENTING THE 1963 CONSTITUTION

The Constitution was followed by the 'Instruction for the orderly implementation of the Constitution on the Sacred Liturgy'. It is dated 26 September 1964 and bears the signature of the President of the Advisory Commission for Implementing the Constitution on the Sacred Liturgy, Cardinal Lercaro, and of the Prefect of the Sacred Congregation of Rites, Cardinal Larraona. The Instruction reveals that some of the principal declarations of the Constitution are now to be put into practice. We would draw attention to the following points:

The high altar is to be removed from the back wall and arranged in such a way that the faithful can see it to be the focal point of the whole church. It must be possible to walk right round it and to celebrate facing the people. The bishop may give permission for the tabernacle to be placed not on the high altar but in another special place in the church. But celebration facing the people is also allowed, even when there is a small tabernacle on the high altar. There should only be a small number of side altars; if possible, these should be placed in side chapels. The cross and candlesticks (with permission from the bishop) need not be placed on the altar but near to it. The Constitution recommends that an ambo or even two ambos should be set up for reading the lections; these must be placed in such a position that the readers can be clearly seen and heard. The celebrant is also to listen to whatever is read or sung by the deacon, sub-deacon, or the choir and no longer needs, as at one time, to read the texts privately to himself.

The practice of kissing the celebrant's hand whenever anything was handed to him or when he handed it back, and the habit of kissing the objects handed to the celebrant has been dispensed with altogether. By abandoning this, the process has fortunately been begun of reducing the number of elements of court ceremonial within the liturgy.

Psalm 42 has been removed from the prayers said at the foot of the altar. If there is any other liturgical action which comes directly before the mass, then all the prayers at the foot of the altar are to be dispensed with. The 'Oratio super oblata' (i.e. the Secret) is to be sung at high mass or else to be said aloud like the other prayers. At the end of the Canon the words from 'Per ipsum' to 'Per omnia saecula saeculorum' are to be sung or said aloud; during this the chalice and the host are to be elevated, and the signs of the cross have been eliminated. On this occasion also the celebrant does not genuflect until the people have replied 'Amen'. It is now permitted for the people to say the Pater-noster with the celebrant in their own tongue and the embolism which follows is to be said or sung aloud. In administering communion the celebrant says 'Corpus Christi' to each communicant without making the sign of the cross and the communicant replies 'Amen'. The Last Gospel has disappeared altogether.

The vernacular is permitted (provided the local conference of bishops agrees) for the lections, the newly introduced Intercessory Prayers, the Kyries, Gloria, Credo, Sanctus, Paternoster, Agnus Dei, and for the antiphons at the Introit, Offertory, and Communion, for the chants between the lections, and for the 'Ecce agnus dei', 'Domine non sum dignus', and 'Corpus Christi'. Other texts which are said or sung by the celebrant only may not be said in the vernacular without special permission from the Holy See.

The full consequences of demanding that all the congregation take part in the service and that all linguistic barriers that have hitherto obtained be set aside have not, as one can see, yet had their full effect. In particular, the Canon still continues to be recited in Latin. It follows from this that the much (and in my opinion unjustly) criticized parallel Latin and vernacular texts must in future be done away with. In the same way, the practice must be avoided of the faithful, who have no knowledge of Latin, bowing their heads over their Missals and reading the Canon while it is being recited at the altar instead of listening to and watching the celebrant.

On all Sundays and feast-days, there is to be a sermon at each mass. Care should be taken in the course of the sermons that the homily forms a part of the liturgy of the day.

Marriage, except in exceptional circumstances, ought always to be solemnized within the celebration of the mass. And the nuptial blessing must still be given.

The putting into practice of the thoroughgoing reform of the liturgy demanded by the Vatican Council has thus been enthusiastically begun. We can look forward with confidence to the announcement soon of some further reforms.

EXTRACT FROM THE 1963 CONSTITUTION

1. This sacred Council has several aims in view: it desires to impart an ever-increasing vigour to the Christian life of the faithful; to adapt more suitably to the needs of our own times those institutions which are subject to change; to foster whatever can promote union among all who believe in Christ; to strengthen whatever can help to call the whole of mankind into the household of the Church. The Council, therefore, sees particularly cogent reasons for undertaking the reform and promotion of the liturgy.

14. Mother Church earnestly desires that all the faithful should be led to that full, conscious, and active participation in liturgical celebrations which is demanded by the very nature of liturgy. Such participation by the Christian people as a 'chosen race, a royal priesthood, a holy nation, a redeemed people' (I Pet. 2.9; cf. 2.4–5) is their right and duty as a result of their baptism.

In the restoration and promotion of the sacred liturgy, this full and active participation by all the people is the aim to be considered above all else; for it is the primary and indispensable source from which the faithful are to derive the true Christian spirit; and, therefore, pastors of souls must zealously strive to achieve it, by means of the necessary instruction, in all their pastoral work.

21. In order that the Christian people may more certainly derive an abundance of graces from celebrating the liturgy, holy Mother Church desires to undertake with great care a general restoration of the liturgy itself. For the liturgy is made up of immutable elements divinely instituted, and of elements subject to change. These not only may, but ought to be changed with the passage of time if they have suffered from the intrusion of anything out of harmony with the inner nature of the liturgy or have become unsuited to it.

23. So that sound tradition may be retained and yet the way remain open to legitimate progress, a careful investigation is always to be made

into each part of the liturgy which is to be revised. This investigation should be undertaken from the theological, historical, and pastoral points of view. Also the general laws governing the structure and meaning of the liturgy must be studied.

25. The liturgical books are to be revised as soon as possible: experts are to be employed on the task and bishops from various parts of the world are to be consulted.

30. To promote active participation, the people should be encouraged to take part by means of acclamations, responses, psalmody, antiphons, and hymns, as well as by actions, gestures, and bodily attitudes. A reverent silence should also be observed at the proper time.

34. The rites should be distinguished by a noble simplicity; they should be short, clear, and unencumbered by any useless repetitions; they should be within the people's powers of comprehension, and normally should not require much explanation.

35. More passages from Holy Scripture should be included in sacred celebrations, and they should be more varied and suitable.

36. (2) Since the use of the mother tongue is frequently of great assistance to the people in the mass, the administration of sacraments, and other parts of the liturgy, the occasions on which it may be used should be increased.

APPENDIX II

GUIDING PRINCIPLES FOR DESIGNING AND BUILDING A CHURCH IN THE SPIRIT OF THE ROMAN LITURGY

(Compiled in 1947 by order of and with the assistance of the Liturgical Commission and published in 1949 by the Aschendorff Press in Münster)

(a) BASIC PRINCIPLES

1. A Christian church is a consecrated building and, even without the eucharist, a place where God is specially present and in which the people of God hold their assemblies. They assemble here for the following purposes (we give them in order of priority):

(a) First and foremost, to celebrate and make new the sacrificial offering of Christ for our redemption;

(b) Secondly, to receive the fruits of Christ's redemptive sacrifice in the holy sacraments;

(c) Thirdly, to hear the Word of God;

(d) Fourthly, to pay their devotions to Christ, present in the eucharistic bread;

(e) Fifthly, to take part in extra-liturgical devotions.

2. A Christian church, however, is not merely a place where people assemble for liturgical and extra-liturgical services, but is also a place where the individual Christian can make his or her own private devotions.

3. It follows from what we have said about the nature and purpose of a Christian church that it is deserving of an honour and dignity which it shares with no other building, because:

(a) A Christian church is first of all in a very special way the 'tabernacle of God amongst men' (Apoc. 21.3), i.e. the place where God guarantees that He may be found by His faithful; it is 'our Father's House' (cf. Luke 15.17); it is 'God's royal palace' (*basilica*).

(b) Secondly, a Christian church is a place where the Church, the Body of Christ, is moulded and developed and hence it is itself a living symbol of this Body;

(c) Thirdly, a Christian church is the place in which God's ultimate union with his people is anticipated, and for this reason, therefore, the church has rightly been described as the 'heavenly Jerusalem, coming down from heaven to earth' (cf. Apoc. 21.2).

4. On the other hand, however, it follows that, by reason of the many kinds of functions which a church fulfils, its manner of construction opens up a variety of problems. The kind of building needed for the celebration of the eucharist, for example, is different from that required for the administration of the sacraments of baptism and penance. So, too, one would need one kind of building for administering the sacraments, another for preaching sermons, one for the veneration of the sacrament, another for conducting popular devotions, and yet another for people's private devotions. It is the task of the Church and her architects to find a solution to the problem of how this variety of usages to which a church is put can be fulfilled in the most fitting manner possible.

5. The offering of the eucharistic sacrifice, the administration of the sacraments, the preaching of the Word, and the veneration of Our Lord in the Sacrament are not performed in exactly the same way in every Christian church in the world. Over the centuries a variety of methods of performing these tasks, called 'liturgies' or 'rites', has been evolved. Far and away the most important of these liturgies are the Roman and the Byzantine, the former proper to the sees of the West, and the latter to the churches of the East.

Though in essentials these two rites are wholly in agreement, Roman and Byzantine churches are characterized by certain differences in their outward forms. Hence a church in which the Roman liturgy is to be celebrated cannot be identical with one which has to serve the purposes of the Byzantine liturgy.

6. A church is meant for the people of God of our own day. Hence it ought to be designed in such a way that people today may feel that it speaks to their own particular condition. In it, the deepest needs of contemporary man should find their fulfilment, his desire to live in community, his demand to know what is true, what is genuine, his desire to escape from what is merely peripheral and to occupy himself with issues of fundamental importance, his passion for clarity, enlightenment, and lucidity, and his longing for peace and quiet, warmth and shelter.

(b) CONCLUSIONS

1. It would be incorrect to build our church and school, local hos-

pital and office for social services, parish hall and parish library, presbytery and sacristans' house all in different places, unless we had very good reason for doing so.

The ideal we ought to strive after would be to join all these institutions together in one place in a single harmonious unit, so that people could see clearly the close connection between the church and its clergy, the eucharist and the administration of charity, and between the sacraments and education.

2. It would not be a good idea to situate a church (without good reason) right on the edge of a noisy main thoroughfare, however necessary it may be to direct the attention of modern man, such as he is in the eyes of this world, very firmly towards the eternal God.

It would be a good idea if the faithful on their way to church were to pass through some place where they could be quiet and assemble to gether, i.e. a kind of walled forecourt or a proper *atrium*, thus preparing themselves to enter the silence of the holy place where God is present.

3. It would be incorrect to make the exterior of a church, in proportion, outline, structure, and decoration, so like contemporary secular buildings in the immediate vicinity that it appeared to be just another secular building. It would be just as wrong to put up advertising slogans on the wall of the church to attract the attention of passers-by in the street.

Our efforts ought to be directed towards pointing out the wholly other, supernatural, and divine aspect of what goes on in the interior of the church in a way which is both dignified and expressive and to structure the church in such a manner that it tones in suitably with its immediate environment.

4. We should not be well advised, in dealing with the position of the entrance to the church, to think only of the problem of how to protect people from the weather or how to regulate the flow of people in and out.

We ought rather to return once more to constructing church entrances (especially the main entrance) in an impressive manner so that the attention of the faithful is drawn to seeing the parallel between the doorway of the church and the gate of heaven.

5. It would be a mistake not to plan the interior of a church with a view to making it suitable for the offering of the Eucharistic sacrifice, but rather with a view to making it fit for the veneration of the eucharistic presence of Christ. This would be wrong, because in our scale of

purposes for which a church is used, the veneration of Christ in the Sacrament does not assume first place.

This problem concerning the conflict between the variety of functions which a church has to fulfil can only be solved in a satisfactory manner if, where possible, there is a place for the offering of the eucharistic sacrifice separate from that where the Sacrament is venerated, and also, if possible, separate places should be provided for the sacraments of baptism and penance. If this is done, each section can be architecturally designed to suit its own particular purposes.

6. Equally incorrect is the widespread opinion that the thing to strive for is an altar positioned centrally in the middle of the congregation of the faithful and that, therefore, a centrally orientated church is the only satisfactory form of building.

A church is first and foremost a building designed for the offering of the eucharistic sacrifice. This ceremony, however, according to the Western Roman concept of the liturgy, is an action—primarily the action of Christ Himself and of His representative, the celebrating priest, but also an action performed by the whole congregation. The principal parts taken by the congregation in this sacred action are the responses which precede the preface and the 'Amen' at the end of the Canon; and also the offertory procession and the procession to receive communion, the first of which, it is true, seldom appears in the liturgy today. In order that all these actions may be suitably performed one needs a building with the altar as its focal point, where priest and people, leader and chorus are situated directly opposite one another with space left for an aisle for processions up and down. Ideally one would want a church fulfilling all these requirements of the Roman liturgy (i.e. interior with the altar at its focal point, priest and people situated directly opposite one another, making practicable the orderly conduct of processions up and down) without at the same time creating too great a distance between the sanctuary and the far end of the nave.

7. The altar, according to its original meaning, is the place where earth is raised up to heaven. In a Christian context the altar is considered to be the table where the people of God offer sacrifice and hold their meal, and at the same time the place where God appears amongst us in His eucharistic presence. Since, however, through the consecration, the God-Man becomes present on the altar, the altar, even when it has no tabernacle, is also the Throne of Christ. And because the altar is the throne of Christ, the Fathers of the Church considered

that it represented Christ Himself, for the throne indeed represents the Ruler. From all this it follows that it is very wrong to make the altar look like a shelf set up against the wall or to construct it as if its sole or primary function were to be a support for the tabernacle, crucifix, candles, reliquaries, pictures, and small statues.

In an ideal church the altar should be set in an isolated position, raised up in proportion to the rest of the building, and arranged in such a way that people can walk right round it; its carefully planned design and the equally careful way in which the material of which it is made has been selected, its monumentality in comparison with the proportions of the rest of the building, the way in which the perspectives of the interior neatly converge upon it, the fact that it is placed in the most brightly lit part of the church, and may also have a tabernacle—all this should show clearly that the altar, perhaps emphasized by a ciborium is the holiest place in the church, the very heart and centre of everything in the church. The altar in fact should be the starting point from which the ideal church should be planned and structured, both as to its interior as to its exterior design.

8. It would be a mistake to abandon without good reason the venerable tradition of building our churches to face East.

We should rather help the faithful to understand and to become aware once more of the profound and beautiful symbolism of turning East for prayer, thereby bringing to life once more the direction in which churches today are orientated. There are many indications today which point to the fact that in the church of the future, priests everywhere will once more celebrate from behind the altar, facing the people, as at one time they always did, and as is still done in the ancient Roman basilicas today; for indeed the fact that people in many quarters want the community aspect of the eucharist as a gathering of the faithful round a table to be given clearer expression seems to demand just such a resolution of the problem. Nor indeed would the rule of turning East for prayer stand in the way of such a development. For, ideally, the object of turning East is to face God and His only begotten Son, who like the sun, are thought of as enthroned in the East and coming from the East. Now, however, this 'coming' or 'advent' of God in His Theophany takes place on our altars; hence in a Christian church, the object of turning East for prayer is to face the altar; and, therefore, both priest and people have to turn towards the altar.

9. In larger churches it would be equally wrong to situate the altar for no particular reason at the very end of the building as so often

happened in early Christian times in churches built in the form of a hall ('single-room churches').

One would be more in accordance both with tradition and with the present-day circumstances if one were to make a separate sanctuary or choir for the altar, rectangular, hemi-spherical, or polygonal in shape (a 'two-room church').

10. It would be a mistake to fill the back wall of the sanctuary with windows so that these cause our eyes to be distracted from the altar itself. It would be just as much a mistake to fill up the back wall with sacred pictures which have no connection with the eucharistic sacrifice, and which are not suitable for the whole of the liturgical year.

Ideally, the architecture and decoration of the sanctuary should be chosen in such a way that our attention is not drawn to these in themselves but rather to the altar and to the sacred action which is being performed there. For the danger in putting up pictures and images in the sanctuary is that they distract from the world of imagery created by the solemn eucharistic prayer (i.e. the text of the mass between the 'Sursum corda' and the concluding doxology). In any case, people ought not in these matters to have recourse to historical precedent, but should rather choose themes of lasting significance.

11. It would be incorrect to construct the interior of a church in such a way that the congregation loses its sense of being a unity, a family gathered together for worship. It would, on the other hand, be just as incorrect if the interior were constructed so that there was not a single corner left for people to pray in private.

The ideal solution to this situation would probably be a church in which on the one hand there was always available a space adequate to contain large congregations on Sundays and feast-days and also the smaller week-day congregations, and which would serve to emphasize the unity of the assembled congregation; and on the other hand it would still have just the kind of corner for devotion that the individual would want for making his or her own private devotional exercises.

12. It would be a pity if in the building used for worship our attention were distracted from the altar by side altars, statues, stations of the Cross, confessionals, clumsily placed candle-stands, and pews, which all serve to distract the attention of the faithful from the holy things themselves.

All superfluous additions should be dispensed with, and necessary structures, e.g. side altars and confessionals, should, where possible, be relegated to side chapels or to a crypt. What remains in the main body of the church should be constructed and arranged so as not to interrupt the gentle flow of the interior up to the altar.

13. It would be a mistake not to situate the sacristy right next to the sanctuary and to place it, as in early Christian times, at one side of the west front of the church. It would, on the other hand, be a good idea if a connecting passage were constructed between the sacristy and the entrance to the church so that on Sundays and feast-days the clergy could process solemnly through the congregation up to the altar, the Introit chant of the eucharistic liturgy ('Introitus') thereby regaining its full significance.

14. The spaciousness of cathedral churches, shrines, and large city churches has made it necessary for preaching to be done not from the sanctuary but from a tall pulpit which is normally set in the centre of the church to one side or close against the wall. Under the influence of these great churches, it has unfortunately become an almost universal custom to situate the pulpit in such a way that the preacher always has his back to part of the congregation.

The liturgical sermon (i.e. that which is inserted and forms an integral part of the very structure of the eucharistic celebration) ought to be primarily a continuation and exposition of the Word of God which has been proclaimed in the two readings from scripture. Like the Epistle and Gospel, therefore, the sermon ought, where possible, to be preached from the sanctuary, perhaps from an ambo on the edge of the choir.

15. The choir which provides the music has a clearly defined function to fulfil in the liturgy. Its task is to lead the congregation in prayer, responses, and music, to take part in the antiphonal chants with the people, and from time to time to perform on behalf of the congregation. It follows, therefore, that it is a mistake to place the choir high up in a gallery at the back in a place where they cannot be seen by the congregation.

In an ideal church, organized and structured in accordance with the best liturgical interests, the choir should be given a place in the nave, right next to the sanctuary. If galleries at the back are not abandoned altogether, they should be used for the organ, the liturgical function of which does not consist in filling in the 'pauses' in the sacred action with solo music, but rather in supporting the singing of the choir and congregation, and, on occasions, in lending weight to the festal mood of the people at the beginning and end of the service. (The gallery at the back would also be the normal place for the four-part polyphonic choir and orchestra, though the last of these is quite clearly alien to strictly liturgical services.)

16. At holy baptism we are born again as children of God and at the same time made members of the Church, the body of Christ. It is lamentable that in parochial life today, this fundamental meaning of the sacrament of baptism is scarcely expressed at all, and that, as a result, the font is one of the most neglected features of the church.

In an ideal church, a place specially partitioned off ought to be given to the font, which itself should be monumental in form and situated near the entrance to the church. There is a venerable tradition which directs that this space should be either round or polygonal in shape. If we reflect a moment on the baptismal rite itself, then we shall come to the same conclusions concerning the structure of the baptistry. For the very heart of the baptismal rite is not so much that man is performing an action, but rather that he is the object and recipient of the secret activity of God. For a rite with this kind of content, a long building, which suggests symbolically a building meant for action, is inappropriate and one requires rather a building with its focal point at the centre, its axis running vertically up and down, thus symbolizing a place where the grace of God is received.

17. It would be a mistake if we were to structure and decorate our churches in imitation of the comfort of the houses of the well-to-do or the bareness of the houses of the poor.

The interior of an ideal church ought to convey the impression of being neither middle-class nor working-class. It should do something to convey the majesty of God, which is far removed from all secular or earthly standards, and thus lift all who enter out of their private lives, while at the same time allowing them to sense the 'human kindness of Our Redeemer' (Titus 3.4).

18. It would be wrong if, as has mostly been the case in the recent past, people should be content to leave the decoration of the church and its fittings with pictures and ornaments, in particular the decoration of the porch, the sanctuary, the altar, the font, and the pulpit to the whims of the parish priest, the founder of the church, or simply to chance.

In any attempt to construct a model church, one should not only work out a plan for the building itself, but also a plan of how the church is to be fitted out from the aesthetic point of view, a plan moreover which has been well thought out both theologically and catechetically. Such a plan will consequently ensure that when the church is completed, its decorations will present the faithful not merely with fragments of the spiritual life, but in a certain sense, with the spiritual life as a whole, set out in a logical order with the emphasis in the right place.

19. In the planning of new churches there is a general tendency to build them only just so large as money and building space will allow. Larger churches are erroneously thought to be better simply because of their size.

There is in fact an optimum size for churches. Ideally, a church should be just so large that the priest at the altar can be clearly understood and seen without the help of technical equipment even by those sitting in the back rows of the congregation, and so that communion may be given to all in church without disrupting the celebration of the mass itself. This optimum size should not be exceeded without good reason. (It is obvious, though, that cathedrals and churches at shrines need to be of somewhat larger proportions.)

20. It would be incorrect to equip a parish church of average proportions with a sanctuary big enough to take as many clergy as one would find in the chancel of a cathedral. It would be just as wrong to build a sanctuary so short that the altar steps came right up to the altar rails.

Ideally, the size of the sanctuary should be proportionate to the size of the rest of the building, and the pavement between the altar steps and the altar rails should be wide and deep enough to provide room enough for solemn mass with a deacon to be celebrated quite smoothly.

21. It would be a mistake to fill up the nave with pews to such an extent that the front ones came right up to the altar or communion rails, and that the side ones reached nearly to the wall.

In an ideal church, provision should be made for sufficiently wide gangways to be kept in the centre, at the sides, in front of the altar rails, and at the entrance, so that if several hundred wish to come to the Lord's Table, there is no unedifying crush, and that processions ordered for certain liturgical occasions (i.e. the Introit procession on Sundays and feast-days and the processions on Candlemas and Palm Sunday, etc.) may be performed without people being cramped for space.

Those entrusted with the task of building a church have indeed a heavy responsibility laid upon them. The success of their work depends on whether the faithful love their parish church or do not love it, whether they come to it willingly or unwillingly. One can never be too conscientious, therefore, or too thorough in the planning of a new church.

THE HYMN OF THE ANGELS

Glory be to God on High
And on earth, peace to men of good will,
We praise Thee
We bless Thee
We worship Thee
We glorify Thee
We give thanks to Thee for Thy great glory
Lord God, Heavenly King, God the Father Almighty.
O Lord, the only begotten Son, Jesus Christ
O Lord, God, Lamb of God, Son of the Father
Who takest away the sins of the world, have mercy upon us
Who takest away the sins of the world, receive our prayer
Who sittest at the right hand of God the Father; have mercy
    upon us
For Thou alone art the Holy One
Thou only art the Lord
The only art the most high, O Jesus Christ
With the Holy Ghost in the glory of God the Father.

Amen.

THE DEACON'S HYMN OF PRAISE
AT THE LIGHTING OF THE PASCHAL CANDLE

Now let the angelic heavenly choirs exult; let joy pervade the unknown beings who surround God's throne; and let the trumpet of salvation sound the triumph of this mighty King. Let earth, too, be joyful, in the radiance of this great splendour. Enlightened by the glory of her eternal King, let her feel that from the whole round world the darkness has been lifted. Let mother Church likewise rejoice, wearing the radiance of this great Light; let this temple echo with the multitude's full-throated song.

Dear brethren, who are present at this wondrous lighting of the holy frame, I pray you join with me and invoke the mercy of almighty God, that he who, not for any merit of mine, has deigned to number me among his Levites, may shed his own bright light upon me and enable me to glorify with perfect praise this candle; through our Lord Jesus Christ, his Son,—who is God, living and reigning with him in the unity of the Holy Spirit:

For ever and ever—Amen.

The Lord be with you—and with thy spirit.—Lift up your hearts— We lift them up to the Lord—Let us give thanks to the Lord our God —It is right and fitting.

Just is it indeed and fitting with all the ardour of our heart and mind and with the service of our voice to hymn God, the invisible almighty Father and his only begotten Son, our Lord Jesus Christ who repaid Adam's debt for use to his eternal Father, and with his dear blood wiped out the penalty of that ancient sin. This is the paschal feast wherein is slain the true Lamb whose blood hallows the doorposts of the faithful. This is the night on which thou didst first cause our forefathers, the sons of Israel, in their passage out of Egypt, to pass dry-shod over the Red Sea. This is the night which purged away the blackness of sin by the light of the fiery pillar. This is the night which at this hour throughout the world restores to grace and yokes to holiness those who believe in Christ, detaching them from worldly vice and all the murk of sin. On this night Christ burst the bonds of death and rose victorious from the grave. Without redemption, life itself had been no boon. How wonderful the condescension of thy mercy towards us; how far beyond all reckoning thy loving kindness! To ransom thy slave thou gavest up thy Son! O truly necessary sin of Adam, that Christ's death blotted out; and happy fault that merited such a Redeemer! Blessed indeed is this the sole night counted worthy to know the season and the hour in which Christ rose again from the grave. It is this night of which the scripture says: And the night shall be bright as day. And the night shall light up my joy. By this night's holiness, crime is banished and sin washed away; innocence is restored to the fallen, and gladness to the sorrowful. It drives forth hate, brings peace and humbles tyranny.

In thanksgiving for this night, then, holy Father, receive the evening sacrifice of this flame, which Holy Church, by the hands of her ministers, renders to thee in the solemn offering of this wax candle wrought by bees. For now we see the splendour of this column, kindled to the glory of God from shining flame. A flame which though it be divided into parts, yet suffers no loss of light, being fed from the ever melting wax that the mother-bee brought forth to form the substance of this precious candle. Blessed indeed is the night, which despoiled the Egyptians and enriched the Hebrews! The night on which heaven is wedded to earth, the things of God to those of man!

We therefore pray thee, Lord, that this candle, hallowed in honour of thy name, may continue unfailingly to scatter the darkness of this night. May it be received as a sweet fragrance, and mingle with the lights of heaven. May the morning-star find its flame alight, that Morning-Star which knows no setting, which came back from limbo and shed its clear light upon mankind. We pray thee, Lord, to grant us a season of peace at this time of Easter gladness. Deign to preserve us thy servants, and all the clergy and faithful people, together with our Holy Father N. and our Bishop N. Guide and keep them all under thy continual protection. Look also upon those in power who are our rulers, and with the gift of thy love and mercy that is beyond all telling, direct their thoughts to justice and peace, so that when their toil on earth is over, they and all thy people may come at last to their heavenly home; through the same Jesus Christ, thy Son, our Lord. Amen.

APPENDIX IV

POSTSCRIPT 1978, BY JOHN HALLIBURTON

Students of the development of the modern Roman liturgy since 1965 would do well to consult *Vatican Council II—The Conciliar and Post-conciliar Documents*, edited by Austin Flannery, OP. Documents of liturgical interest are collected in pp. 1–281. On 4 December 1963 the Constitution on the Sacred Liturgy (Sacrosanctum Concilium) was promulgated (see Appendix I) and on 26 September 1964 came the First Instruction for its implementation. Parishes all over the world began to feel the first impact of the reforms and particular care was taken to ensure the liturgical education of the clergy. Two further Instructions were to follow. The second ('Tres abhinc annos . . .') in 1967 considered responses from the dioceses and without changing the existing liturgical books enabled some modifications by means of simple rubrical directions. Meanwhile, on 3 April 1969, the eve of the fourth centenary of the first edition of Pius V's *Missale Romanum*, an *Apostolic Constitution* was issued, heralding the new *Missale Romanum* and highlighting its main features. There were to be three new eucharistic prayers, a new and more representative lectionary and a revised *Ordo Missae* (some elements having been simplified and clarified, e.g. the offertory, and some restored to their former vigour and significance, e.g. the homily, the Prayer of the Faithful and the penitential rite). The new *Missale Romanum* was published on 26 March 1970, prefaced by a General Instruction (reprinted by the CTS). There are three main parts to the revised liturgy: the *Introductory Rites* (entrance chant, greeting of the people, penitential rites, Kyries, if not included in the act of penitence, Gloria, when appointed, and the Collect.) Next, the *Liturgy of the Word* (scripture readings, chants between the readings, the homily—ordered on Sundays and recommended on weekdays—the profession of faith and the Prayer of the Faithful). Third, the *Liturgy of the Eucharist*, also in three parts: the preparation of the gifts, encouraging the participation of the people, who bring the gifts to the altar and take part in the offertory prayers; then the eucharistic prayer—the celebrant today has four from which to choose—in which the people take their part in the introductory dialogue, the

Sanctus, the acclamations after the Institution Narrative and in the final *Amen*; finally the Communion Rite which comprises the Lord's Prayer, the fraction with embolism and doxology, the exchange of the sign of peace, the commixture, the invitation to communion, the distribution of communion, a pause for silent prayer and the Post-communion prayer. At the end, the celebrant gives the people his blessing and dismisses the congregation.

The Third Instruction on the Correct Implementation of the Constitution on the Sacred Liturgy was issued on 5 September 1970. Care had been taken since the Second Instruction not to intervene too frequently during a six-year period of adjustment to the new liturgy. The time had come however to establish reasonable bounds, and while preserving an essential pluriformity to allow for cultural diversity and pastoral need, now it was judged appropriate to affirm a right sense of liturgical unity. (See also the *Circular Letter* of April 1973, prohibiting the use of eucharistic prayers other than those provided and the *Note on the Obligation to use the New Roman Missal* of October 1974.)

BIBLIOGRAPHY

A. ABBREVIATIONS

I give only abbreviations that might present difficulties in interpretation.

AC	*Antike und Christentum* (Münster)
ArchLw	*Archiv für Liturgiewissenschaft*
CSEL	*Corpus scriptorum ecclesiasticorum latinorum* (Vienna)
DACL	*Dictionnaire d'archéologie chrétienne et de liturgie* (Paris)
EphL	*Ephemerides liturgicae* (Rome)
J.	P. Jaffé, *Regesta pontificum romanorum*, 2 vols. (Leipzig, 1885)
JbAC	*Jahrbuch für Antike und Christentum* (Münster)
JbLHymn	*Jahrbuch für Liturgik und Hymnologie*
JbLw	*Jahrbuch für Liturgiewissenschaft* (Münster)
LexThK	*Lexikon für Theologie und Kirche*
LitJb	*Liturgisches Jahrbuch* (Münster)
PG	Migne, *Patrologia graeca*
PL	Migne, *Patrologia latina*
RAC	*Reallexikon für Antike und Christentum* (Stuttgart)
RevScR	*Revue des sciences religieuses* (Strasbourg)
RGG	*Religion in Geschichte und Gegenwart*
RHE	*Revue d'histoire ecclésiastique* (Louvain)
RM	*Mitteilungen des Deutschen Archäologischen Instituts, Römische Abteilung*
RQS	*Römische Quartalschrift* (Freiburg)
ThLZ	*Theologische Literaturzeitung* (Leipzig and Berlin)
ZKG	*Zeitschrift für Kirchengeschichte* (Stuttgart)
ZKTh	*Zeitschrift für katholische Theologie* (Innsbruck)

B. GENERAL
The term 'liturgy' and its definition

H. Strathman and R. Meyer, 'Λειτουργέω', etc., in *ThWb* 4 (1942) pp. 221–38.

J. A. Jungmann, 'Was ist Liturgie?' in *Gewordene Liturgie* (Innsbruck, 1941), pp. 1–27.

J. A. Jungmann, 'Liturgie und *pia exercitia*' in *LitJb* 9 (1959), pp. 79–86.

B. Fischer, 'Liturgie' in *LexThK* 6 (1961), p. 1085.

The nature and characteristics of the liturgy

E. Lengeling, 'Liturgie' in *Handbuch theologischer Grundbegriffe* 2 (Munich, 1963), pp. 865–80.

A. Stenzel, '*Cultus publicus*. Ein Beitrag zum Begriff u. ekklesiologischen Ort der Liturgie' in *ZKTh* 75 (1953), pp. 174–214.

A. Baumstark, 'Das Gesetz der Erhaltung des Alten in liturgisch hochwertiger Zeit' in *JbLw* 7 (1927), pp. 1–23.

———. *Liturgie comparée. Principes et méthodes pour l'étude historique des liturgies chrétiennes* (3rd ed. Chevetogne-Paris, 1953). [Translated into English as *Comparative Liturgy*, London, 1958.]

In the second of these two books, B. directs our attention on pp. 67–9 to three further laws of liturgical prayer. This develops (1) from being simple to becoming more elaborate, (2) from being unbiblical to becoming more biblical, (3) from being asymmetrical to becoming symmetrical, and (4) from being unbiased to becoming positively didactic. The universal validity of these laws is open to debate.

J. Daniélou, *Bible et liturgie. La théologie biblique des sacraments et des fêtes d'après les pères de l'Église* (Paris, 1951). [Translated into English as *The Bible and the Liturgy* (London, 1960).]

C. Vaggagini, *Il senso teologico della liturgia* (Rome, 1957). [Translated into German as *Theologie der Liturgie* (Einsiedeln, 1959).]

Systematic accounts of the liturgy as a whole
(which for the most part deal also with liturgical history)

L. Eisenhofer, *Handbuch der katholischen Liturgik*, 2 vols. (2nd ed., Freiburg, 1941).

G. Rietschel (and B. Graff), *Lehrbuch der Liturgik*, 2 vols. (1st ed., Berlin, 1900; 2nd ed., Göttingen, 1951.)

J. Lechner, *Liturgik des römischen Ritus*, begründet von L. Eisenhofer (6th ed., Freiburg, 1953). Short and concise. [Translated into English as *The Liturgy of the Roman Rite*, London/Freiburg, 1961.]

L. A. Winterswyl, *Laienliturgik* (1st ed., Kevalaer, 1938; 2nd ed., Cologne, 1948).

A. G. Martimort (ed.), *L'église en prière. Introduction à la liturgie* (Paris, 1961). [Translated into German as *Handbuch der Liturgiewissenschaft*, 2 vols. (Freiburg, 1963).]

Leiturgia. Handbuch des evangelischen Gottesdienstes, ed. K. F. Müller and W. Blankenburg, vol. 2, *Gestalt und Formen* (Kassel, 1955).

J. A. Jungmann, *Der Gottesdienst der Kirche auf dem Hintergrund seiner Geschichte* (1st ed., Innsbruck, 1955; 2nd ed., 1962).

Systematic and historical studies of the liturgy in general

L. Duchesne, *Les origines du culte chrétien* (1st ed., Paris, 1889; 5th ed., 1923.) A classic study. [Fifth edition translated into English as *Christian Worship* (London, 1923).]

A. Baumstark, *Vom geschichtlichen Werden der Liturgie* (*Ecclesia orans* 10, Freiburg, 1923).

A. Baumstark, *Liturgie comparée.*

W. Nagel, *Geschichte des christlichen Gottesdienstes* (Sammlung Göschen, 1202/1202a, Berlin, 1962).

G. Dix, *The Shape of the Liturgy* (1st ed., London, 1945). Several new editions have followed.

R. Stählin, 'Die Geschichte des christlichen Gottesdienstes' in *Leiturgia. Handbuch des evangelischen Gottesdienstes*, ed. K. F. Müller and W. Blankenburg, vol. 1 (Kassel, 1954), pp. 1–81.

M. Righetti, *Manuale di storia liturgica*, 4 vols. (Milan, 1950–3).

L. Schuster, *Liber sacramentorum, note storiche e liturgiche sul messale romano*, 10 vols. (3rd ed., Turin, 1928 ff.). German edition published in Regensburg, 1929 ff. [Translated into English as *The Sacramentary* (London, 1924–30).] Didactic interests take pride of place.

T. Klauser, *Die abendländische Liturgie von Aeneas Silvius Piccolomini bis heute. Erbe und Aufgabe* (Vorträge der Aen. Silv.-Stiftung, ed. 1., Basle, 1962.)

Systematic and historical studies of the eucharist

A. Baumstark, *Die Messe im Morgenland* (Sammlung Kösel 8, Kempten, n. d.

P. Batiffol, *Leçons sur la messe* (1st ed., Paris, 1916; 8th ed., 1920).

A. Baumstark, *Missale Romanum. Seine Entwicklung, ihre wichtigsten*

Urkunden und Probleme (Eindhoven-Nijmegen, 1929). Cf. *JbLw* 10 (1930), pp. 211–15.

J. Brinktrine, *Die hl. Messe in ihrem Werden und Wesen* (1st ed., Paderborn, 1931; 3rd ed., 1950).

J. A. Jungmann, *Missarum Sollemnia. Eine genetische Erklärung der römischen Messe*, 2 vols. (1st ed., Vienna, 1948; 5th ed., 1962). A standard work. [Translated into French as *Missarum Sollemnia* (Paris, 1950). It is with a certain hesitation that we recommend the English edition, *The Mass of the Roman Rite* (New York, 1950).]

B. Capelle, 'Précis d'histoire de la messe', in *idem., Travaux liturgiques* 2 (1962), pp. 10–30.

J. A. Jungmann, *Wortgottesdienst im Lichte von Theologie und Geschichte* (1st ed., Regensburg, 1939; 4th ed., 1965), originally entitled *Die liturgische Feier, grundsätzliches und geschichtliches.*

J. Pascher, *Eucharistia, Gestalt und Vollzug* (1st ed., Münster, 1947; 3rd ed., 1953).

Systematic and historical studies of the liturgy of the other sacraments

A. Stenzel, *Die Taufe* (Innsbruck, 1958).

Baptism ought one day to be dealt with exhaustively after the manner of Jungmann's *Missarum Sollemnia.*

J. A. Jungmann, *Die lateinischen Bussriten in ihrer geschichtlichen Entwicklung* (Innsbruck, 1932).

L. Andrieux, *La première communion, histoire et discipline* (*Textes et documents*, Paris, 1911). See also J. Baumgärtler, *Die Erstkommunion der Kinder* (Munich, 1929).

Deals with the subject only as far as the Middle Ages.

B. Kleinheyer, *Die Priesterweihe im römischen Ritus* (*Trierer theologische Studien* 12, Trier, 1962).

V. Raffa, 'Partecipazione colletiva dei vescovi alla consacrazione episcopale' in *EphL* 78 (1964), pp. 105–40.

M. Andrieu, 'Les ordres mineurs dans l'ancien rit romain' in *RevScR* 5 (1925), pp. 232–78.

B. Binder, *Geschichte des feierlichen Ehesegens von der Entstehung der Ritualien bis zur Gegenwart* (Metten, 1938). See also K. Ritzer, *Eheschliessung. Formen, Riten und religiöses Brauchtum des ersten Jahrtausends*, 2 vols. (Munich, 1951; new edition, revised, 1962), vol. 38 of *Liturgiegeschichte. Quellen und Forschungen.*

R. Metz, *La consécration des vierges dans l'église romaine* (Bibl. Inst. Droit. Canon., Strasbourg, 4; Paris, 1954).

D. Stiefenhofer, *Die Geschichte der Kirchweihe vom 1.–7. Jahrhundert* (Munich, 1909).

J. Pascher, *Die Liturgie der Sakramente* (1st ed., Münster, 1951; 3rd ed., 1961).

Systematic and historical studies of the liturgy of the hours of prayer

S. Bäumer, *Geschichte des Breviers* (Freiburg, 1895). [Translated into English as *History of the Roman Breviary* (London, 1905).]

P. Batiffol, *Histoire du bréviaire romain* (1st ed., Paris, 1893; 3rd ed., 1911). [Translated into English as *History of the Roman Breviary* (London, 1912).]

J. Brinktrine, *Das römische Brevier* (Paderborn, 1932).

P. Salmon, *L'office divin. Histoire de la formation du bréviaire (Lex orandi* 27, Paris, 1959).

J. Pascher, *Das Stundengebet der römischen Kirche* (Munich, 1954).

R. J. Hesbert, *Corpus antiphonalium officii* 1 ff. (Rome, 1963 ff.). See also V. Raffa in *EphL* 78 (1961), pp. 521–4.

The history of buildings used for worship

See under Chapter IV, Section v.

The history of liturgical dress and insignia

See under Chapter I, Section vi.

The history of the altar and its furnishings

J. Braun, *Der christliche Altar in seiner geschichtlichen Entwicklung,* 2 vols. (Munich, 1924).
   This book is both reliable and exhaustive as to its details but is inadequate in its historical treatment of the subject.

J. Braun, *Das christliche Altargerät in seinem Sein und in seiner Entwicklung* (Munich, 1932).

The history of liturgical language

See under Chapter I, Sections iii and vii.

The history of liturgical gestures

See under Chapter III, Section v.

The history of liturgical singing and music

E. Werner, *The sacred bridge. The interdependence of liturgy and music in synagogue and church during the first millennium* (London/New York, 1959). See also A. Stuiber in *ZKG* 111 (1961), pp. 384–6.

W. Apel, *Gregorian chant* (Bloomington, 1958). I have not in fact seen this book.

O. Ursprung, *Die katholische Kirchenmusik* (Potsdam, 1931).

K. G. Fellerer, *Geschichte der katholischen Kirchenmusik* (2nd ed., Essen, 1949).

J. Gelineau, *Chant et musique dans le culte chrétien* (Paris, 1961). [Translated into German as *Die Musik im christlichen Gottesdienst* (Regensburg, 1965).]

H. Hucke, 'Kirchenmusik' in *Concilium* I (1965), pp. 102–24.

Collected studies of the history of the liturgy

E. Bishop, *Liturgica historica* (Oxford, 1918).

J. A. Jungmann, *Gewordene Liturgie. Studien und Durchblicke* (Innsbruck, 1941).

Miscellanea liturgica in honorem L. C. Mohlberg, 2 vols. (Rome, 1948).

Vom christlichen Mysterium. Gesammelte Arbeiten zum Gedächtnis von O. Casel (Düsseldorf, 1951).

J. A. Jungmann, *Liturgisches Erbe und pastorale Gegenwart. Studien und Vorträge* (Innsbruck, 1960).

B. Capelle, *Travaux liturgiques de doctrine et d'histoire*, 2 vols. (Louvain, 1955 and 1962).

W. Dürig (ed.), *Liturgie. Gestalt und Vollzug* (Festschrift J. Pascher: Munich, 1963).

Collections of sources

J. Beckmann, *Quellen zur Geschichte des christlichen Gottesdienstes* (Gutersloh, 1956).

The most important sources, translated into German.

P. Rado, *Enchiridion liturgicum, complectens theologiae sacramentalis et dogmata et leges iuxta novum codicem rubricarum* (Rome, 1961).

H. Kraft, *Texte zur Geschichte der Taufe, besonders der Kindertaufe in der alten Kirche* (Kleine Texte 174, Berlin, 1955).

E. C. Whitaker, *Documents of the baptismal liturgy* (London, 1960).

J. Quasten, *Monumenta eucharistica et liturgica vetustissima* (Florilegium Patristicum, 7, 1–7; Bonn, 1935–7).

C. SPECIAL READING FOR EACH PERIOD

Chapter I—Creative Beginnings

Section i: Outline of the period

Jesus as founder of the liturgy

W. Nagel, *Geschichte des christlichen Gottesdienstes* (Sammlung Göschen 1202–1202a; Berlin, 1962), pp. 7–11.

E. Lohmeyer, *Kultus und Evangelium* (Göttingen, 1942).

Jewish elements in the liturgy

I. Elbogen, *Der jüdische Gottesdienst in seiner Entwicklung* (2nd ed., Frankfurt, 1924; 4th ed., Hildesheim, 1961).

J. Leipoldt, *Der Gottesdienst der ältesten Kirche: jüdisch? griechisch? christlich?* (Leipzig, 1937).

W. Bousset, 'Eine jüdische Gebetssammlung im 7. Buch der Apostolischen Konstitutionen' in *Nachr. Gott. Ges. der Wissensch.*(1915), pp. 435–89.

A. Baumstark, *Vom geschlichtlichem Werden der Liturgie* (Freiburg, 1923), pp. 12–21, 'Das Erbe der Synagoge'. See also W. O. E. Oesterley, *The Jewish background of the Christian liturgy* (Oxford, 1925); and C. W. Dugmore, *The influence of the synagogue upon the divine office* (Oxford, 1944; 2nd ed., London, 1964.)

G. Dix, *Jew and Greek. A study in the primitive Church* (London, 1953).

E. Lohse, *Die Ordination in Spätjudentum und im NT* (Göttingen, 1951). See also A. Ehrhardt, 'Jewish and Christian ordination' in

J.E.H. 5 (1954), pp. 125–38. J. M. Robinson, 'Die Hodajot-Formel in Gebet und Hymnus des Frühchristentums' in *Apophoreta, Festschrift E. Haenchen* (Berlin, 1964), pp. 194–223.

J. P. Audet, 'Esquisse historique du genre littéraire de la 'bénédiction' juive et de l'eucharistie chrétienne' in *Revue biblique* 65 (1958), pp. 371–99. See also A. Stuiber, 'Doxologie' in *RAC* 4 (1959), pp. 210–26; and *idem*, 'Eulogia' in *RAC* 6 (1966), pp. 900–28.

C. P. Price, 'Jewish morning prayers and early Christian anaphoras' in *Anglican Theological Review* 43 (1961), pp. 153–68.

B. J. Van der Veken, 'De primordiis liturgiae paschalis' in *Sacris erudiri* 13 (1962), pp. 461–501.

J. van Goudoever, *Biblical calendars* (2nd ed., Leyden, 1961).
This deals with the connection between Jewish feasts and the Christian festival of Easter.

A. Baumstark, 'Trishagion und Qeduscha' in *JbLw* 3 (1923), pp. 18–32.

T. Klauser, 'Akklamation' in *RAC* 1 (1950), pp. 216–33.

H. Engberding, 'Alleluja' in *RAC* 1 (1950), pp. 293–9. See also A. Stuiber, 'Amen' in *JbAC* 1 (1958), pp. 153–9.

L. Gougaud, 'Étude sur les "Ordines commendationis animae"' in *EphL* 49 (1935), pp. 3–27.
In these Ordines we encounter the most important 'paradigmatic prayers' that are still in use. The earlier evidences for the 'paradigmatic prayers' are assembled in K. Michel's *Gebet und Bild in frühchristlicher Zeit* (Leipzig, 1902), pp. 1–48.

J. Coppens, *L'Imposition des mains et les rites connexes dans le Nouveau Testament et dans l'Église ancienne* (Wetteren-Paris, 1925).

G. Bornkamm, 'Lobpreis, Bekenntnis und Opfer' in *Apophoreta, Festschrift E. Haenchen* (Berlin, 1964), pp. 46–63. Explains the two meanings of 'confession' in Hebrew, Greek, and Latin.

Hellenistic elements

A. Baumstark, *Vom geschichtlichem Werden der Liturgie* (Freiburg, 1923), pp. 21–9, 'Der hellenistische Einschlag'.

O. Perler, 'Arkandisziplin' in *RAC* 1 (1950), pp. 667–76.

F. J. Dölger, *Sol salutis* (*Liturgiegeschichtliche Forschungen* 4/5; 2nd ed., Münster, 1925).
Investigations into the basis of the ancient practice of turning east for prayer. See also E. Peterson, *Frühkirche Judentum und Gnosis* (Rome-Freiburg-Vienna, 1959), especially pp. 1–14, 'Die ge-

schichtliche Bedeutung der jüdischen Gebetsrichtung'; and pp. 15–35, 'Das Kreuz und das Gebet nach Osten'.

N. A. Dahl, *Anamnesis* (Lund, 1948).

J. Laager, 'Epiklesis' in *RAC* 5 (1962), pp. 577–99. See also J. P. de Jong, 'Epiklese' in *LexThK* 3 (2nd ed., 1959), cols. 933–7.

E. Peterson, Εἷς Θεός. *Epigraphische, vorgeschichtliche und religionsgeschichtliche Untersuchungen* (Göttingen, 1926).

Some basic investigations into the hellenistic forms of acclamation. See also T. Klauser, 'Akklamation' in *RAC* 1 (1950), pp. 216–33. In this article the fact was overlooked that 'Deo gratias' is also hellenistic or at least Roman in origin. Texts to prove this are provided in G. Appel, 'De Romanorum precationibus' (*Religionsgeschichtliche Versuche und Vorarbeiten*, 7, 2; Giessen, 1909), pp. 182–3.

F. J. Dölger, 'Der Exorcismus im altchristlichen Taufritual' (*Studien zur Geschichte und Kultur des Altertums* 3, 1/2; Paderborn, 1909).

Basic to any understanding of the rites of baptism.

H. Conzelmann, 'Christus im Gottesdienst der neutestamentlichen Zeit' in *Bild u. Verkündigung, Festgabe Hanna Jursch* (1962), pp. 21–30.

The author maintains that worship is a factor in the event of our salvation, not however because it possesses a cultic quality but because God imparts His salvation by His Word.

The development of the liturgy to the time of Gregory the Great

H. Lietzmann, 'Die Entstehung der christlichen Liturgie nach den ältesten Quellen' in *Vorträge Bibl. Warburg* 5 (1925/26), pp. 45–66.

J. M. Nielen, *Gebet und Gottesdienst im Neuen Testament* (1st ed., Freiburg, 1937; 2nd ed., 1965). See also G. Delling, *Der Gottesdienst im Neuen Testament* (Berlin, 1952), and *ArchLw* 6.1 (1959), pp. 223–7.

W. Rordorf, 'Der Sonntag. Geschichte des Ruhe- und Gottesdiensttages im ältesten Christentums' in *Abhand. z. Theol. des Alten u. Neuen Testaments*, 43 (Zurich, 1962).

N. Nedbal, 'Sabbat und Sonntag im Neuen Testament' (unpublished dissertation, Vienna, 1956).

N. Adler, 'Das erste christliche Pfingstfest' (*Neutestamentliche Abhandlungen* 18, 1; Münster, 1938).

K. Völker, *Mysterium und Agape* (Gotha, 1927). See also W. Goossens, *Les origines de l'eucharistie* (Gembloux, 1931).

> According to both Völker and Goossens, the eucharist and agape were always separate institutions. See too, H. Chirat, *L'assemblée chrétienne à l'âge apostolique* (Paris, 1949). This deals with the separation of the eucharist from the agape between the years AD 60 and 80.

A. Arnold, 'Der Ursprung des christlichen Abendmahls im Lichte der neuesten liturgiegeschichtlichen Forschung' in *Freiburg. Theolog. Studien* 44 (2nd ed., Freiburg, 1939). See also H. Schürmann, 'Der Abendmahlsbericht Luc. 22.7.–38 als Gottesdienstordnung, Gemeindeordnung, Lebensordnung' in *Botschaft Gottes*, NT 1 (Leipzig, 1958); and H. Kosmala, 'Das tut zu meinem Gedächtnis' in *Novum Testamentum* 4 (1960), pp. 81–94; and H. Schürmann, 'Die Gestalt der urchristlichen Eucharistiefeier' in *Münchener Theologische Zeitschrift* 6 (1955), pp. 107–31.

E. von Severus, 'Brotbrechen' in *RAC* 2 (1963), pp. 620–6.

O. Cullmann, *Urchristentum und Gottesdienst* (4th ed., Zürich, 1962), pp. 29–34. [Translated into English as *Early Christian Worship* (London, 1966).]

> The author challenges the fact that the Service of the Word and the eucharist proper were originally independent of one another. Apart from the letter of Pliny, however, there is much else to vouch for the fact that both of these were services in their own right.

G. Dix, 'Primitive consecration prayers' in *Theology* 37 (1938), pp. 261–83.

O. Casel, 'Prophetie und Eucharistie' in *JbLw* 9 (1929), pp. 1–19. See also E. Dekkers, 'Van profetie tot Canon' in *Tijdsch. v. Liturgie* 25 (1946), pp. 8–25; and R. P. C. Hanson ,'The liberty of the bishop to improvise prayer in the eucharist' in *Vig. Chr.* 15 (1961), pp. 173–6.

A. Adam, 'Ein vergessener Aspekt des frühchristlichen Herrenmahles' in *ThLZ* 88 (1963), pp. 9–20.

> Did the liturgy of the temple influence Christian worship? See also E. Käsemann, 'Der gottesdienstliche Schrei nach der Freiheit' in *Apophoreta, Festschrift E. Haenchen* (Berlin, 1964), pp. 142–53. Deals with the text of Rom. 8.26, 27.

H. Wenschkewitz, 'Die Spiritualisierung der Kultusbegriffe, Tempel, Priester und Opfer in Neuen Testament' in *Angelos*, Beiheft 4 (Leipzig, 1932).

H. Lietzmann, 'Messe und Herrenmahl. Eine Studie zur Geschichte der Liturgie' in *Arbeiten zur Kirchengeschichte* 8 (1st ed., Berlin, 1926; 3rd ed., 1955). [Translated into English as *Mass and Lord's Supper*, with an Introduction and an Essay by R. D. Richardson (Leyden, 1964).]

A. Clark, 'The offertory rite' in *EphL* 67 (1953), pp. 242–7.

W. Bauer, *Der Wortgottesdienst der ältesten Christen* (Tübingen, 1930). See also H. Urner, 'Die ausserbiblische Lesung im christlichen Gottesdienst, Ihre Vorgeschichte und Geschichte bis zur Zeit Augustins' in *Veröffentl. der Evangelischen Gesellschaft für Liturgie-forschung* 6 (Göttingen, 1952); and B. de Gaiffier, 'La lecture des "actes des martyrs" dans la prière liturgique de l'Occident' in *Anal. Bolland.* 72 (1954), pp. 134–66.

A. Kurfess, 'Plinius und der urchristliche Gottesdienst' in *ZNW* 35 (1936), pp. 295–8. See also L. C. Mohlberg, '"Carmen Christo quasi Deo"' in *Riv. di archeol. christ* 14 (1937), pp. 92–123.

G. Delling, 'Zum gottesdienstlichen Stil der Johannes-Apokalypse' in *Novum Testamentum* 3 (1959), pp. 107–37.

B. Reicke, 'Diakonie, Festfreude und Zelos in Verbindung mit der altchristlichen Agapenfeier' in *Uppsala Univ. Arsskr.* 5 (Uppsala, 1951); cf. *ArchLw* 6 (1959), pp. 248–50.

N. Adler, 'Taufe und Handauflegung. Eine exegetisch-theologische Untersuchung von Apg. 8, 14–17' in *Neutestamentliche Abhandlungen* 19, 3 (Münster, 1951).

K. G. Eckhart, 'Urchristliche Tauf- und Ordinationsliturgie (Col. 1.9–20; Act. 28.18)' in *Theol. viatorum* 8 (1961–2), pp. 23–37.

E. Stommel, 'Christliche Taufriten und antike Badesitten' in *JbAC* 2 (1959), pp. 5–14.

F. Fransen, 'Firmung' in *LexThK* 4 (2nd ed., 1960), pp. 145–52.

C. Callewaert, 'Initia officii canonici' in *EphL* 52 (1938), pp. 490–8. See also J. A. Jungmann, 'Altchristliche Gebetsordnung im Lichte des Regelbuches von En Fescha' in *ZKTh* 75 (1953), pp. 215–19; and J. H. Walker, 'Terce, Sext and None—an apostolic custom?' in *Studia Patristica* 5 (1962), pp. 206–12.

See too P. de Puniet, 'L'antique office des vigiles et la dévotion au psautier' in *Revue grégorienne* 23 (1939), pp. 172–85; J. M. Hanssens, 'Aux origines de la prière liturgique, nature et genèse de l'office des matines' in *Analecta Gregoriana* 57 (1952); A. Baumstark, 'Abendgebet' in *RAC* 1 (1950), pp. 9–12.

P. Salmon, 'Les origines de la prière des heures d'après le témoignage de Tertullien et de S. Cyprien' in *Mélanges Ch. Mohrmann* (Utrecht, 1963), pp. 202–10.

J. Stadhuber, 'Das Stundengebet des Laien im christlichen Altertum' in *ZKTh* 71 (1949), pp. 129–83.

B. Fischer, *Die Psalmenfrömmigkeit der Märtyrerkirche* (Freiburg, 1949). [Translated into French as 'Le Christ dans les psaumes' in *La Maison Dieu* 27 (1951), pp. 186–9.]

P. Blanchard, 'Le correspondance apocryphe du pape S. Damase et de S. Jérome sur le psautier et le chant de l'Alleluia' in *EphL* 63 (1949), pp. 376–88.

R. Zerfass, 'Die Rolle der Lesung im Stundengebet' in *LitJb* 13 (1963), pp. 159–67.

Section ii: The Roman Church Order of Hippolytus

E. Schwartz, 'Über die pseudoapostolischen Kirchenordnungen' in *Schriften der Wissenschaftlichen Gesellschaft in Strassburg* 6 (1910). See also R. H. Connolly, 'The so-called Egyptian Church Order and derived documents' in *Texts and Studies* 8, 4 (Cambridge, 1916).

G. Bovini, 'Dant' Ippolito dottore e martire del III. secolo' (Rome, 1943).

R. Lorentz, 'De egyptische Kerkordening en Hippolytus van Rome' (Leiden, 1929). See also H. Engberding, 'Das angebliche Dokument römischer Liturgie aus dem Beginn des 3. Jahunderts' in *Miscellanea liturgica L. C. Mohlberg* 1 (Rome, 1948), pp. 47–71.
    Lorentz and Engberding cast doubts on the theses maintained by Schwartz and Connolly.

H. Elfers, 'Die Kirchenordnung Hippolyts von Rom' (Paderborn, 1938). See also O. Casel in *ArchLw* 2 (1952), pp. 115–30. Elfers opposes the theory of Lorentz. See also B. Botte, 'L'authenticité de la tradition apostolique de S. Hippolyte' in *Recherches théol. anc. et med.* 16 (1949), pp. 177–85.

H. Elfers, 'Neue Untersuchungen über die Kirchenordnung Hyppolyts von Rom' in *Abhandlungen über Theol. u. Kirche, Festschr. K. Adam* (1952), pp. 181–98.
    Strengthens his defence of the Schwartz/Connolly thesis.

D. van den Eynde, 'Nouvelle trace de la "traditio apostolica" d'Hippolyte dans la liturgie romaine' in *Miscellanea liturg. Mohlberg* I (Rome, 1948), pp. 409–11.

A. Salles, 'La "Tradition Apostolique", est-elle un témoin de la liturgie romaine?' in *Rev. Hist. Rel.* 148 (1955), pp. 181–213. Questions the Roman origins of the baptismal liturgy of Hippolytus. See also J. M. Hanssens, 'La liturgie d'Hippolyte, ses documents, son titulaire, ses origines et son caractère' in *Or. Christ. Analecta* 155 (Rome, 1959). The author considers the Church Order of Hippolytus to be the work of the Church of Alexandria.

G. Kretschmar, 'Bibliographie zu Hippolyt v. Rom' in *JbLHymn* I (1955), pp. 90–5.

B. Botte (ed.), 'Tradition Apostolique de S. Hippolyte' in *Liturgiegeschichtl. Quell. und Forsch.* 39 (Münster, 1963).

B. Capelle, 'L'introduction du catechuménat à Rome' in *Recherches théol. anc. et méd.* 5 (1933), pp. 129–54.

B. Botte, 'Competentes' in *RAC* 3 (1957), pp. 266–8.

E. Dick, 'Das Pateninstitut im altchristlichen Katechumenat' in *ZKTh* 63 (1939), pp. 1–49.

H. Scheidt, 'Die Taufwasserweihegebete im Sinne vergleichender Liturgiegeschichte untersucht' in *Liturgiegeschichtl. Quell. u. Forsch.* 29 (Münster, 1937). See also A. Oliver, 'Vom Ursprung der römischen Taufwasserweihe' in *ArchLw* 8, 1 (1963), pp. 62–78; J. P. de Jong, 'Benedictio Fontis. Eine genetische Erklärung der römischen Taufwasserweihe' in *ArchLw* 8, 1 (1963), pp. 21–46; E. Stommel, 'Studien zur Epiklese der römischen Taufwasserweihe' in *Theophaneia* 5 (Bonn, 1950).

A. Stenzel, *Die Taufe. Eine genetische Erklärung der Taufliturgie* (Innsbruck, 1958).

B. Botte, 'Note sur le symbole baptismal de S. Hippolyte' in *Mélanges J. de Ghellinck* (Gembloux, 1951), pp. 189–200.

P. M. Gy, 'Die Segnung von Milch und Honig in der Osternacht' in *Paschatis sollemnia*, ed. B. Fischer and J. Wagner (Basle, 1959), pp. 206–12.

T. Klauser, ' " Taufet in lebendigem Wasser!" Zum religions- und kulturgeschichtlichen Verständnis von Didache 7, 1–3' in *Pisciculi F. J. Dölger dargeboten* (Münster, 1939), pp. 157–64.

J. Daniélou, 'Le symbolisme de l'eau vive' in *RevScR* 32 (1958), pp. 335–46.

F. J. Dölger, 'Die Sonne der Gerechtigkeit und der Schwarze' in *Liturgiegeschitchtl. Forsch.* 2 (Münster, 1918). Explains the renunciations and the baptismal promise in the rite of baptism. See also H.

Kirsten, 'Die Taufabsage. Eine Untersuchung zu Gestalt und Geschichte der Taufe nach den altkirchlichen Taufliturgien' (1960).

F. J. Dölger, 'Heidnische Begrüssung und christliche Verhöhnung der Heidentempel. *Despuere* und *exsufflare* in der Dämonenbeschwörung' in *AC* 3 (1933), pp. 192–205; see also B. Botte, 'La sputation, antique rite baptismal?' in *Mélanges Chr. Mohrmann* (Utrecht, 1963), pp. 196–201.

F. J. Dölger, 'Der Kuss im Tauf- und Firmungsritual nach Cyprian v. Karthage und Hippolyt v. Rom' in *AC* 1 (1929), pp. 186–96.

O. Stegmüller, 'Diptychon' in *RAC* 3 (1957), pp. 1143–8. Deals among other things with the baptismal register.

O. Heggelbacher, *Die christliche Taufe als Rechtsakt nach dem Zeugnis der frühen Christenheit* (Freiburg, 1953).

J. Jeremias, *Die Kindertaufe in den ersten vier Jahrhunderten* (Göttingen, 1958). [Translated into English as *Infant baptism in the first four centuries* (London, 1960).]
The author suggests that the baptism of children goes right back to the NT period. *idem,* 'Nochmals die Anfänge der Kindertaufe, Eine Replik auf K. Alands Schrift' in *Theolog. Existenz heute, NF* 101 (Munich, 1961); K. Aland, 'Die Säuglingstaufe im Neuen Testament und in der alten Kirche. Eine Antwort an J. Jeremias' in *Theolog. Existenz heute, NF* 86 (1st ed., Munich, 1961; 2nd, 1963).
The author suggests that the baptism of infants did not take place until the year 200. Cf. A. Strobel, 'Säuglings- und Kindertaufe in der ältesten Kirche. Eine kritische Untersuchung der Standpunkte von J. Jeremias und K. Aland' in *Begründung und Gebrauch der hl. Taufe.* (Part of the proceedings of a study conference published in Berlin and Hamburg in 1963), pp. 7–69. Finally W. Michaelis, article in *ThLZ* 89 (1964), pp. 196–9.

H. Lietzmann, 'Messe und Herrenmahl' in *Arbeiten zur Kirchengeschichte* 8 (Bonn, 1926), pp. 158–86; 197–210. [Translated into English as *Mass and the Lord's Supper* (London, 1964).]
The author deals among other things with the eucharist and the agape in Hippolytus.

F. J. Dölger, 'Unterschungen zum abendlichen Lichtsegen in Antike und Christentum' in *AC* 5 (1956), pp. 1–43.

C. C. Richardson, 'The so-called epiclesis in Hippolytus' in *Harv. Theol. Rev.* 40 (1947), pp. 101–98. See also B. Botte, 'L'epiclèse de l'anaphore d'Hippolyte' in *Recherches théol. anc. et méd.* (1947), pp 241–51.

> Richardson and Botte question the authenticity of the epiclesis in Hippolytus.

J. B. Bauer, 'Die Früchtesegnung in Hippolyts Kirchenordnung' in *ZKTh* 47 (1953), pp. 71–5.

L. Brou, 'Le "Sancta sanctis" en occident' in *JTS* 46 (1946), pp. 11–29. Some further observations on this subject in *Sacris erudiri* 4 (1952), p. 238.

> The author inquires as to whether this summons of the deacon, though not found in Hippolytus, was nevertheless as much a feature of the western liturgy as it was of the eastern.

Justinus, 'Apologia' 61, 65–7.

> In his Apology for the Christian religion, written in Rome in *c.* 150, the philosopher and martyr gives the following information concerning the liturgy of his day. 1. Baptism (para 61): the candidates for baptism who confessed their faith and promised to change their way of life prepared themselves for baptism by prayer and fasting; the congregation also prayed and fasted with them (hence the origins of the season of fasting, Lent). At the baptismal 'bath' (which was in fact a 'washing'), the name of the Father and of the Son and of the Holy Ghost was pronounced over the candidates. The effect of this ceremony of washing was 'regeneration' and 'illumination'. 2. The eucharist (65–6): the newly baptized were led immediately into the midst of the assembled congregation, and began their life as fully fledged members by taking part in the Intercessory Prayer and also sharing in the Kiss of Peace which came at the end of this prayer. Then bread and a vessel containing water and wine were brought to the 'president' and the president pronounced over these a prayer of praise and thanksgiving 'according as he was able' (i.e. this was a piece of charismatic improvisation) in which he called upon the Son and the Holy Ghost. The congregation ended the prayer with the acclamation 'Amen'. The effect of this prayer of thanksgiving was to consecrate the 'food' which was also called the 'eucharist', i.e. to transform it into the flesh and blood of the incarnate Lord. The 'deacons' then communicated all present with this food, and also the absent members of the congregation. This ritual action, says Justin, went back to the express command of Jesus when he instituted the eucharist, an event which is also

described by Saint Paul. 3. The Service of the Word (67): on Sunday, the day of the creation of the world and of the Resurrection of Jesus, there took place an assembly of the people. At this assembly, the 'memories' of the apostles or the writings of the prophets were read, for so long as time allowed. After this, the president gave a brief address, based on the scriptures that had been read. The eucharist proper (which we have already described) followed immediately after the Service of the Word. And at this the faithful presented their gifts to the president, according to their means; and from these the president supplied the needy of all kinds.

E. C. Ratcliffe, 'The Sanctus and the pattern of the early Anaphora' in *Journ. Eccl. Hist.* 1 (1950), pp. 29–36; 125–34.

Some reflections on the untrustworthiness of the text of the Canon. See also W. C. van Unnik, 'I Clem. 34 and the "Sanctus" ' in *Vig. Chr.* 5 (1951), pp. 204–48.

More about the development of the Sanctus is given below in the bibliography to Section iii of Chapter IV. A summary account of the traces of the Roman liturgy in I Clement (*c.* AD 98) is given in O. Koch, 'Eigenart und Bedeutung der Eschatologie im theologischen Aufriss des 1. Clemensbriefs' in *Theophaneia* 17 (Bonn, 1964), pp. 56–64.

Section iii: The change to Latin as the language of the liturgy

G. Bardy, *La question des langues dans l'Église ancienne* (Paris, 1948). See also O. Rousseau, 'Les langues liturgiques de l'Orient et de l'Occident' in *Irénikon* 14 (1957), pp. 1–20, 113–30.

T. Klauser, 'Der Übergang der römischen Kirche von der griechischen zur lateinischen Liturgiesprache' in *Miscellanea G. Mercati* (*Studi e Testi*, 121; Rome, 1946), pp. 467–82.

A. Baumstark, 'Ein Übersetzungsfehler im Messkanon' in *Studia Catholica* 5 (1929), pp. 378–82. See also R. le Déaut, 'Le titre de "Summus sacerdos" donné a Melchisédech est-il d'origine juive?' in *Rech. Sc. R.* 50 (1962), pp. 222–9; B. Botte, 'Histoire des prières de l'ordinaire de la messe' in *L'ordinaire de la messe* by B. Botte and C. Mohrmann (eds.); 'Texte critique, traduction, et études' in *Études liturgiques* 2 (Paris-Louvain, 1953), 18. Contains information about the Melchisedech prayer in the Canon.

C. Mohrmann, 'Le latin liturgique' in *L'ordinaire de la messe* by B. Botte and C. Mohrmann (Paris-Louvain, 1953), pp. 29–48. See also C. Mohrmann, *Études sur le latin des chrétiens*, 2 vols. (2nd ed., Rome, 1961).

B. Botte, 'L'ange du sacrifice' in *Rech. théol. anc. et méd.* 1 (1929), pp. 285–308; see also E. Peterson, 'Das Buch von den Engeln. Stellung und Bedeutung der hl. Engel im Kultus' (Leipzig, 1934). Reprinted in E. Peterson, *Theologische Traktate* (Munich, 1951), pp.323–407.

H. Lietzmann, 'Messe und Herrenmahl' in *Arbeiten zur Kirchengeschichte* 8 (Bonn, 1926). [Translated into English as *Mass and Lord's Supper* (Leyden, 1964).]

> The author gives an exposition of those elements in the liturgy which have become integral to its tradition. On pp. 24–9, he deals with the institution narrative; on pp. 50–67 with the anamnesis; on pp. 68–80, 93–113, 117–22, with the epiclesis; on pp. 81–93 with the oblation.–There is an important text in Commodian (Instr. 2, 35, 14–16, in *CSEL* 15, p. 107) which relates to the 'Sursum corda' in the introductory dialogue, in which the habit of talking in services is denounced. 'When the priest of the Lord summons us to "Lift up our hearts", in order that silence may be observed during the Canon which is just about to begin, then you answer quite clearly, but you do not make your response at any one particular time (i.e. in reality you begin to chatter again immediately afterwards).' The summons to 'Lift up our hearts' therefore has also this very practical and trivial sense; though the necessity for such a summons is shown by Liberius in Ambrose's *De virginitate*: cf. Ambrose, Exp. in Ps. 1.4.

O. Casel, 'Das Gedächtnis des Herrn in der altchristlichen Liturgie' in *Ecclesia Orans* 2 (Freiburg, 1918); see also J. A. Jungmann, 'Das Gedächtnis des Herrn in der Eucharistie' in *Theol. Quart. Schr.* 133 (Stuttgart, 1953), pp. 385–99; and B. Botte, 'Problèmes de l'anamnèse' in *Journ. Eccl. Hist.* 5 (1954), pp. 16–24.

O. Casel, 'Die λογικὴ θυσία der antiken Mystik in christlich-liturgischer Umdeutung', in *JbLW* 4 (1924), pp. 37–47. *idem,* 'Ein orientalisches Kultwort in abendländischer Umschmelzung' in *JbLw* 11 (1931), pp. 1–19. See also B. Botte, 'Rationabilis' in *L'ordinaire de la messe* by B. Botte and C. Mohrmann (Paris-Louvain, 1953), pp. 117–22.

F. Skutsch, 'Ein neuer Zeuge der altchristlichen Liturgie' in *Archiv. f. rel. Wiss.* 13 (1910), pp. 291 ff.

He is dealing here with a text by Firmicus Maternus, which, so far as its language is concerned, is closely related to the Latin Canon. Firmicus Maternus, however, was not a Christian and this is a fact that has been overlooked by the author.

See also G. Morin, 'La nouvelle édition des *Consultationes Zacchaei* et son interêt au point de vue liturgique' in *JbLw* 13 (1933), pp. 185–8.

The author is justified in pointing out the linguistic parallels with the Canon, but his theory that the author of this text is Firmicus Maternus is not in fact substantiated.

G. Morin, 'Depuis quand un canon fixe à Milan? Restes de ce qu'il a remplacé' in *Rev. bénéd.* 51 (1939), pp. 101–9.

C. Callewaert, 'Histoire positive du Canon romain. Une epiclèse à Rome?' in *Sacris erudiri* 2 (1949), pp. 95–110.

He proposes that the Canon came into being in Rome and not in Milan.

E. Dekkers, 'Tertullianus en de geschiedenis der liturgie' in *Catholica* 6.2 (Brussels/Amsterdam, 1947).

The texts carefully collected in this work seem to show that at that time in Carthage the liturgy was already being celebrated in Latin. Unfortunately Dekkers has not dealt with this question of language in isolation from the rest of his study.

P. Winninger, 'Langues vivantes et liturgie' in *Rencontres* 59 (Paris, 1961). [Translated into German as 'Volkssprache und Liturgie' (Trier, 1961).] See also L. Lentner, 'Volkssprache und Sakralsprache. Geschichte einer Lebensfrage bis zum Ende des Konzils v. Trient' in *Wiener Beitr. z. Theologie* 5 (Vienna, 1964); and T. Klauser, *Die abendländische Liturgie von Aeneas Silvius Piccolomini bis heute. Erbe und Aufgabe* (Basel, 1961), pp. 30–3.

This work contains a discussion of the reasons for and against the use of the vernacular in the liturgy. Reference is made to the fact that the best way of taking part in the liturgy, both from the theological as from the catechetical point of view, is that people should listen to it and not read it while it is being celebrated.

B. Opfermann, 'Die Erforschung des röm. Messkanons. Ein Bericht' in *Theologie und Glaube* 44 (1954), pp. 263–79.

L. Eizenhöfer, *Canon missae Romanae* 1. *Traditio textus* (Rome, 1954).

A. Baumstark, 'Antik-römischer Gebetsstil im Messkanon' in *Miscell.*

liturg. L. C. Mohlberg 1 (Rome, 1948), pp. 300–31. See also C. Mohrmann, 'L'évolution du stylistique du canon de la messe romaine' in *Vig. Chr.* 4 (1950), pp. 1–19.

B. Capelle, 'L'évolution du "Qui pridie" de la messe romaine' in *Rech. théol. anc. et méd.* 22 (1955), pp. 5–16.

E. Peterson, 'Dona, munera, sacrificia' in *EphL* 46 (1932), pp. 75–7.
Under these three headings we are meant to distinguish between the offerings for the dead, the offerings for the living, and the oblations of those taking part in the eucharist; but this is scarcely correct. We should however take note of the parallels in the Liturgy of St. Mark (ed. Brightman, 129, 20).

B. Capelle, 'L'intercession dans la messe romaine' in *Rev. bénéd.* 65 (1955), pp. 181–91; and *idem, Travaux liturgiques* 2 (1962), pp. 248–57.

B. Capelle, 'Omnibus orthodoxis atque apostolicae fidei cultoribus' in *Miscellanea hist. A. de Mayer* 1 (Louvain, 1946), pp. 137–50 (in *idem, Travaux liturgiques* 2 (1962), pp. 258–68).

A. Stuiber, 'Die Diptychon-Formel für die *nomina offerentium* im römischen Messkanon' in *EphL* 68 (1954), pp. 129–46).

B. Capelle, 'Innocent I et le Canon de la messe' in *Rech. théol. anc. et. méd.* (1952), pp. 15–16; and *idem, Travaux liturgiques* 2 (1962), pp. 236–47.
In a letter to Decentius of Gubbio the Pope directs that the names of those who are to be remembered in the intercession are to be inserted and read in the Canon.

A. Baumstark, 'Das Communicantes u. seine Heiligenliste' in *JbLw* 1 (1921), pp. 5–33.

V. L. Kennedy, 'The Saints of the Canon of the Mass' in *Studi de antichità cristiana* 14 (Vatican City, 1963).
The author draws conclusions from the lists of the saints about the time at which the prayers were compiled.

B. Capelle, 'Problèmes du "Communicantes" de la messe' in *Riv. Liturgica*, pp. 187–95; in *idem, Travaux liturgiques* 2 (1962), pp. 269–75.

L. Eizenhöfer, 'Te igitur und Communicantes im römischen Messkanon' in *Sacris erudiri* 8 (1956), pp. 14–75.

V. L. Kennedy, 'The pre-Gregorian "Hanc igitur"' in *EphL* 50 (1936), pp. 349–58.

T. Michels, 'Woher nahm Gregor d. Gr. die Kanonbitte, "diesque nostros in tua pace disponas"?' in *JbLw* 13 (1933), pp. 188–90.

T. Michels, 'Mysterium fidei im Einsetzungsbericht' in *Catholica* 6 (1937), pp. 81–8.

> The author is of the opinion that Leo the Great originated this insertion in the Canon. It is difficult, however, to be absolutely sure of this.

N. J. Abercrombie, ' "Nobis quoque" in the Roman "Canon missae" ' in *Journ. Theol. Studies*, NS 4 (1933), pp. 49–50.

A. Stuiber, 'Refrigerium interim. Die Vorstellungen vom Zwischenzustand und die frühchristliche Grabeskunst' in *Theophaneia* 11 (Bonn, 1957).

> The author maintains that 'refrigerium' is the word used both for the place where the departed are awaiting, and also to describe this intermediary state itself.

C. Callewaert, 'La finale du canon de la messe' in *Rev. Hist. Eccl.* 39 (1943), pp. 5–21.

H. Fine, 'Die Terminologie der Jenseitsvorstellungen bei Tertullian' in *Theophaneia* 12 (Bonn, 1958).

> Confirms (p. 168) Stuiber's observations on the word 'refrigerium'.

J. Brinktrine, 'Über die Herkunft und die Bedeutung der römischen Messe, "Per quem haec omnia" ' in *EphL* 62 (1948), pp. 365–9.

Section iv: Casel's doctrine of the mysteries

T. Filthaut, *Die Kontroverse über die Mysterienlehre* (Diss., Munich, Warendorf, 1947).

> A systematic exposition of this doctrine. On pp. 122–5, he gives a list of Casel's innumerable works, almost up to the time of his death; we include here only the most important.

O. Casel, *Das christliche Kultmysterium* (4th ed., Regensburg, 1960); *idem*, *Das christliche Festmysterium* (Paderborn, 1941); *idem*, 'Glaube, Gnosis, Mysterium' in *JbLw* 15 (1941), pp. 155–305; *idem*, 'Das Mysteriengedächtnis der Messliturgie im Lichte der Tradition' in *JbLw* 6 (1926), pp. 113–204; *idem*, 'Neue Zeugnisse für das Kultmysterium' in *JbLw* 13 (1933), pp. 99–171.

V. Warnach, 'Taufe und Christusgeschehen nach Röm. 6' in *ArchLw* 3.2 (1954), pp. 284–366; *idem*, 'Die Tauflehre des Römerbriefes in der neueren theologischen Diskussion' in *ArchLw* 5.2 (1958), pp. 274–332.

B. Neunheuser, 'Ende des Gesprächs um die Mysteriengegenwart' in *ArchLw* 4.2 (1956), pp. 316–29.

B. Neunheuser (ed.), *Opfer Christi und Opfer der Kirche. Die Lehre vom Messopfer als Mysteriengedächtnis in der Auseinandersetzung mit der modernen Theologie* (Dusseldorf, 1960).

In connection with this analysis of Casel's teachings, mention should be made of one or two further investigations, namely:

K. Prüm, ' "Mysterion" von Paulus bis Origenes' in *ZKTh* 61 (1937), pp. 391–425.

G. Söhngen, 'Symbol und Wirklichkeit im Kultmysterium' in *Grenzfragen zwischen Theologie und Philosophie* 4 (1st ed., Bonn, 1937; 2nd ed., 1940); *idem*, 'Der Wesensaufbau des Mysteriums' in *Grenzfragen*, etc., 6 (Bonn, 1938).

R. Schnackenburg, *Das Heilsgeschene bei der Taufe nach dem Apostel Paulus* (Munich, 1950).

G. Fittkau, 'Der Begriff des Mysteriums bei Johannes Chrysostomus, Eine Auseinandersetzung mit dem Begriff des "Kultmysteriums" in der Lehre O. Casels' in *Theophaneia* 9 (1953).

J. Betz, *Die Eucharistie in der Zeit der griechischen Väter*, 2 vols. so far (Freiburg, 1955, 1961).

W. Diezinger, 'Effectus in der römischen Liturgie. Eine kultsprachliche Untersuchung' in *Theophaneia* 15 (Bonn, 1961).

The author deals here, on pp. 137–46, with Casel's theme concerning the 'making present of our salvation' in the Roman prayers. He also takes to pieces Casel's exegesis of the Secret for the ninth Sunday after Pentecost.

G. Wagner, *Das religionswissenschaftliche Problem von Röm. 6, 9–11* (Zürich, 1962).

Casel's research into liturgical language and the meaning of symbols. 'Oblatio rationabilis' in *Theol. Quart.-Schr.* 99 (1917–18), pp. 429–439. 'Vom heiligen Schweigen' in *Bened. Mon.-Schr.* (1921), pp. 417–25. 'Actio in liturgischer Verwendung' in *JbLw* 1 (1921), pp. 34–9; 'Die Lichtsymbolik in der Liturgie' in *Zeitschr. f. christl. Erz. Wiss.* 14 (1921), pp. 33–7.

'Zur Feuerweihe' in *JbLw* 2 (1923), pp. 90–1. 'Die Perle als religiöses Symbol' in *Bened. Mon.-Schr.* 6 (1924), pp. 321–7. 'Die λογικὴ θυσία der antiken Mystik in christlichliturgischer Umdeutung' in *JbLw* 4 (1929), pp. 37–47; 'Der österliche Lichtgesang der Kirche' in *Liturgische Zeitschr.* 4 (1931–2), pp. 179–91. Λειτουργία-munus in *Oriens Christ.* 3, 7 (1932), pp. 289–302.

See also H. Frank in *JbLw* 13 (1933), pp. 184–5. [See also the English translation of selected articles, *The Mystery of Christian Worship* (London, 1962).]

Section v: The position of Christ in the liturgy

J. A. Jungmann, 'Die Stellung Christi im liturgischen Gebet' in *Liturgiewiss. Quellen u. Forsch.* 19–20 (1st ed., Münster, 1925; 2nd ed., 1962).

J. Lebreton, 'La forme primitive du Gloria in excelsis; prière au Fils ou priere au Père? in *RechScR* 13 (1923), pp. 322–9.

K. Adam, *Christus unser Bruder* (Regensburg, 1930). [Translated into English as *Christ our Brother* (London, 1931).]

The author deals here with the 'mediatorial ending' (through Christ our Lord) on pp. 47–94.

L. A. Wynterswyl, *Laienliturgik* (Cologne, 1948). The passage we have quoted in the text is contained on pp. 106–7 of this excellent little book.

Section vi: Liturgical dress, liturgical insignia, and liturgical privileges

J. Braun, *Die liturgische Gewandung im Occident und Orient nach Ursprung und Entwicklung, Verwendung und Symbolik* (Freiburg, 1907; second impression, Darmstadt, 1964).

A wonderful collection of material; the historical side is dealt with too briefly. According to the opinion expressed on p. 773, vestments and insignia were made by the express command of the Church—he probably means 'of the bishops of Rome'.

A. Alföldi, 'Die Ausgestaltung des monarchisches Zeremoniells am römischen Kaiserhofe' in *RM* 49 (1934), pp. 1–118; *idem*, 'Insignien und Tracht der römischen Kaiser' in *RM* 50 (1935), pp. 1–171.

Alföldi's investigations are of fundamental importance.

T. Klauser, 'Der Ursprung der bischöflichen Insignien und Ehrenrechte. Rede gehalten bei Antritt des Rektorats der Rheinischen Friedrich-Wilhelms-Universität zu Bonn am 11. Dezember 1948' in *Bonner Akademische Reden* 1 (2nd ed., Krefeld, 1948).

The notes to this lecture contain references to all insignia and privileges. For further reading see:

T. Klauser, 'Bischöfe auf dem Richterstuhl' in *JbAC* 5 (1962).
The text of Saint Hilary dealt with in this account reveals the
concern of an important bishop that having to act as judges in
secular courts will have a corrupting effect on the episcopal office.
At the same time it reveals that bishops were not compelled to
accept office as a judge.

A. Steinwenter, 'Audientia episcopalis' in *RAC* 1 (1950), pp. 915–17.
See also S. Calderone, *Constantino e il cattolicesimo* (Florence, 1961).
He deals on pp. 230 ff. with the bishop's activity as judge; on
pp. 296 ff. with the 'dignitates';
and *idem*, 'Sulla "manumissio in ecclesia" ' in *Annuario Scolast.
Liceo Ginnasio G. La Farina* (Messina, 1962/3), pp. 5–22.

E. Stommel, 'Die bischöfliche Kathedra im christlichen Altertum' in
Münchener Theol. Zeitschr. 3 (1952), pp. 17–32; *idem*, 'Bischofs-
stuhl und hoher Thron' in *JbAc* 1 (1958), pp. 52–78.
In his researches Stommel uncovers the differences between
the original episcopal *cathedrae* and those conferred by the
Emperor.

D. R. Dendy, 'The use of lights in Christian worship' in *Alcuin Club
Collections* 41 (London, 1959).

E. G. C. F. Atchley, 'A history of the use of incense in divine worship'
in *Alcuin Club Collections* 13 (London, 1909).

S. Eitrem, *Opferritus und Voropfer der Griechen und Römer* (Chris-
tiania, 1915), pp. 198–260.
Of fundamental importance for an understanding of the history
of the religious and ritual use of incense. The author suggests that
the use of incense in court ceremonial stands in direct line of
succession to its use in emperor worship (pp. 237–40).

C. Callewaert, 'Introitus' in *EphL* 52 (1938), pp. 484–9.
He establishes the fact that the Introit must have developed for
the first time in the fourth century but fails to take account of the
rank granted to bishops in the reign of Constantine.

T. Klauser, 'Mitra' in *LThK* 7 (2nd ed., 1962), pp. 490–1.
Sketches the development of the *camelaucum* into the mitre.

H. Kruse, 'Studien zur offiziellen Geltung des Kaiserbildes im römischen
Ritus' in *Studien z. Gesch. u. Kultur d. Altert.* 19, 3 (Paderborn,
1934).
It is well known that in the titular churches of Rome pictures of
the Pope and the cardinal concerned were hung on the west wall
of the church. Kruse however has explored the connection

between the emperor's right to have his picture hung in public buildings and churches, but not the connection between this and modern church practice today.

P. Salmon, *Étude sur les insignes du pontife dans le Rit Romain. Histoire et liturgie* (Rome, 1953). [Translated into German as *Mitra und Stab* (Mainz, 1960).]

Concerned mainly with the development that took place in the Middle Ages. The author does not go very deeply into the question of their origins.

See also *idem*, 'Aux origines de la crosse des évêques' in *Mélanges M. Andrieu* (Strasbourg, 1956), pp. 373–83.

The pastoral staff is first mentioned by Isidore of Seville. It is conceivable that this insignia was originally given to the bishops when Rome and Italy had already severed their ties with Constantinople. In any case, the pastoral staff seems not to have been introduced from Spain into France until the eleventh century and thence brought into Italy with the Frankish edition of the Roman liturgy. The pastoral staff therefore would appear to be the peculiar contribution of those who composed the liturgy of the Franco-German church; we shall have more to say about these in Section vi of Chapter 2. Salmon, however, does not explicitly deny the secular origin of the pastoral staff.

O. Nussbaum, *Das Brustkreuz des Bischofs* (Mainz, 1964).

Shows that the pectoral cross arose out of the popular custom of wearing first an amulet and then a cross on the breast. When the pectoral cross became an official insignia of the bishops, the rite of consecration of bishops had already been given its final form. Hence the pectoral cross finds no place in this rite.

V. Labhart, 'Zur Rechtssymbolik des Bishofsrings' in *Rechtshistor. Arbeiten* 2 (Cologne/Graz, 1963).

The author has found the earliest evidence for the ring as a symbol of episcopal dignity in Isidore of Seville and at the 4th Council of Toledo. It did not occur to her, however, to look for the origins of this insignia in Constantinople (cf. the note on Salmon's book).

A. Grabar, 'L'empereur dans l'art byzantin' Recherches sur l'art officiel de l'Empire de l'Orient' in *Public. Fac. Lettres Strasb.* 75 (Paris, 1936), pp. 189–261.

Shows how the iconographical representations of the emperors have a bearing on the images of Christ. This theme is followed up and developed in J. Kollwitz, 'Christusbild' in *RAC* 3 (1957), pp. 15–24.

H. U. Instinsky, *Bischofsstuhl und Kaiserthron* (Munich, 1955). Investigates among other things the connection between the enthronement of the emperors and that of bishops. See also, and for a criticism of Klauser's 'Insignia', S. Mazzarino in *Jura* (1956), pp. 345–52.

Section vii: Characteristics of the Roman liturgy

F. L. Cross, 'Pre-Leonine elements in the Proper of the Roman Mass' in *Journ. Theol. Studies* 50 (1949), pp. 191–7.

C. Callewaert, 'S. Léon le Grand et les texts du Léonien' in *Sacris erudiri* 6 (1954), pp. 282–326; and E. Dekkers, 'Autour de l'oeuvre liturgique de s. Léon le Grand' in *Sacris erudiri* 10 (1958), pp. 363–398; also A. P. Lang, *Leo d. Gr. und die Texte des Altgelasianums mit Berücksichtigung des Sacr. Gregorianums* (Steyl, 1957): *idem*, 'Anklänge an liturgische Texte in Epiphaniesermonen Leos d. Gr.' in *Sacris erudiri* 10 (1958), pp. 43–126; *idem*, 'Leo d. Gr. und die liturgischen Texte des Oktavtages von Epiphanie' in *Sacris erudiri* 11 (1959), pp. 12–135; and *idem*, 'Anklänge an Orationen der Ostervigil in Sermonen Leos d. Gr.' in *Sacris erudiri* 13 (1962), pp. 281–325; and 14 (1963), pp. 1–22 (Beilage).

B. Capelle, 'Messes du pape S. Gélase dans le Sacramentaire Léonien' in *Rev. bénéd.* 36 (1945/6, pp, 12–41 (in *idem, Travaux liturgiques* 2 (1962), pp. 79–105); *idem*, 'L'oeuvre liturgique de S. Gélase' in *Journal Theol. Studies* NS 2 (1951), pp. 129–44 (in *idem, Travaux liturgiques* 2 (1962), pp. 146–60); see also C. Coebergh, 'Le pape Saint Gélase Ier, auteur de plusieurs messes et préfaces du soi-disant Sacramentaire Léonien' in *Sacris erudiri* 4 (1952), pp. 46–102; and G. Pomarès, 'Gélase Ier, Lettre contre les Lupercales et 18 messes du Sacramentaire Léonien' in *Sources chrét.* 65 (Paris, 1959). Also A. Chavasse, 'Messes du pape Vigile 537–55 dans le Sacramentaire Léonien' in *EphL* 64 (1905), pp. 161–213; 66 (1952), pp. 145–219.

T. Klauser, 'Die abendländische Liturgie von Aeneas Silvius Piccolomini bis heute. Erbe und Aufgabe' in *Vorträge der Aen. Silv. Stiftung an der Univ. Basel* 1 (Basle, 1962). The purpose of this lecture is to present our liturgical inheritance in its true light as one of the classic creations of mankind and the author considers, therefore, that a series of lectures bearing the name of a great humanist are a suitable occasion on which to speak about the liturgy.

P. Bruylants, *Les oraisons du Missel Romain*, 2 vols. (Louvain, 1952). The author traces the tradition of the Easter Collect 'Deus, qui hodierna die' (vol.2, pp. 96–7).

G. Manz, 'Ausdrucksformen der lateinischen Liturgiesprache bis ins 11. Jh.' in *Texte und Arbeiten*, Beiheft 1 (Beuron, 1941).

In section 4 he deals with the phrase 'aditus aeternitatis'; unfortunately he does not take into account the expression 'devicta morte'.

E. Norden, *Agnostos Theos. Untersuchungen zur Formengeschichte religiöser Rede* (1st ed., Leipzig, 1912; 2nd ed., Darmstadt, 1956).

On pages 143–76 he comments on the various styles of predication, including relative predication; according to the opinion expressed on pp. 201–7, relative predication was not unknown in Judaism;

see also A. Quacquarelli, 'Retorica e liturgia antenicene' in *Richerche patristiche* 1 (Rome-Paris-Tournai, 1960).

The contents are not exactly what one might expect from the title. Cf. J. A. Jungmann in *ZKTh* 82 (1060), pp. 491–2; and T. Klauser, in *Gnomon* 33 (1961), pp. 713–16.

A. Stuiber, 'Libelli sacramentorum romani' in *Theophaneia* 6 (Bonn, 1950).

On pp. 63–4 he deals with the prayers in the so-called Leonine Sacramentary, which reveal anti-Pelagian tendencies; they are assigned to the period 440–530.

H. Lausberg, *Handbuch der literarischen Rhetorik* (Munich, 1960).

F. Stummer, 'Vom Satzrhythmus in der Bibel und in der Liturgie der lateinischen Christenheit' in *ArchLw* 3 (1953/4), pp. 233–8; see also M. G. Haessly, *Rhetoric in the Sunday collects of the Roman Missal* (Cleveland, 1938).

I have not seen this article, but am acquainted with its contents via the *Rev. Et. Lat.* 17 (1939), pp. 414–16; H. Rheinfelder, 'Zum Stil der lateinischen Orationen' in *JbLw* 11 (1931), pp. 20–34; and P. Salmon, 'Les protocoles des oraisons du Missel Romain' in *EphL.* 45 (1930), pp. 140–7.

O. Casel, 'Beiträge zu römischen Orationen' in *JbLw* 11 (1931), pp. 35–45.

Deals with antithetical pairs of ideas.

A. Schott, *Messbuch der hl. Kirche* (1st ed., Freiburg, 1884); see also D. Zähringer, *Funfundsiebzig Jahre Schott* (Freiburg, 1959); and U. Bomm, *Volksmessbuch* (1st ed., Einsiedeln, 1927).

The works of Schott and Bomm have been appearing in increasingly improved editions and both have made important contributions to the spread of liturgical ideas in Germany. The simplified Klosterneuburg texts have had the same effect.

H. Ashworth, 'On translating the missal' in *EphL* 78 (1964), pp. 145–6.

W. Dürig, 'Die Erforschung der lateinisch-christlichen Sakralsprache' in *LitJb* 1 (1951), pp. 32–47.

A. Pfliegler, *Liturgicae orationis concordantia verbalia* 1 ff. (Rome, 1964 ff.).

M. P. Ellebracht, 'Remarks on the vocabulary of the ancient orations in the Missale Romanum' in *Latinitas christiana primaeva* 18 (Nijmegen, 1963). See also A. Stuiber, in *RQS* 59 (1964), pp. 119–21.

O. Casel, 'Actio in liturgischer Verwendung' in *JbLw* 1 (1921), pp. 34–9; *idem*, 'Actio' in *RAC* 1 (1950), pp. 82–3.

H. Wagenvoort, 'Caerimonia' in *RAC* 2 (1953), pp. 820–2.

H. Petre, 'Caritas' in *Spicileg. Sac. Lovaniense* 22 (Louvain, 1948).

O. Casel, 'Castigatio vocis' in *JbLw* 7 (1927), pp. 139–41.

B. Droste, ' "Celebrare" in der römischen Liturgiesprache. Eine liturgietheologische Untersuchung' in *Münchener theol. Studien* 2 26 (Munich, 1963). See also A. Stuiber in *RQS* 59 (1964), pp. 121–2; and W. Nagel in *ThLZ* 90 (1965), pp. 148–9.

B. Capelle, 'Collecta' in *Rev. bénéd.* 42 (1930), pp. 197–204 (in *idem*, *Travaux liturgiques* 2 (1962), pp. 192–9).

He maintains that *collecta* means *colligere orationem* and is Gallic in origin.

M. Herz, 'Sacrum commercium. Eine begriffsgeschichtliche Studie Zur Theologie der römischen Liturgiesprache' in *Münchener theol. Studien* 15 (Munich, 1958).

The same opinion is put forward by S. Poque, 'Christus mercator. Notes augustiniennes' in *RechScR* 40 (1960), pp. 564–77.

B. Botte, 'Confessor' in *Archiv. lat. med. aevi* 16 (1941), pp. 137–48; see also H. Rheinfelder, 'Confiteri, confessio, confessor im Kirchenlatein und in den romanischen Sprachen' in *Die Sprache* 1 (1949), pp. 56–7.

H. Hoppenbrouwers, 'Conversatio' in *Graecitas et latinitas christianorum primaeva*, Suppl. 1 (Nijmegen, 1964), pp. 45–95.

A. Daniels, 'Devotio' in *JbLw* 1 (1921), pp. 40–60; supplemented by K. Winkler and A. Stuiber, 'Devotio' in *RAC* 3 (1957), pp. 849–62. The authors draw mostly on non-Christian material.

W. Dürig, 'Disciplina. Eine Studie zum Bedeutungsumfang des Wortes in der Sprache der Liturgie und der Väter' in *Sacris erudiri* 4 (1952), pp. 245–79.

V. Morel, 'Disciplina', in *RAC* 3 (1957), pp. 1213–29.

M. Steinheimer, 'Die δόξα τοῦ θεοῦ in der römischen Liturgie' in *Münch. theol. Studien* 2, 4 (Munich, 1951).

Deals primarily with the word *gloria*, but also with *claritas*, *maiestas*, *splendor*, and *adventus*.

A. Vermeulen, *The semantic development of 'gloria' in early Christian Latin* (Utrecht, 1956).

E. Peterson, 'Zur Bedeutungsgeschichte von παρρησία' in *Festschrift R. Seeberg*, 1 (Leipzig, 1929), pp. 283–97; *idem*, 'Fiducia in den altrömischen Sakramentaren' in *Liturg. Leben* 1 (1934), pp. 224–31. See also L. Engels, 'Fiducia dans la Vulgate, le problème de traduction παρρησία-Fiducia', in *Graecitas et latinitas christianorum primaeva*, Suppl. 1 (1964), pp. 97–141.

W. Dürig, 'Imago. Ein Beitrag zur Terminologie und Theologie der römischen Liturgie' in *Münch. theol. Stud.* 2, 5 (Munich, 1952).

B. Botte, 'Paschalibus initiata mysteriis' in *EphL* 61 (1947), pp. 77–87. In the secret for Easter Sunday we should not think that *initiare* signifies 'initiation into the mysteries'; the word here means rather to introduce, to make a beginning, to found or to constitute. The 'mysteria paschalia', i.e. the glorious sacrificial death of Jesus on the Cross has introduced or laid the foundation for the eucharistic liturgy of Easter (*preces populorum cum oblationibus hostiarum*); and may these therefore (the *preces cum oblationibus*) suffice for us unto 'aeternitatis medela'. This is an example of a Roman prayer which is too complicated in its mode of expression. See also R. Berger, 'Die Wendung "offerre pro" in der röm. Liturgie' in *Liturgiegeschichtl. Quellen u. Forsch.* 41 (Münster, 1965).

O. Casel, 'Λειτουργία-Munus' in *Oriens Christ.* 3 Ser. 7 (1932), pp. 289–302. See also the comments of H. Frank in *JbLw* 13 (1935), pp. 181–5; also B. Botte, 'Secundi meriti munus' in *Questions liturg. et paroiss.* 21 (1936), pp. 84–8.

'Meritum' can also mean 'dignity', 'rank', or 'office', e.g. 'sacerdotale meritum' (as in Masses of the Dead). 'Secundum meritum' here means the second rank of the church's 'munera' (sc. offices or services). By this is meant the office of the presbyterate.

C. Mohrmann, 'Missa' in *Vig. Ch.* 12 (1958), pp. 67–92.

I. Carton, 'A propos des oraisons du carême. Note sur l'emploi du mot "observantia" dans les homélies de s. Léon' in *Vig. Ch.* 8 (1954), pp. 104–14.

H. Wagenvoort, 'Orare, precari' in *Verbum. Essays . . . dedicated to H. W. Olbink* (1964), pp. 101–11.

C. Mohrmann, 'Pascha, Passio, Transitus' in *EphL* 66 (1952), pp. 37–52.

W. Dürig, *Pietas liturgica. Studien zum Frömmigkeitsbegriff und zur Gottesvorstellung der abendländischen Liturgie* (Regensburg, 1958).

T. Klauser, 'Studien zur Entstehungsgeschichte der christlichen Kunst' II, in *JbAC* 2 (1959), pp. 115–45.
Examines the 'Pietas' inscriptions frequently found on coins, examines the meaning of this concept and the iconography with which it is associated ('Orans').

C. Mohrmann, 'Sur l'histoire de "praefari-praefatio"' in *Vig. Ch.* 7 (1953), pp. 1–15. See also E. Dekkers, 'Προφητεία-Praefatio' in *Mélanges Chr. Mohrmann* (Utrecht, 1963), pp. 190–5.
Following the investigations of Christine Mohrmann, Dekkers shows how the prophetic eucharistic prayer of the charismatics may have given rise to the expression 'praefatio', i.e. a solemn, authoritative speech.

C. Mohrmann, 'Rationabilis-λογικός' in *Revue intern. des droits de l'antiquité* 5 (1950), pp. 225–34.

P. de Puniet, 'Intus reformari' in *EphL* 52 (1938), pp. 125–40.

H. Finé, 'Die Terminologie der Jenseitsvorstellungen bei Tertullian' in *Theophaneia* 12 (Bonn, 1958). Important for the expressions 'refrigerium', 'solatium', and 'requies'.

L. Koep, ' "Religio" und "Ritus" als Problem des frühen Christentums' in *JbAC* 5 (1962), pp. 43–59.
The author maintains that 'religio' = religious conviction, and 'ritus' = the external form of worship.

B. Botte, 'Prima resurrectio. Un vestige de millénarisme dans les liturgies occidentales' in *Rech. théol. anc. et méd.* 15 (1948), pp. 5–17.

F. J. Dölger, 'Sacramentum militiae' in *AC* 2 (1930), pp. 268–80; see also A. Kolping, *Sacramentum Tertullianeum* 1. *Untersuchungen über die Anfänge des christlichen Gebrauchs der Vokabel sacramentum*

(Münster, 1948); and C. Mohrmann, 'Sacramentum dans les plus anciens textes chrétiens' in *Harvard Theol. Rev.* 47 (1954), pp. 141–52.

J. Pascher, ' "Servitus religiosa" seit Augustinus' in *Festschrift E. Eichmann* (Paderborn, 1940), pp. 335–52.

H. Linssen, 'Θεὸς σωτήρ. Entwicklung und Verbreitung einer liturgischen Formelgruppe' in *JbLw* 8 (1928).

> Deals also with the corresponding Latin terms, *salvator* and *redemptor mundi.*

B. M. Serpilli, *L'offertorio della Messa dei defunti* (Rome, 1946). Cf. *EphL* 61 (1947), pp. 245–52.

Bonif. Fischer, 'Praeceptis salutaribus moniti' in *ArchLw* 1 (1950), pp. 124–7.

> Maintains that the adjective *salutaris* is a replacement of the noun *salvatoris.*

F. J. Dölger, 'Sphragis. Eine altchristliche Taufbezeichnung in ihren Beziehungen zur profanen und religiösen Kultur des Altertums' in *Studien z. Gesch. u. Kultur des Altertums* 5, 3–4 (Paderborn, 1912).

> Shows how it came to be used as the *signaculum* to describe baptism.

G. E. M. de Sainte Croix, 'Suffragium: from vote to patronage' in *Brit. Journ. Sociol.* 5 (1954), pp. 33–48.

R. Guardini, *Vom Geist der Liturgie* in *Ecclesia orans* 1 (1st ed., Freiburg, 1918; many editions since).

E. Bishop, *The genius of the Roman rite* in idem, *Liturgica historica* (Oxford, 1918), pp. 1–19. Translated into French and annotated by A. Wilmart, as *Le génie du rit romain* (Paris, 1920); and into German as *Der Geist des römischen Ritus* in *Liturg. Zeitschr.* (1931–2), pp. 393–417.

A. Stuiber, 'Libelli sacramentorum romani. Untersuchungen zur Entstehung des sog. Sacr. Leonianum' in *Theophaneia* 6 (Bonn, 1950), pp. 65–71.

P. Salmon, 'Les "Amen" du canon de la messe' in *EphL* 42 (1928), pp. 496–506. Cf. G. Ellard, 'Interpolated Amen's in the Canon of the mass' in *Theol. Studies* 6 (1945), pp. 380–94.

J. A. Jungmann, *Missarum Sollemnia* (5th ed., Vienna, 1962), pp. 179–85.

> Deals with the confusion of signs of the cross that are directed to be made over the oblations during the Canon.

Chapter II: Franco-German Leadership

Section i: Outline of the period

H. Lietzmann (ed.), 'Das Sacramentarium Gregorianum nach dem Aachener Urexemplar' in *Liturgiegeschichtl. Quellen* 3 (Münster, 1921).

See Section iii of this chapter for our comments on the position of this sacramentary in the general framework of liturgical history; also for our comments on the Gelasian and mixed sacramentaries.

K. Gamber, 'Das Sonntagsmessbuch von Jena u. die Neufassung der Sonntagsmessen durch Gregor. d. Gr.' in *Traditio* 15 (1959), pp. 107–61.

Maintains the thesis that the material of the sacramentary was collected by Gregory, but not finally codified until the pontificate of Honorius I (625–38).

See also B. Capelle, 'La main de S. Grégoire dans le Sacramentaire Grégorien' in *Revue. bénéd.* 49 (1937), pp. 23–8, in *idem, Travaux liturgiques* 2 (Louvain, 1962), pp. 161–75; C. Callewaert, 'S. Grégoire, les scrutins et quelques messes quadragésimales' in *EphL* 53 (1939), pp. 191–203; *idem,* 'L'oeuvre liturgique de s. Grégoire. La Septuagésime et l'Alleluia' in *Sacris erudiri* (1940), pp. 635–54.

A. Chavasse, 'Peut-on dater le Sacramentaire Grégorien?' in *EphL* 67 (1953), pp. 108–11.

Like Mohlberg he thinks that he can establish the year of the Sacramentary's origin as 595 from the way the Sundays have been arranged in the Calendar of the Saints. Not wholly convincing.

T. Klauser, 'Das römische Capitulare evangeliorum. Untersuchungen zu seiner ältesten Geschichte' 1 in *Liturgiegeschichtl. Quellen u. Forsch.* 28 (Münster, 1935).

Puts forward the theory that the marginal notes came before the lists. The oldest list can be traced back to 645. Also contains an edition of the texts.

A. Chavasse, 'Les plus anciens types du lectionnaire et de l'antiphonaire romaines de la messe, rapports et dates' in *Rev. bénéd.* 62 (1952), pp. 3–94.

R. J. Hesbert, *Antiphonale missarum sextuplex* (Brussels, 1935).

An edition of the earliest MSS. In the prologue Gregory is named as the editor.

H. Hucke, 'Entstehung und Aufgabe der römischen Schola cantorum' in *Die Musikforschung* 11 (1958), pp. 399–405.

S. J. P. Van Dijk, 'Gregory the Great, founder of the urban Schola cantorum' in *EphL* 77 (1963), pp. 345–56.

J. Gelineau, *Antiphona. Recherches sur les formes liturgiques de la psalmodie aux premiers siècles* (Paris, 1963).

A. Dohmes, 'Der pneumatische Charakter des Kultgesanges nach frühchristlichen Zeugnissen' in *Vom christl. Mysterium* (1951), pp. 35–53.

M. Andrieu, *Les Ordines Romani* 1 ff. (Louvain, 1931 ff.). We deal with the Ordines more thoroughly in Section iv of this chapter.

H. Ashworth, 'Did St. Augustine bring the Gregorianum to England?' in *EphL* 72 (1958), pp. 39–43. See also H. Frank, 'Die Briefe des hl. Bonifatius und das von ihm benutzte Sakramentar' in *St. Bonifatius, Festschrift* (Fulda, 1954), pp. 58–88.

As is well known, Saint Boniface was an Anglo-Saxon; hence the importance of this question.

T. Klauser, 'Die liturgischen Austauschbeziehungen zwischen der römischen und der fränkish-deutschen Kirche vom 8. bis zum 11. Jh.' in *Histor. Jahrb.* 53 (1933), pp. 169–89.

I deal with the travels of the Roman liturgy in Section v of this chapter.

K. Gamber, 'Sakramentartypen. Versuch einer Gruppierung der Handschriften und Fragmente bis zur Jahrtausendwende' in *Texte und Arbeiten* 1, 49–50 (Beuron, 1958).

A survey of the full complement of the MSS. of the sacramentaries. Unfortunately, the serviceability of this guide to the sources and literature of the sacramentaries is limited by too bold an attempt at systematization. The Gelasian sacramentary of the eighth century is dealt with on pp. 99–119. A more useful book by the same author is 'Codices liturgici latini antiquiores' in *Spicileg. Friburg. subsid.* 1 (Friburg, Switzerland, 1963); see also F. Dell, 'Oro' in *EphL* 79 (1965), pp. 58–66.

A. Baumstark, 'Advent', in *RAC* 1 (1950), pp. 112–25.

C. Lambot, 'Le "Pater" dans la liturgie apostolique d'après S. Grégoire' in *Rev. bénéd.* (1930), pp. 265–9; see also J. A. Jungman, 'Das Paternoster im Kommunionritus' in *idem, Gewordene Liturgie* (1941), pp. 137–64.

'Amalarii episcopi opera liturgica omnia', ed. J. M. Hanssens, 3 vols., *Studi e Testi*, 138–40 (Vatican City, 1948–50).

In the introduction to vol. 1, Hanssens proves that there was only one Amalarius. See also:

P. Duc, *Étude sur l'Expositio missae de Florus de Lyon, suivie d'une édition critique du texte* (Belley, 1937); and A. Kolping, 'Amalar v. Metz u. Florus v. Lyon, Zeugen eines Wandels im liturgischen Mysterienverständnis in der Karolingerzeit' in *ZKTh* 73 (1951), pp. 424–64.

E. Dumoutet, *Le Christ selon la chair et la vie liturgique au moyen-âge* (Paris, 1932).

I shall be returning later to this theme (in Chapter III, Section ii).

Section ii: The decline of the 'Prayer of the Faithful'

F. J. Dölger, 'Das erste Gebet der Täuflinge in der Gemeinschaft der Brüder' in *AC* 2 (1930), pp. 142–55.

He suggests that in these mostly non-Roman sources what is meant by the 'first prayer' is the Lord's prayer, but this would scarcely seem to be a correct assessment.

B. Capelle, 'Collecta' in *Rev. bénéd.* 42 (1930), pp. 197–204.

Suggests that *collecta* was a gallic term, and that the original Roman expression was *oratio*.

T. Klauser, 'Diakon' in *RAC* 3 (1957), pp. 888–999.

In column 901 I describe the deacon's task of 'addressing the people'; and in columns 906–7, touch on the deacon's pagan forerunner, the herald of the mystery cults.

B. Capelle, 'Le Kyrie de la messe et le pape Gélase' in *Rev. bénéd.* 46 (1934), pp. 126–44; *idem*, 'Le pape Gélase et la messe romaine' in *RHE* 35 (1939), pp. 22–34; see also C. Callewaert, 'Les étapes de l'histoire du Kyrie' in *RHE* 38 (1942), pp. 20–45; F. J. Dölger, 'Sol salutis. Gebet und Gesang im christlichen Altertum' in *Liturgiegeschtl. Quellen* 4/5 (2nd ed., Münster, 1925), pp. 60–103.

The author shows that the acclamation 'Kyrie eleison' was taken over from the surrounding Hellenistic culture, and that on occasions the people said this a hundred times and more.

A. Baumstark, 'Das Gesetz der Erhaltung des Alten in liturgisch hochwertiger Zeit' in *JbLw* 7 (1927), pp. 1–23.

V. Thalhofer, 'Vom Pronaus, speciell von den an die Pfarrpredigt sich anschliessenden Gebeten und Verkündigungen' in *Theol. praktisch. Quartalschrift* 38 (1885), pp. 25–42.

He maintains that the 'Pronaus' found in German ecclesiastical circles corresponds to the 'prières du prône' encountered in the French-speaking world.

Section iii: The liturgical books

A. Chavasse, *Le sacramentaire Gélasien* in *Bibl. de la théol.* 4, 1 (Paris, 1957); see the review by J. A. Jungmann in *ZKTh* (1959), pp. 236–9.

J. P. Kirsch, 'Die römischen Titelkirchen im Altertum' in *Studien zur Geschichte und Kultur des Altertums* 9, 1/2 (Paderborn, 1918); and *idem*, 'Die Stationskirchen des Missale Romanum' in *Ecclesia orans* 19 (Freiburg, 1926).

L. Eizenhöfer, 'Untersuchungen zum Stil und Inhalt der römischen Oratio super populum' in *EphL* 52 (1938), pp. 258–311; cf. on the same theme A. Stuiber, 'Libelli sacramentorum romani. Untersuchungen zur Entstehung des sogenannten Sacramentarium Leonianum' in *Theophaneia* 6 (Bonn, 1950), pp. 71–5.

A. Chavasse, 'L'oraison "super sindonem" dans la liturgie romaine' in *Rev. bénéd.* 70 (1960), pp. 313–23.

K. Mohlberg and A. Baumstark, 'Die älteste erreichbare Gestalt des Liber sacramentorum anni circuli der römischen Kirche' (Cod. Pad. D.47, fol. 11r–100r) in *Liturgiegeschichtl. Quellen* 11/12 (Münster, 1927).

J. Zettinger, 'Die Berichte über Rompilger aus dem Frankenreiche bis zum Jahre 800' in *RQS* Suppl. 11 (Rome, 1900).

Section iv: The Roman bishop's mass *c.* AD 700

M. Andrieu, *Les Ordines Romani du haut moyen-âge*, 5 vols. in *Spicileg. Sacrum Lovan.* 11, 23, 24, 28, 29 (Louvain, 1931, 1948, 1951, 1956, 1961).

T. Michels, 'Beiträge zur Geschichte des Bishofsweihetages' in *Liturgiegeschichtl. Quellen* 10 (Munich, 1927).
He observes that the ordinations took place on the evening of the Ember Saturday and that the consecration of bishops came last. Since Saturday evening was in fact the beginning of Sunday, the old tradition of ordaining bishops on a Sunday was thus respected. Cf. M. Andrieu, *Les Ordines Romani du haut moyen-âge* 24, pp. 535–56, 582–3.

M. Andrieu, 'La cérémonie appelée "Diligentia" à S. Pierre de Rome au début du IXe siècle' in *RevScR* 1 (1921), pp. 62–8.

C. Vogel and R. Elze, *Le Pontifical Romano-Germanique du dixième siècle*, 2 vols., *Studi e Testi*, pp. 226–7 (Vatican City, 1963). There is a third volume to follow. The descendants of this pontifical are dealt with in:

M. Andrieu, *Le Pontifical Romain au moyen-âge*. 1. *Le Pontifical Romain du XIIe siècle*. 2. *Le Pontifical de la Curie Romaine*. 3. *Le Pontifical de Guillaume Durand*. 4. *Tables*. *Studi e Testi*, 86, 87, 88, 89 (Vatican City, 1938, 1940, 1940, 1941).

J. Lauer, *Le palais du Latran* (Paris, 1911).

F. W. Deichmann, *Frühchristliche Kirchen in Rom* (Basle, 1948). Plans and pictures of some of the more important Roman basilicas.

R. Hierzegger, 'Collecta und Statio. Die römischen Stationsprozession im frühen Mittelalter' in *ZKTh* 60 (1936), pp. 511–54; see also C. Mohrmann, 'Statio' in *Vig. Ch.* 7 (1953), pp. 221–45.

E. Jerg, 'Die sustentatio in der römischen Liturgie vor dem Hintergrund des kaiserlichen Hofzeremoniells' in *ZKTh* 80 (1958), pp. 316–24.

J. Braun, *Die liturgische Gewandung in Occident und Orient* (Freiburg, 1907; reprinted, Darmstadt, 1964).
Cf. the remarks we have made in Section vi of Chapter I.

O. Casel, 'Castigatio vocis' in *JbLw* 7 (1927), pp. 139–41; he deals with the meaning of the Amice which to begin with was designed to cover the head. This was already worn at Rome in the offering of pagan sacrifices; it was a means of preventing one's eyes and ears from being distracted during the sacred action.

T. Klauser, *Der Ursprung der bischöflichen Insignien und Ehrenrechte* (Rektoratsrede, Bonn, 11, December 1948; published at Krefeld in the same year).
Cf. what we have said in Section vi of Chapter I.

J. A. Jungmann, 'Fermentum. Ein Symbol kirchlicher Einheit und sein Nachleben im Mittelalter' in *Colligere fragmenta. Festschr. A. Dold* (Beuron, 1952), pp. 185–90.

F. J. Dölger, 'Der Altarkuss' in *AC* 2 (1930), pp. 190–221.

C. Vogel, ' "Versus ad orientem". L'orientation dans les Ordines romani du haut moyen-âge' in *Studi medievali* 3, 1 (Spoleto, 1960), pp. 447–69.

A. M. Schneider, 'Ambo' in *RAC* 1 (1950), pp. 363–5.
Suggests that the word derives from ἀναβαίνω to climb up. The practice of having two ambos is somewhat later and always

exceptional. The ambo corresponds to the *pulpitum* (pulpit) of the ancient orator, reciter, or singer.

T. Klauser and J. A. Jungmann, 'Entlassungsruf' in *RAC* 5 (1962), pp. 457–61.

L. Völkl, 'Apophoretum, Eulogie u. Fermentum als Ausdrucksformen der frühchristlichen Communio' in *Miscellanea G. Belvederi* (Vatican City, 1954), pp. 391–414.

V. H. Elbern, *Der eucharistische Kelch im frühen Mittelalter* (Berlin, 1964).

F. Eckstein and A. Stuiber, 'Brotformen' in *RAC* 2 (1954), pp. 626–30. See also F. Eckstein and T. Klauser, 'Brotstempel' in ibid., cols. 630–31.

L. Haberstroh, 'Der Ritus der Brechung und Mischung nach dem Missale Romanum' in *St. Gabrieler Studien* 5 (St. Gabriel, 1937). See also B. Capelle, 'Fraction et commixtion' in *Maison Dieu* 35 (1953), pp. 79–94 (reprinted in *idem, Travaux liturgiques* 2 (1962), pp. 319–31). M. Andrieu, 'Immixtio et consecratio. La consecration par contact dans les documents liturgiques du moyen-âge' in *Univ. de Strasbourg, Bibl. de L'Inst. de Droit Canonique* (Paris, 1924).

T. Klauser, 'Festankündigung', Musterartikel des *RAC* 7 (1968).

K. Wessel, *Abendmahl und Apostelkommunion* (Recklinghausen, 1964). This delightful little book contains reproductions of the most important representations of the Apostles' communion, e.g. patens from Riha and Stuma, codexes from Rossano and Florence. From these one can see how communion was given at Rome *c.* AD 700.

T. Klauser, 'Die konstantinischen Altäre in der Lateranbasilika' in *Röm. Quartalschr.* 43 (1935), pp. 179–86. The 'altars' mentioned in this article are in fact offertory tables which were found at the end of the 'gangways' (aisles) along which the faithful used to bring their gifts. These 'gangways' also made it easier for the faithful to come up to receive communion.

A. Stuiber, 'Apophoretum' in *JbAC* 3 (1960), pp. 155–9. The term 'apophoretum', which is so interesting from the historico-liturgical point of view, comprises also the piece of eucharistic bread which the faithful used to take home with them as well as the 'fermentum' and 'blessed' bread.

T. Klauser, *Der Ursprung der Insignien*, etc. (see above), pp. 23–8. Contains an analysis of the 'Donation of Constantine'.

Section v: The development of the Roman liturgy

T. Klauser, 'Die liturgischen Austauschbeziehungen zwischen der römischen und der fränkisch-deutschen Kirche vom 8.–11. Jh.' in *Histor. Jahrbuch* 53 (1933), pp. 169–89.

See also C. Vogel, 'Les échanges liturgiques entre Rome et les pays francs jusqu'à l' époque de Charlemagne' in *Settimane di studio del centro Italiano di studi sull' alto medioevo* (Spoleto, 1960), pp. 185–330. Deals with some details in the general sketch provided by Klauser (up to the reign of Charlemagne); and H. Hucke, 'Die Einführung des gregorianischen Gesangs im Frankenreich' in *RQS* 49 (1954), pp. 172–87.

T. Zwölfer, *Sankt Peter, Apostelfürst und Himmelspförtner. Seine Verehrung bei Angelsachsen und Franken* (Stuttgart, 1929); see also E. Ewig, 'Der Petrus- und Apostelkult im spätrömischen und fränkischen Gallien' in *ZKG* 71 (1960), pp. 215–51.

E. Bourque, *Étude sur les sacramentaires romains* 2, 1: *Le Gélasien du VIIIe siècle* (Quebec, 1952).

K. Gamber, 'Heimat und Ausbildung der Gelasiana saec. VIII' in *Sacris erudiri* 14 (1963), pp. 99–129.

H. Lietzmann (ed.), *Das Sacramentarium Gregorianum nach dem Aachener Urexemplar; Liturgiegeschichtl. Quellen* 3 (Münster, 1921).

G. Ellard, *Master Alcuin, liturgist* (Chicago, 1956); see also R. Amiet, 'Le prologue "Hucusque" et la table des Capitula du supplément d'Alcuin au sacramentaire grégorien' in *Scriptorium* 7 (1953), pp. 177–209; idem, 'Le plus ancien témoin du supplément d'Alcuin: le missel "excarpsus" composé à Gellone vers 810' in *EphL* 72 (1958), pp. 97–110.

G. Ferrari, *Early Roman monasteries. Notes for the history of the monasteries and convents at Rome from the Vth through the Xth century. Studi di antichità christ.* 23 (Vatican City, 1957).

M. Andrieu, 'Les ordres mineurs dans l'ancien rit romain' in *RevScR* 5 (1925), pp. 232–74. Evidence of Frankish elements in the Roman rite of ordination in the eleventh century.

B. Capelle, 'L'introduction du symbole à la messe' in *Mélanges J. de Ghellinck* 2 (Gembloux, 1951), pp. 1003–27. The speech by Berno mentioned in the text is contained in his 'De quibusdam rebus ad missae officium spectantibus' 2 (in *PL* 142, cols. 1060–61).

Section vi: The Franco-German contribution

M. Andrieu, *Les Ordines Romani du haut moyen-âge* 3 (Louvain, 1951), pp. 265–73.

> Audrieu groups under Ordo XXIII the observations of a Frankish priest of the eighth century on the subject of his experiences of the veneration of the Cross on Good Friday in Rome (cf. No. 11/9 of this Ordo; the liturgy described in this section comprises a procession with the relic of the Cross to S. Croce, the prostration, the kissing of the cross, and some lections).

H. Barré, *Les homiliaires carolingiens de l'école d'Auxerre. Studi e Testi* 225 (Vatican City, 1962).

F. Wiegand, *Erzbischof Odilbert v. Mailand über die Taufe* (Leipzig, 1899).

> On pp. 23–5 he gives Charlemagne's questions and such answers as are still preserved by the six archbishops, including also some further reactions.

L. Eisenhofer, *Handbuch der kathol. Liturgik* 1 (2nd ed., Freiburg, 1941), pp. 120–1.

A. Chavasse, 'Le carême romain et les scrutins prébaptismaux avant le IXe siècle' in *RechScR* 35 (1948), pp. 361–75.

> Apart from the actual baptismal ceremonies, the Frankish clergy took trouble over the *scrutinia*, i.e. the 'questioning' of the candidates for baptism, even though most of them were children by that time. The Roman texts gave either three or seven *scrutinia*. Chavasse reconstructs their history.

H. Hucke, 'Gregorianischer Gesang in altrömischer u. fränkischer Uberlieferung' in *Archiv f. Musikwiss.* 12 (1955), pp. 74–87.

J. Hrbata, 'De expositione missae Walafridi Strabonis' in *EphL* 63 (1949), pp. 145–65.

T. Klauser, 'Eine Stationsliste der Metzer Kirche aus dem 8. Jh.' in *EphL* 44 (1930), pp. 162–93; see also P. Maranget, 'Les stations de carême à Paris' in *Miscellanea G. Belvederi* (Vatican City, 1954/55), pp. 47–54; M. Andrieu, 'Règlement d'Angilramne de Metz (768–791) fixant les honoraires de quelques fonctions liturgiques' in *RevScR* 10 (1930), pp. 349–69.

M. Andrieu, *Les Ordines Romani* 2 (Louvain, 1948), pp. 380–447 and 3 (Louvain, 1951), pp. 263–532.

> These sections contain the Ordines XI and XXIII–XXXIII which deal with Holy Week and the Easter Vigil. In his com-

mentary, Andrieu carefully separates the Roman and Frankish elements. On Tenebrae, the putting out of the candles, and the new fire, see 3, 311–22.

A. Baumstark, *Liturgie comparée* (3rd ed., Chevetogne-Paris, 1953). He deals in this book among other things with the 'Adoratio crucis' (on pp. 157–67).

A. Baumstark, 'Orientalisches in den Texten der abendländischen Palmenfeier' in *JbLw* 3 (1923), pp. 148–52; cf. *idem*, 'La solemnité des palmes dans l'ancienne et la nouvelle Rome' in *Irenikon* 13 (1936), pp. 1–24; see also H. Gräf, 'Palmenweihe und Palmen-prozession in der lateinischen Liturgie' *Veröffentlichungen des Missionspriestersem. St. Augustin* 5 (Kaldenkirchen, 1959).

A. Baumstark, 'Der Orient und die Gesänge der Adoratio crucis' in *JbLw* 2 (1922), pp. 1–17.

H. Kruse, 'Studien zur offiziellen Geltung des Kaiserbildes' in *Studien z. Gesch. u. Kultur d. Altert.* 19, 3 (Paderborn, 1924), pp. 76–9. Suggests that the 'Adoratio crucis' is to be explained by the fact that the Cross came to be looked upon as Christ's standard; and therefore just as people used to venerate the decorated standard of the emperor, so now they venerated the Cross.

F. J. Dölger, 'Das Karsamstags-Feuer aus der Kristall-Linse' in *AC* 6 (1950), pp. 286–96; see also R. Kottje, 'Über die Herkunft der österlichen Feuerweihe' in *Trierer theol. Zeitschr.* 72 (1962), pp. 109–12.

B. Capelle, 'La procession du Lumen Christi au samedi saint' in *Rev. bénéd.* 44 (1932), pp. 105–19; see also O. Casel, 'Der österliche Lichtgesang der Kirche' in *Liturgische Zeitschrift* 4 (1931/2), pp. 179–91; and F. J. Dölger, ' "Lumen Christi". Untersuchungen zum abendländischen Lichtsegen in Antike und Christentum' in *AC* 5 (1936), pp. 1–43.

B. Capelle, 'Le rite des cinq grains d'encens' in *Questions liturgiques et paroissales* 17 (1932), pp. 1–11.

Bonif. Fischer, 'Ambrosius der Verfasser des österlichen Exsultet?' in *ArchLw* 2 (1952), pp. 61–74. Fischer is probably right in challenging Capelle's thesis that Ambrose is in fact the author. See also O. Benoit and G. Castelli, 'Le "Praeconium Paschale" ' in *EphL* 67 (1953), pp. 309–34; and H. Lausberg, 'Exsultet, etc.' in *LexThK* 3 (1959), cols. 1318–19. An explanation of the Exsultet from the point of view of the hymnologist.

R. Kottje, *Studien zum Einfluss des Alten Testaments auf Recht und Liturgie des frühen Mittelalters*, Bonner histor. Forschungen 23 (Bonn, 1964).

A. Olivar, 'Vom Ursprung der römischen Taufwasserweihe' in *ArchLw* 6 (1959/60), pp. 62–78; see also E. Stommel, 'Studien zur Epiklese der römischen Taufwasserweihe' in *Theophaneia* 5 (Bonn, 1959).

> On pp. 20–34 he attempts to distinguish between the Roman and Gallo-Frankish elements in the rite of blessing baptismal water; further information in S. Benz, 'Zur Vorgeschichte des Textes der römischen Taufwasserweihe' in *Rev. bénéd.* 66 (1956), pp. 218–53.

G. Ellard, *Ordination anointings in the Western church before* AD *1000*. (*Monographs of the Medieval Academy of America* 8, Cambridge, Mass., 1933). Reviewed by T. Klauser in *JbLw* 13 (1933), pp. 348–52; see also M. Andrieu, 'Le sacre épiscopal d'après Hincmar de Reims' in *RHE* 48 (1953), pp. 22–73; B. Kleinheyer, *Die Priesterweihe im römischen Ritus. Eine liturgie-historische Studie* (*Trier theol. Stud.* 12, Trier, 1962); reviewed by A. Stuiber in *ThLZ* (1963), pp. 936–8; C. A. Boumann, 'Sacring and Crowning' (*Bijdragen van het Instituut voor Middeleeuwse Geschiedenis Univ. Utrecht* 30, Groningen, 1957); and *idem*, 'De vorsprong van de rituele zalving der Koningen. De stand van een probleem' in *Dancwerc aan Th. Enklaar* (Groningen, 1958), pp. 64–85.

E. Kantorowicz, *Laudes regiae. A study in liturgical acclamations and medieval ruler worship* (Berkley, 1946); see also B. Opfermann, *Die liturgischen Herrscherakklamationen im Sacrum Imperium des Mittelalters* (Weimar, 1953).

S. Benz, 'Zur Geschichte der römischen Kirchweihe nach den Texten des 7. bis 9. Jahrhunderts' in *Enkainia* (Düsseldorf, 1956), pp. 62–109.

G. Schille, *Frühchristliche Hymnen* (Berlin, 1965).

> Deals with the hymns of the New Testament period.

B. Capelle, 'Le texte du "Gloria in excelsis" ' in *RHE* 44 (1949), pp. 439–57 (reprinted in *idem*, *Travaux liturgiques* 2 (1962), pp. 176–91); see also W. Stapelmann, *Der Hymnus angelicus. Geschichte und Erklärung des Gloria* (Heidelberg, 1948).

W. Bulst, *Hymni latini antiquissimi* (Heidelberg, 1956); see also C. Blume, *Unsere liturgischen Lieder. Das Hymnar der altchristlichen Kirche* (Regensburg, 1932).

> Texts, translations, and commentary.

W. von den Steinen, 'Die Anfänge der Sequenzdichtung' in *Zeitschr.
f. schweizer. Kirchengeschichte* 40 (1946), pp. 190–212, 241–68; and
in 41 (1947), pp. 1–9, 48, 122–62.

E. Kähler, *Studien zum Te Deum und zur Geschichte des 24. Psalms in
der Alten Kirche* (*Veröffentlich. d. ev. Ges. f. Liturgieforsch.* 10,
(Göttingen, 1958). Reviewed by A. Stuiber in *ZKG* 71 (1960),
pp. 340–1.

J. Kroll, 'Die christliche Hymnodik bis zu Klemens von Alexandria' in
*Verzeichnis der Vorlesungen an der Akademie zu Braunsberg Sommer-
Semester* 1921 *u. Winter-Semester* 1921/22 (Königsberg, 1921, 1922).
Of fundamental importance. See also the investigations by
J. Robinson referred to above.

Section vii: The Calendar

T. Klauser, 'Capitulare evangeliorum I' (*Liturgiegeschichtl. Quellen u.
Forsch.* 26; Münster, 1935).
See especially pp. 184–5 for a survey of the development of the
lists of feasts.

W. Rordorf, *Der Sonntag. Geschichte des Ruhe- u. Gottesdiensttages im
ältesten Christentum* (*Abhandl. z. Theol. des Alten und Neuen Testaments* 43; Zurich, 1962). Reviewed by J. van Goudoever in *Vig. Ch.*
18 1964), pp. 57–8; also by R. Kittje in *RQS* 59 (1964), pp. 107–11.
See also W. Rordorf, 'Zum Ursprung des Osterfestes am Sonntag'
in *Theol. Zeitschr.* 18 (1962), pp. 167–89; H. Schürmann, 'Die
Anfänge christlicher Osterfeier' in *Theol. Quartalschrift* 131 (1951),
pp. 414–25; J. van Goudoever, 'The celebration of the resurrection
in the NT' in *Studia evangelica* 3 (1964), pp. 254–9; C. W. Dugmore,
'Lord's day and Easter' in *Neotestamentica et Patristica, Freundes-
gabe O. Cullmann* (*Nov. Test. Suppl.* 6; Leiden, 1962), pp, 272–81;
and O. Casel, 'Art und Sinn der ältesten christlichen Osterfeier' in
JbLw 14 (1938), pp. 1–78.

A. Baumstark, 'Nocturna laus. Typen frühchristlicher Vigilienfeier
und ihr Fortleben' (*Liturgiegeschichtl. Quellen u. Forsch.* 32; Münster, 1957). Reviewed by G. Kretschmar in *JbLHymn* 5 (1960), pp.
75–9.
Baumstark suggests that the Easter vigil is the starting point of all
further vigil celebrations.

B. Lohse, *Das Passafest der Quartodecimaner* (Gütersloh, 1953). In
the East Christians over a wide area were in the habit of keeping

Easter on the old Jewish Passover, the 14th Nisan; hence these conservative Christians were called the 'Quartodecimans'. The altercations with this group constitute what is generally known as the Paschal controversy.

G. Kretschmar, 'Himmelfahrt und Pfingsten' in *ZKG* 66 (1954/55), pp. 209–53; see also J. Boeckh, 'Die Entwicklung der altkirchlichen Pentekoste' in *JbLHymn* 5 (1960), pp. 1–45.

H. Delehaye, *Les origines du culte des martyrs* (*Subsidia hagiographica* 20, Brussels, 1933). This is a classic work of fundamental importance. See also J. Jeremias, *Heiligengräber in Jesu Umwelt. Eine Untersuchung zur Volksreligion zur Zeit Jesus* ((Göttingen, 1958); supplement in *Zeitschr f. NT Wiss.* 52 (1961), pp. 95–101; but see T. Klauser, 'Christlicher Märtyrerkult, heidnischer Heroenkult und spätjüdische Heiligenverehrung' (in *Arbeitsgemeinschaft für Forschung des Landes NRW Jahresfeier*, 1960, Cologne and Opladen, 1960), pp. 43–54. I investigate the extent to which the Jewish cult of the martyrs described by Jeremias actually gave rise to its Christian counterpart.

H. Lietzmann (ed.), *Die drei ältesten Martyrologien* (*Kleine Texte* 2; Bonn, 1911).

On pages 3–4 there is a text of the Roman 'depositio martyrum'. See also J. P. Kirsch, *Der stadtrömische christliche Festkalendar im Altertum* (*Liturgiewiss. Quellen* 7/8; Münster, 1924). The author succeeds in extracting from the so-called Martyrologium Hieronymianum a somewhat earlier edition of the Roman calendar. Also:

H. Stern, *Le Calendrier de 354. Étude sur son texte et ses illustrations* (*Bibl. archéol. et histor.* 55; Paris, 1953).

A basic work on the civil calendar which draws principally on the history of art for its illustrations.

A. Stuiber, 'Heidnische und christliche Gedächtniskalender' in *JbAC* 3 (1960), pp. 24–33.

Shows that the Christian calendar is but the continuation of a pre-Christian tradition.

H. Usener, *Religionsgeschichtliche Untersuchungen über das Weihnachtsfest* (1st ed., Bonn, 1889; 2nd ed., 1911).

K. Holl. 'Das Ursprung des Epiphanienfestes' in *Sitz.-Ber. Akademie Berlin* 19 (1917), pp. 402–38; (in K. Holl, *Gesammelte Aufsätze* 2 (1928), pp. 123–54).

The investigations of Holl and Usener are certainly along the right lines but they do not provide us with any conclusive facts, as may be shown from the following titles:

B. Botte, *Les origines de la Noël et de l'Épiphanie* (Louvain, 1932; reprinted 1962). H. Frank, 'Frühgeschichte und Ursprung des römischen Weihnachtsfests im Licht neuerer Forschung' in *ArchLw* 2 (1952), pp. 1–24; H. Engberding, 'Der 25. Dezember als Tag der Feier der Geburt des Herrn' in *ArchLw* 2 (1952), pp. 25–43.

> According to this author, the feast ought not to be thought of as replacing the pagan feast of the Sun God, but rather as being the product of mathematical speculations as to the actual day of Jesus' birth. L. Fendt, 'Der heutige Stand der Forschung über das Geburtsfest Jesu am 25. XII, und über Epiphanias' in *ThLZ* 78 (1953), pp. 1–10; O. Cullmann, *Der Ursprung des Weinachtsfestes* (2nd ed., Zurich, 1960).

> The author suggests that the feast of Christmas became split off from the earlier feast of the Epiphany, a feast however which comprised all the ideas relating to the feast of Christmas.

H. Lietzmann, *Petrus und Paulus in Rom. (Arbeiten z. Kirchengeschich.* 1; 2nd ed., Berlin, 1927).

> Deals with the 'natales episcoporum', the feast of Saint Peter's Chair, the feast of Saint Peter on the 29 June and the feasts around Christmas in chs. 2, 4, 6–9.

See also A. Baumstark, 'Begleitfeste' in *RAC* 2 (1954), pp. 78–92.

> The author places the feasts around Christmas, Epiphany, and Easter within the context of the traditions followed in antiquity.

T. Klauser, *Die Cathedra im Totenkult der heidnischen und christlichen Antike (Liturgiegeschichtl. Forschungen* 9; Münster, 1927).

> Follows the development of the Feast of Saint Peter's Chair from its origins in the cult of the dead to its becoming the feast commemorating the occasion of the Apostle taking up his office. See further, A. Chavasse, 'Les fêtes de s. Pierre (29.6) et de s. Paul (30.6) au VIIe–VIIIe siècle' in *Eph.L* 74 (1060), pp. 166–7.

Balth. Fischer, 'Formen der Tauferinnerung im Abendland' in *LitJb* 9 (1959), pp. 87–94, 157–66.

C. Callewaert, 'La durée et le caractère du carême ancien dans l'Église latine' in *Sacris erudiri* (1940), pp. 449–506.

A. Chavasse, *Le sacramentaire Gélasien* (Tournai, 1958), pp. 569–80.

> Deals with the origins of the prayers for Thursdays in Lent constructed in Rome in the eighth century; he suggests that these were taken from the presbyters' sacramentary.

L. Fischer, *Die kirchlichen Quatember* (*Veröffentlichungen des kirchen-hist. Sem. München* 5, 3; Munich, 1914).

K. A. H. Kellner, *Heortologie oder die geschichtliche Entwicklung des Kirchenjahres und der Heiligenfeste* (3rd ed., Freiburg, 1911; re-printed 1964).

> Almost every section of this book has long since been super-seded, but as yet nothing better as a whole has replaced it.

A. Baumstark, 'Advent' in *RAC* 1 (1950), pp. 112–25. Cf. J. A. Jung-mann, 'Advent und Voradvent' in *ZKTh* 61 (1937), pp. 341–90. Full and complete edition of this in *idem, Gewordene Liturgie* (Inns-bruck, 1941), pp. 232–94.

> See also A. Chavasse, 'L'avent romain du VIe au VIIIe siècle' in *EphL* 67 (1953), pp. 297–308; and W. Croce, 'Die Adventsliturgie im Lichte ihrer geschichtlichen Entwicklung' in *ZKTh* 76 (1954), pp. 257–96 and 440–72.

B. Botte, 'La première fête mariale de la liturgie romaine' in *EphL* 47 (1933), pp. 425–30. See the remarks on this by T. Klauser in *JbLw* 13 (1933), pp. 356–7.

B. Capelle, 'Les origines de la préface romaine de la vierge' in *RHE* 38 (1942), pp. 46–58.

W. Delius, *Geschichte der Marienverehrung* (Munich, 1963). Delius's account of the liturgical devotion to Our Lady is too brief.

A. Frolow, *La relique de la vraie croix. Recherches sur le développe-ment d'un culte* (*Arch. de L'Orient Chrétien* 7; Paris, 1961).

G. Kretschmar, 'Kirchenjahr' in *RGG* 3 (1959), pp. 1440–2; see also J. Pascher, *Das liturgische Jahr*. (Munich, 1963).

J. A. Jungmann, 'Wochentage' in *LexThK* 10 (1965).

R. H. Bainton, 'Die Ursprünge des Epiphaniasfestes' in *Bild und Verkündigung, Festgabe Hanna Jursch* (1962), pp. 9–20. Maintains that from the second century onwards 6 January counted as the day of Jesus' nativity.

Chapter III—The Period of Expansion

Section i: Outline of the Period.

G. Morin, *Études, textes, découvertes* 1 (Maredsous-Paris, 1913).

> On pages 457–65, he gives the text of Gregory's 'Regula canoni-corum', at the very beginning of which are to be found some observations made by the Pope himself.

J. No. 4840–1.

In these two letters of 1074, Gregory VII commands the kings of Leon, Castille, and Aragon to adopt the Roman liturgy which came into their hands for the first time as a result of the attack of the Saracens.

F. Kempf, 'Gregorianische Reform' in *LexThK* 4 (1960), pp. 1196–201. The article shows that the liturgical centralism introduced by Gregory VII was the inevitable consequence of the earlier measures he took in an attempt to correct the existing ecclesiastical administration.

A. A. King, *Liturgies of the past* (London, 1959).

He describes the Western liturgies which have fallen into disuse, namely the liturgies of Aquileia, Benevento, Gaul, etc.

P. Borella, *Il rito ambrosiano* (Brescia, 1964).

S. J. P. van Dijk and J. H. Walker, *The origins of the modern Roman liturgy: the liturgy of the papal court and the Franciscan Order in the 13th century* (London, 1960). See also S. J. P. van Dijk, *Sources of the modern Roman liturgy. The 'Ordinals' of Haymo of Faversham and related documents (1243–1307)* (*Studia et Documenta Franciscana* 1/2; Leiden, 1963). Reviewed by H. Ashworth in *EphL* 78 (1964), pp. 525–6.

T. Klauser, 'Ein Kirchenkalendar aus der römischen Titelkirche der heiligen Vier Gekrönten' in *Scientia sacra. Theologische Festgabe für K. J. Kardinal Schultz* (Cologne and Düsseldorf, 1935), pp. 11–40.

R. Klauser, 'Zur Entwicklung des Heiligsprechungsverfahrens bis zum 13. Jh.' in *Zeitschr. der Savigny-Stiftung, Kanonist Abt.* 71 (1954), pp. 85–101.

Not Alexander III but Innocent III before him claims for the Holy See the sole right to canonize.

J. Leclercq, 'Formes anciennes de l'Office marial' in *EphL* 74 (1960), pp. 89–102. See also L. Gougaud, 'Pourquoi le samedi a-t-il été consacré à la Sainte Vierge?' in *idem, Dévotions et pratiques ascétiques du moyen-âge* (Paris, 1925), pp. 65–73.

P. Lefèvre, 'La signification de la liturgie franciscaine' in *RHE* 58 (1963), pp. 857–62. According to Lefèvre, the Church's liturgy became impoverished as a result of its conforming more and more to the liturgy of the papal court.

O. Nussbaum, 'Kloster, Priestermönch und Privatmesse' in *Theophaneia* 14 (Bonn, 1961).

O. d'Angers, 'La messe publique et privée dans la piété de s. François' in *Études francisc.* 49 (1937), pp. 475–86. See also *ArchLw* 2 (1952), p. 253.

E. Dumoutet, *Le Christ selon la chair et la vie liturgique au moyen-âge* (Paris, 1932).

Using medieval monuments as evidence, the author throws light on and gives a definitive description of medieval piety and its development.

Section ii: The dissolution of the liturgical community

G. Nickl, *Der Anteil des Volkes an der Messliturgie im Frankenreiche von Chlodwig bis Karl d. Gr. (Forschungen z. Gesch. d innerkirchl. Lebens* 2; Innsbruck, 1930).

J. R. Geiselmann, *Die Abendmahlslehre an der Wende der christlichen Spätantike zum Frühmittelalter* (Munich, 1933).

Examines the change in ideas concerning the moment of consecration. See also J. A. Jungmann, 'Der Kanon unter der Einwirkung der Eucharistielehre des frühen Mittelalters' in *idem, Gewordene Liturgie* (Innsbruck, 1941), pp. 120–36.

J. A. Jungmann, 'Praefatio und stiller Kanon' in *idem, Gewordene Liturgie*, pp. 55–119.

J. P. Kirsch and T. Klauser, 'Altar (christlich)', in *RAC* 1 (1950), pp. 334–54, especially p. 350; see also J. Braun, *Der christliche Altar*, 2 vols. (Munich, 1924); and O. Nussbaum, 'Der Standort des Liturgen am christlichen Altar vor dem Jahre 1000' (*Theophaneia* 18; Bonn, 1965).

Section iii: The development of the private mass and its consequences

J. Wagner, 'Altchristliche Eucharistiefeier im kleinen Kreis'. Unpublished dissertation, Bonn, 1949.

O. Nussbaum, 'Kloster, Priestermönch und Privatmesse' (*Theophaneia* 14; Bonn, 1961).

J. N. Hanssens, 'Fungiturne minister missae privatae diaconi et subdiaconi vicibus?' in *EphL* 48 (1934), pp. 406–12.

Draws out attention to some important texts of the ninth to eleventh centuries.

J. A. Jungmann, *Missarum sollemnia* 1 (5th ed., Vienna, 1962), pp. 531–5. Deals with the question of the 'Epistle' and 'Gospel' sides.

B. Luykx, 'Essais sur les sources de l'Ordo missae de Prémontré' in *Analecta Praem.* 22/23 (1946/47), pp. 35–90; *idem*, 'Die orsprong van het gewone der mis' in *De eredienst der Kerk* 3 (Utrecht, 1956). I have not had access to this article and am acquainted with it only through a reference in S. J. P. van Dijk's *The origins of the modern Roman liturgy* (London, 1960), pp. 49–51. It is however printed in German in 'Priestertum und Mönchtum' (*Liturgie und Mönchtum*, Laacher Hefte 29, 1961, pp, 72–119).

S. J. P. van Dijk and J. H. Walker, *The origins of the modern Roman liturgy. The liturgy of the Papal Court and the Franciscan Order in the 13th century* (London, 1960), pp. 292–301. The Ordo which Haymo laid before the General Chapter for its approval in 1243 begins with the words 'Indutus planeta'. We have as yet no knowledge of its origins.

L. Oliger, 'Der päpstliche Zeremonienmeister, Johannes Burckard v. Strassburg' in *Archiv f. elsäss. Kirchengesch.* 9 (1934), pp. 199–232.

B. Luykx, 'Missale' in *LexThK* 7 (1962), pp. 449–51.

W. Dürig, *Geburtstag u. Namentag: Eine liturgiegeschichtliche Studie* (Munich, 1954); and *idem*, 'Die Geburtstagsmesse des Cod. Vat. Reg.' 3–16 in *Münchener theol. Zeitschr.* 4 (1953), pp. 46–64.

K. Rahner, *Die vielen Messen und das eine Opfer* (Freiburg, 1951).

Section iv: The decline of the offertory procession

T. Klauser, 'Die Liturgie der Heiligsprechung' in *Hl. Überlieferung, I. Herwegen dargeboten* (Münster, 1938). On pages 217–20, I deal with the early Christian offertory procession; in addition, I deal in this investigation with the offertory procession in the liturgy of canonization.

K. J. Merk, *Abriss einer liturgiegeschichtlichen Erklärung des Messstipendiums* (Stuttgart, 1928); *idem*, 'Das Messstipendium' in *Theol. Quart. Schr.* 136 (1956), pp. 199–288.

J. A. Jungmann, *Missarum sollemnia* 2 (5 ed., Vienna, 1962), pp. 3–34. Gives a complete picture of the development of the offertory procession from the beginning to its dissolution on account of the practice of giving mass stipends on the one hand, and the collection of alms on the other.

B. Capelle, 'Charité et offertoire' in *Maison Dieu* 24 (1930), pp. 121–38 (in *idem*, *Travaux liturgiques* 2 (1962), pp. 222–35).

An inquiry into whether the contributions brought as 'material for the offertory' were in fact the ordinary liturgical oblations, and nothing to do with the gifts offered for charity.

T. Klauser, 'Eine rätselhafte Exultetillustration aus Gaëta' in *Corolla L. Curtius dargebracht* (Stuttgart, 1937).

See pp. 168–76 and Plate 61 for an account of the offertory procession.

K. J. Merk, *Die messliturgische Totenehrung in der röm. Kirche* (Stuttgart, 1926).

A. Kolping, 'Der aktive Anteil der Gläubigen an der Darbringung des eucharistischen Opfers. Dogmengeschichtliche Untersuchung frühmittelalterl. Messerklärungen' in *Divus Thomas* 27 (1949), pp. 369–80 and 18 (1950), pp. 79–110, 147–70.

H. Chirat, 'Ψώμια διαφορά in *Mélanges E. Podechard* (Lyons, 1945), pp. 121–34.

Deals with way in which allegory crept into the rite of the offertory procession.

M. ten Hompel, *Das Opfer als Selbsthingabe* (Freiburg, 1920).

Section v: The meaning of genuflexion

C. Sittl, *Die Gebärden der Griechen und Römer* (Leipzig, 1890), pp. 156–61, 177–9.

A. Alföldi, 'Die Ausgestaltung des monarchischen Zeremoniells am römischen Kaiserhofe' in *RM* 49 (1934), pp. 1–118.

Deals with genuflexion to the ruler on pp. 45–62.

L. Koep, ' "Religion" und "Ritus" als Problem des frühen Christentums' in *JbAC* 5 (1962), pp. 43–59.

P. Browe, 'L'atteggiamento del corpo durante la messa' in *EphL* 50 (1936), pp. 402–14.

J. Kramp, 'Von der Kniebeuge vor der Eucharistie' in *ZKTh* 48 (1924), pp. 154–60; see also J. Horst, *Proskynein. Zur Anbetung im Urchristentum nach ihrer religionsgeschichtlichen Eigenart* (*Neutestamentl. Forsch.* 3, 2; Gütersloh, 1932); H. Schlier, 'γόνυ (Kniefall)' in *TheolWb* 1 (1933), pp. 738–40; H. Greeven, 'προσκυνέω' in *TheolWb* 6 (1959), pp. 759–67; and L. Gougaud, 'Les gestes de la prière' in *idem, Dévotions et pratiques ascétiques du moyen-âge* (Paris, 1925), pp. 1–42.

J. A. Jungmann, *Missarum sollemnia* 2 (5th ed., Vienna, 1962), pp. 179–85.

He suggests that the sign of the cross in the Canon can be both
a remembrance of the Cross of Jesus, a demonstrative act, and a
gesture of blessing; see also F. J. Dölger, 'Beiträge zur Geschichte
des Kreuzzeichens' in *JbAC* 1 (1958), pp. 5–19; continued in the
following volumes.

T. Klauser, 'Brust (an die Brust schlagen)' in *RAC* 2 (1954), pp.
655–7.

R. Guardini, *Von heiligen Zeichen* (Mainz, 1923).

Chapter IV—Unification

Section i: Outline of the Period

P. Browe, *Die häufige Kommunion im Mittelalter* (Münster, 1938);
idem, 'Kommunionersatz im Mittelalter' in *EphL* 48 (1934), pp.
534–48.

E. Iserloh, 'Der Kampf um die Messe in den ersten Jahren der Auseinandersetzung mit Luther' in *Kath. Leben und Kämpfen im Zeitalter
der Glaubensspaltung* 10 (Münster, 1952).

N. M. Halmer, 'Der literarische Kampf Luthers u. Melancthons gegen
das Opfer der Messe' in *Divus Thomas* 21 (1934), pp. 63–78.

L. Fendt, *Der lutherische Gottesdienst des 16. Jh.* (Munich, 1923).

J. Pinsk, 'Die Verhandlungen über die "abusus missae" auf dem
Konzil von Trient' in *Schles. Pastoralblatt* 44 (1924), fasc. 1–4.

H. Schmidt, 'Liturgie et langue vulgaire. Le problème de la langue
liturgique chez les premiers réformateurs et au Concile de Trente' in
Analecta Gregor. 22 (Rome, 1950).

J. Beumer, ' "Aufopfern" der hl. Kommunion unliturgisch?' in
Stimmen der Zeit 134 (1938), pp. 331–4; *idem*, 'Die Aufopferung
der hl. Kommunion für andere' in *Liturg. Leben* 2 (1935), pp. 14–18.

E. Keller, 'Anbetung im Geiste und in der Wahrheit. Zur Liturgiere-
form J. H. v. Wessenbergs' in *Erbe u. Auftrag* 38 (1962), pp.
111–23.

F. R. Reichert, 'Die älteste deutsche Gesamtauslegung der Messe,
Nürnberg ca. 1480'. Unpublished dissertation, Trier, 1962.

T. Bogler, *Einleitung zur Faksimile-Ausgabe von Flurheyms Deutschen
Messbuch von* 1529 (Maria Laach, 1964), pp. 10–106.

L. Pralle, 'Die volksliturgischen Bestrebungen des Georg Witzel,
1501–1573' in *Jahrb. d. Bist. Mainz* 3 (1948), pp. 224–42.

A. Vierbach, *Die liturgischen Anschauungen des V. A. Winter. Ein Beitrag zur Geschichte der Aufklärung* (Munich, 1929).

G. Duffrer, *Auf dem Weg zu liturgischer Frömmigkeit. Das Werk des Markus Adam Nickel (1800–1869) als Höhepunkt pastoralliturgischer Bestrebungen im Mainz des 19. Jh.* (Speyer, 1962).

A. L. Mayer, 'Die Stellung der Liturgie von der Zeit der Romantik bis zur Jahrhundertwende' in *ArchLw* 3 (1953/54), pp. 1–77.

F. Zimmerman, *Die Abendmesse in Geschichte und Gegenwart* (Vienna, 1914); see also M. Kaiser and J. Wagner, 'Abendmesse' in *LexThK* 1 (2nd ed., 1957), pp. 35–6; F. Borella, 'La messa vespertina' in *Ambrosius* 29 (1953), pp. 29–35; E. Dekkers, 'L'Église ancienne, a-t-elle connu la messe du soir?' in *Miscellanea liturgica in hon. L. C. Mohlberg* (Vatican City, 1948), pp. 231–59; G. Ellard, *Evening Mass* (Collegeville, Minn., 1954); and E. Dekkers, 'La messe du soir à la fin de l'antiquité et au moyen-âge' in *Sacris erudiri* 7 (1955), pp. 99–130.

Mission et liturgie. Rapports et compte rendu de la première semaine internationale de liturgie missionaire (Nijmegen-Uden, 1959); translated into German as *Mission und Liturgie. Der Kongress von Nijmegen, 1959*, ed. J. Hofinger (Mainz, 1960).

W. Trapp, *Vorgeschichte und Ursprung der liturgischen Bewegung vorwiegend in Hinsicht auf das deutsche Sprachgebiet* (Regensburg, 1940).

O. Rousseau, *Histoire du mouvement liturgique* (*Lex Orandi* 3; Paris, 1945).

Section ii: The guiding principles of the Tridentine commissions for the reform of the liturgy

G. Denzler, *Kardinal Guglielmo Sirleto* (*Münchener theol. Studien* 1, 17; Munich, 1964).

E. Focke and H. Heinrichs, 'Das Kalendarium des Missale Pianum und seine Tendenzen' in *Theol. Quartalschrift* 12 (1939), pp. 383–400, 461–9.

H. Jedin, 'Das Konzil von Trient und die Reform des Röm. Messbuches' in *Liturg. Leben* 6 (1939), pp. 30–66; *idem*, 'Das Konzil von Trient und die Reform der liturgischen Bücher' in *EphL* 59 (1945), pp. 5–38; *idem*, 'Der Abschluss des Trienter Konzils, 1562–63' (*Kath. Leben und Kämpfen* 21, Münster, 1963).

H. Grisar, *Das Missale im Lichte römischer Stadtgeschichte* (Freiburg, 1925).

B. Neunheuser, 'Der Gestaltwandel liturgischer Frömmigkeit', in *Perennitas Th. Michels* (Münster, 1963), pp. 160–91.

> Clarifies the somewhat complicated development of liturgical piety.

Section iii: The Congregation of Rites and its working methods

F. McManus, 'The Congregation of Sacred Rites'. Dissertation, Washington, 1954.

> I have not had access to this work.

J. Braun, *Die liturgische Gewandung im Occident und Orient nach Ursprung und Entwicklung. Verwendung und Symbolik* (Freiburg, 1907; reprinted, Darmstadt, 1964).

> On p. 198 he makes reference to the Synod of Prague.

M. van Bercham and É. Clouzot, *Mosaiques chrétiennes du IVme au Xme siècle* (Geneva, 1924), pp. 200–1.

J. A. Jungmann, *Missarum sollemnia* 2 (5th ed., Vienna, 1962), pp. 161–73, 579–80.

> On the Sanctus and the Benedictus and on the subject of the latter's being separated from the former see also L. Chavoutier, 'Un libellus ps.-ambrosien' in *Sacris erudiri* 11 (1960), pp. 136–92. Important for the beginnings of the Sanctus in the fifth century; cf. also K. Gamber, 'Ein römisches Eucharistiegebet aus dem 4/5. Jh.' in *EphL* 74 (1960), pp. 103–14.

Section iv: The liturgy and the veneration of the Sacrament

P. Browe, *Die Verehrung der Eucharistie im Mittelalter* (Munich, 1933). On pp. 1–11 he deals with the 'everlasting light', on pp. 26–9 with the 'elevation', and on pp. 89–121 with the Corpus Christi procession.

J. Braun, *Der christliche Altar in seiner geschichtlichen Entwicklung* 2 (Munich, 1924).

> Deals with the reservation of the sacrament in the sacristy safe, the 'dove' pyx and the tabernacle on pp. 574–648, with the 're-table' on pp. 277–545 and with sacrament houses on p. 588.

J. R. Geiselmann, 'Berengar von Tours' in *LexThK* 2 (2nd ed., 1958), pp. 215–16.

> He refers here to other works, of which the most important are

the classic studies of the same author of the sacramental theology of Isidore and the pre-scholastics.

V. L. Kennedy, 'The date of the Parisian decree on the elevation of the host' in *Mediaeval Studies* 8 (1946), pp. 87–96. See also H. B. Meyer, 'Die Elevation im deutschen MA und bei Luther' in *KTh* 85 (1963), pp. 65–74.

E. Dumoutet, *Le désir de voir l'hostie et les origines de la dévotion au Saint-Sacrament* (Paris, 1926). See also A. L. Mayer, 'Die heilbringende Schau in Sitte u. Kult' in *Hl. Überlieferung J. Herwegen dargeboten* (Münster, 1938), pp. 243–62.

C. Lambot, 'L'office de la Fête-Dieu. Aperçus nouveaux sur les origines' in *Rev. bénéd.* 54 (1942), pp. 61–123; see also *idem* and I. Fransen, *L'office de la Fête-Dieu primitive. Textes et mélodies retrouvés* (Maredsous, 1946); and J. Cotteaux, 'L'office liégeois de la Fête-Dieu, sa valeur et son destin' in *RHE* 58 (1963), pp. 5–81, 407–59.

J. Braun, *Das christliche Altargerät* (Munich, 1932). Deals on pp. 280–413 with the ciborium and the monstrance; see also M. Andrieu, 'Aux origines du culte du S. Sacrement. Reliquaires, et monstrances eucharistiques' in *Analecta Bolland.* 68 (1953), pp. 22–73.

P. Browe, 'Die Entstehung der Sakramentsandachten' in *JbLw* 7 (1927), pp. 83–103; see also J. Kramp, 'Die eucharistische Huldigung in Gegenwart und Geschichte' in *Stimmen der Zeit* 53 (1923), pp. 161–76; and *idem*, *Eucharistia. Von Ihrem Wesen und ihrem Kult* (2nd and 3rd eds., Freiburg, 1926).

A. L. Mayer, 'Liturgie und Barock' in *JbLw* 15 (1935), pp. 67–154.

Section v: The liturgy and church architecture

R. Grosche, 'Versuch einer Theologie des Kirchbaus' in *Schildgenossen* 17 (1938), pp. 283–91; reprinted in *idem, Et intra et extra* (Düsseldorf, 1958), pp. 99–106.

G. Kunze, *Lehre, Gottesdienst, Kirchenbau in ihren gegenseitigen Beziehungen* (*Veröffentl. d. ev. Ges. f. Liturgieforsch.* 4. 11; 1st ed., Göttingen, 1949; 2nd ed., 1960. Lizenzausgabe der ev. Verlagsanstalt, Berlin, 1959/60). See also W. Jannasch in *ThLZ* 98 (1964), pp. 854–60.

K. Liesenberg, *Der Einfluss der Liturgie auf die frühchristliche Basilika* (Freiburg, 1928).

The author has carried out his research on insufficient material.

C. Heitz, *Recherches sur les rapports entre architecture et liturgie à l'époque carolingienne* (*Bibl. générale de l'École pratique des hautes études* 6; Paris, 1962).

> Deals only with the liturgical use of the west end of the church.

R. Sedlmayr, *Architektur als abbildende Kunst* (*Sitz.-Ber. Akademie Wien. Philos.-hist., Kl.* 225, 3; Vienna, 1948); see also *idem, Die Entstehung der Kathedrale* (Zürich, 1950).

W. E. Gössman, 'Die Kirche als hl. Raum' in *Münchener theol. Zeitschr.* 7 (1956), pp. 129–39.

L. Kitschelt, 'Die frühchristliche Basilika als Darstellung des himmlischen Jerusalem' (dissertation, Munich, 1938). See also the counter-arguments of J. Kollwitz in *Byzant. Zeitschr.* 42 (1942), p. 273.

H. Paulus, *Der Gesinnungscharakter des merowingisch-westfränkischen Basilikenbaues. Ein kunstgeschichtlicher Beitrag zur Entwicklung der abendländischen Kreuzbasilika* (Würzburg, 1944).

> See also A. Strange, *Das frühchristliche Kirchengebäude als Bild des Himmels* (Cologne, 1950); A. Weckwerth, 'Das altchristliche und das frühmittelalterliche Kirchengebäude—ein Bild des Gottesreiches' in *ZKG* 69 (1958), pp. 26–78; and A. Stange, *Basiliken, Kuppelkirchen, Kathedralen. Das himmlische Jerusalem in der Sicht der Jahrhunderte* (Regensburg, 1964).

G. Bandmann, *Mittelälterliche Architektur als Bedeutungsträger* (Berlin, 1951).

> He comments: 'It is a mistake to assume that the variety of differently constituted liturgies were responsible for the many different kinds (of churches)' (p. 170). 'Even if practical considerations determined the building of the transept, nevertheless it can be seen from the example of the cathedrals at Aquileia and Trier, where such motives were not prevalent, that the transept was first and foremost intended to be a throne-room' (p. 180). 'The ancient Christian basilica was not a copy of the city (p. 111). From primitive times the usual miniature pictorial representations of city structures, e.g. of façades with twin towers (as at the city gate) and side doorways, only reappear again in the Middle Ages in the ecclesiastical architecture of the north. Although it is not possible at this stage to make any further morphological connections between the church and the city, yet the transformation of the basilica type of church in this direction

under the influence of the allegorical interpretation of church architecture ("Ecclesia"—"Civitas Dei"—"Nova Jerusalem") is the more convincing explanation of the facts' (pp. 111–12).

J. Sauer, *Symbolik des Kirchengebäudes und seiner Ausstattung in der Auffassung des Mittelalters* (2nd ed., Freiburg, 1924).

O. Nussbaum, 'Zum Problem der rund- und sigmaformigen Altarplatten' in *JbAC* 4 (1961), pp. 18–43.

H. Holtzinger, *Die altchristliche Architektur in systematischer Darstellung* (Stuttgart, 1889).

Still useful. See also G. Dehio and G. Bezold, *Die kirchliche Baukunst des Abendlandes* (Stuttgart, 1884); E. Langlotz and F. W. Deichmann, 'Basilika' in *RAC* 1 (1950), pp. 1225–59; R. Krautheimer, *Corpus basilicarum Romae* 1 ff. (Vatican City, 1937 ff.); F. W. Deichmann, *Frühchristliche Kirchen in Rom* (Basel, 1948); and S. Guyer, *Grundlagen mittelalterlicher Baukunst* (Einsiedeln, 1950).

T. Klauser, 'Die konstantinischen Altäre der Lateranbasilika' in *RQS* 43 (1935), pp. 179–86.

A. M. Schneider, 'Atrium' in *RAC* 1 (1950), pp. 888–9; *idem*, 'Cantharus' in ibid. 2 (1954), pp. 845–7.

T. Klauser, ' "Taufet in lebendigem Wasser". Zum religions- und kulturgeschichtlichen Verständnis von Didache 7, 1–3' in *Pisciculi F. J. Dölger dargeboten* (Münster, 1939), pp. 157–64.

O. Söhngen, 'Der Begriff des Sakralen im Kirchenbau' in *Bild in Verkündigung. Festgabe Hanna Jursch* (1962), pp. 157–74. Amongst other things, the author expresses his objection to the 'two-room' church (p. 168), which does not seem to agree with the ideas set out in the 1963 Constitution.

R. Krautheimer, 'Introduction to an "Iconography of Medieval Architecture" ' in *Journal of the Warburg and Courtauld Institutes* 5 (1942), pp. 1–33.

The author shows that it is difficult to support the association in ideas between the Mausoleum and the baptistry; in contesting this association, he also shows that baptism is not only dying with Christ but also rising again with Christ; hence the reason for the Easter Vigil being the day chosen for baptisms.

idem, 'Il transetto nella basilica paleocristiana' in *Actes du Ve Congr. Int. d'Archéol. Chrét.* (Paris and Rome, 1957), pp. 283–90; see also P. Lemerle, *Philippe et la Macédoine orientale* (Paris, 1945), pp. 375–89; and *idem*, 'Saint-Démétrius de Thessalonique et les problèmes du martyrdom et du transept' in *Bulletin corresp. héllénique* 77 (1953), pp. 660–94.

H. Weigert, 'Das Sakrale in der christlichen Baukunst' in *JbLw* 13 (1952), pp. 178–93. Gives an analysis of rectangular and circular interiors.

A. Grabar, *Martyrium. Recherches sur le culte des réliques et l'art chrétien antique*, 3 vols. (Paris, 1946).

A. Fuchs, 'Kirchenbau' in *LexThK* 6 (2nd ed., 1961), pp. 199–205.
Gives a short but masterly summary of the history of church architecture and deals also with the most recent contributions to this subject.

E. W. Braun and O. Schmitt, 'Beichtstuhl' in *Reallex. z. dr. Kunstgesch.* 2 (1948), pp. 183–94. See also W. Schlombs, *Die Entwicklung des Beichtstuhls in der katholischen Kirche. Ihre Grundlagen und ihre Besonderheiten im alten Erzbistum Köln* (Düsseldorf, 1965).

A. Henze, *Ronchamp. Le Corbusiers erster Kirchenbau* (Recklinghausen, 1956).
He approves, but does not give very good reasons for doing so. See also A. Fuchs, *Die Wallfahrtskapelle Le Corbusiers in Ronchamp kritisch beurteilt* (Paderborn, 1956). The opposite point of view, a most penetrating analysis.

F. Schwarz, *Vom Bau der Kirche* (1st ed., Würzburg, 1938; 2nd ed., Heidelberg, 1947); see also *idem, Kirchenbau, Welt vor der Schwelle* (Heidelberg, 1960).

Appendix I—The 1963 Constitution

Note: There are editions with English or Latin/English texts more suitable for the English-speaking reader.

'Konstitution des II. Vatikanischen Konzils', "Über die heilige Liturgie".' Latin text (and German translation) edited with commentary by Bishop S. K. Landersdorfer, J. A. Jungmann, J. Wagner (Aschendorff, Münster, 1964).

E. J. Lengeling, 'Die Konstitution des II. Vatikanischen Konzils über die heilige Liturgie'.
A Latin-German text with a commentary (Regensberg, Münster, 1964).

'Concilium Vaticanum II. Constitutio de s. Liturgia cum commentario' in *EphL* 78 (1964), pp. 185–420.

Offprints available. The commentary is the work of leading specialists such as C. Vaggagini, A. Haenggi, B. Luykx, P. M. Gy, and others. They have added an index. References to further editions of the text and opinions on the constitution are to be found in *EphL* 78 (1964), pp. 561–72.

The Instruction of 1964

'The Instruction for the orderly implementation of the constitution on the sacred liturgy of the 26th September 1964.' Latin and German text (Pustet, Regensburg, 1964).

Appendix II—Guiding principles for designing and building a church

P. Hammond (ed.), *Towards a church architecture* (London, The Architectural Press, 1962).
> Ten writers think out the problems of church architecture, basing their ideas on the 'Guiding Principles'.

O. Nussbaum, 'Der Kirchenraum und seine liturgische Einrichtung im Licht der Instructio vom 26. September 1964' in *Pastoralblatt für die Diözesen Aachen, Berlin, Essen und Köln* 17 (1965), pp. 102–24.

SELECT SUPPLEMENTARY BIBLIOGRAPHY 1978

B. Botte (*et al.*), *La Parole dans la liturgie* (Paris, 1970).

L. Bouyer, *Eucharist* (Notre Dame, 1968).

J. D. Crichton, *Christian Celebration: The Mass*, G. Chapman, 1973; Christian Classics.

J. G. Davies (ed.), *A Dictionary of Liturgy and Worship*, SCM 1972.

L. Deiss, *Early Sources of the Liturgy*, G. Chapman, 1967.

Doctrine Commissions of the Church of England, *Thinking about the Eucharist*, SCM, 1972; Allenson.

R. P. C. Hanson (ed.), *The Pelican Guide to Modern Theology*, Vol. 2 (ed. J. Daniélou, A. H. Couratin, John Kent).

D. M. Hope, *Leonine Sacramentary*, Oxford U.P., 1971.

R. C. D. Jasper (ed.), *The Eucharist Today*, SPCK 1974.

R. C. D. Jasper and G. Cuming (edd.), *Prayers of the Eucharist, Early and Reformed*, Collins, 1975.

C. P. M. Jones, G. Wainwright and E. J. Yarnold (edd.), *The Study of Liturgy* (published by SPCK, 1978); Oxford U.P.

J. Jeremias, *The Eucharistic Words of Jesus*, SCM, 1966; Fortress.

B. Moreton, *The Eighth Century Gelasian Sacramentary*, Oxford U.P., 1976.

E. C. Ratcliff, *Liturgical Studies* (ed. A. H. Couratin and D. H. Tripp, SPCK 1976.)

A. Schmemann, *Introduction to Liturgical Theology*, Faith Press, 1966; St. Vladimir. *The World as Sacrament*, DLT, 1966.

L. Sheppard (ed.), *The New Liturgy*, DLT, 1970.

R. Taft, *The Great Entrance*, OCA 200, Rome, 1975.

C. Vaggagini, *The Canon of the Mass and Liturgical Reform*, G. Chapman, 1967; Alba, *Theological Dimensions of the Liturgy*, Collegeville, 1959.

A. Verheul, *Introduction to the Liturgy*, Eng. transl. M. Clarke, A. Clarke Books, 1972.

G. Wainwright, *Eucharist and Eschatology*, Epworth, 1971; Allenson.

J. Wilkinson, *Egeria's Travels*, SPCK, 1971; Allenson.

G. G. Willis, *Essays in the Early Roman Liturgy*, SPCK 1964. *Further Essays in the Early Roman Liturgy*, SPCK 1968; Allenson.

Index